Bible Stories

Mother Never Told Me

CL Putnam

Bible Stories Mother Never Told Me

Copyright © by CL Putnam

Published in the United States 2015 by Spooky Eyes Publishing

Paperback ISBN: 978-1508475903

IN DEEPEST APPRECIATION

The following people were extremely helpful in the research, editing and production of this book. My heartfelt thanks to all of them!

Carol Ingelson

Leonard Richardson

John Warmington

Ken Adamson

Patricia Fuhrman

David Mills

Contents   Page

Introduction

A warning to my readers: Some of the stories and descriptions in this book are not suitable for children. They contain graphic images of murder, rape, infanticide, animal cruelty, sexual mutilation and hemorrhoids. And yet, probably every child who ever attended Sunday School has heard these fables, albeit in a highly diluted and pasteurized form that their innocent young minds could comprehend.

I was once one of those children. I can recall, as a little girl, sitting next to my mother, listening to her read those wonderful and inspiring stories from "The Good Book." I learned about the Garden of Eden, and Noah's Ark, and how Moses parted the Red Sea, and how David slew Goliath, and how Jesus loves all the little children, and how he died on the cross and rose from the dead to save our souls. I especially loved Jesus because he was, after all, the whole reason for having Christmas and getting presents.

But the most impressive thing about those stories was my mother's Bible. For one thing, it was the *biggest* book I had ever seen; possibly the biggest book in the whole world! Thirteen inches tall, eleven inches wide and easily five inches thick, that magnificent old Bible was in itself a work of divinely-inspired art. The cover was genuine leather, elegantly tooled in swirling relief. And though worn with age and use, it nevertheless retained its authoritative glory. The edges of the pages were painted with *real gold* (or so I was told). And attached at the top was a shiny red ribbon that could be used as a bookmark. How I loved that beautiful old book, loved to feel its comforting weight on my small lap, loved to gently caress the contours of the cover, loved the dusty "old book" smell, loved the stories contained within, many of them embellished with full-sized color pictures.

Then there were the peculiar little scraps of yellow notebook paper, dozens of them, sticking out from the top; dividers, I presumed, placed there by my mother so she could easily find the next story. At the time, I never questioned why they were there, never asked why she would skip past some sections altogether. The stories she read to me were so marvelous. I had no reason to wonder. No reason to question. I just listened and believed, because that's what children do. Little did I realize that she was practicing her own version of religious censorship.

1

Like most kids raised in a Christian culture I didn't have a choice in the matter. I was a product of my parents' indoctrination. We went to church on Sundays just like everybody else in the world, all the "good" people anyway. I actually liked Sunday School because we sang songs about love and wars and got to make prayer chains out of colored construction paper and shoebox dioramas of the nativity. And again we heard those marvelous stories. Best of all, we got to have cookies and Kool-Aid! Oh yes, we learned our scriptures well...the ones our teachers *wanted* us to learn that is. How could I have known at that tender age that there were *other* stories in the Bible; stories that were never read in Sunday School; stories that were never preached from the pulpit; stories that were not only inappropriate for children, but might shock and horrify adults as well?

I don't recall precisely when the wondering, questioning, doubting part of my brain began to kick in. It might have begun when, to my horror, I learned that Santa Claus wasn't real; that the whole thing had been one colossal lie. (Although I still enjoyed the presents, the cookies and the colored lights.)

Another factor that greatly influenced my eventual departure from religion was my love of science and the natural world. I was particularly fascinated by dinosaurs, and the fact that there are none in the Bible seemed rather odd. (My mother told me they were all killed in the great flood.) Even so, I couldn't get my hands on enough books about them. Funny thing though, these books talked about the age of the Earth in terms of billions of years, not the few thousand we were taught in Sunday School. Also, the books said the dinosaurs died out long before there were any people, yet the church insisted everything, including dinosaurs, was created at the same time. This was all so very confusing. Obviously they could not both be right. But *who* was telling the truth?

I think the final straw (even if I didn't realize it *was* the final straw at the time) came during an afterschool Bible study session. I was about thirteen by then. I casually remarked that I would love to meet people from another planet. Our youth leader, a very sweet young woman, smiled indulgently and said, "There are no people on other planets. We are God's most perfect creation. He wouldn't have any reason to create others." Picture if you will two massive steam locomotives crashing headlong into one another at full speed. That was how I felt inside the moment she said that. I was a *Star Trek* kid. I loved—I *devoured*—anything having to do with space and aliens. I

2

dreamed of becoming an astronaut or at least owning a telescope. For her to quash my childhood fantasies like that was devastating. And at that moment, I knew what it felt like to be completely alone in the universe.

I'm sure the Vietnam War had a lot to do with my intellectual transformation as well. Boys that I had grown up with were coming home in boxes. It seemed as if our high school flag was in a perpetual state of half-mast to commemorate yet another premature death. At memorial services we prayed for those who had been killed. But something always bothered me. Obviously the parents of those young men must have prayed strenuously for their sons' safety. And surely the young men themselves had prayed for their own protection. But they died anyway. So I wondered, what was the point of praying at all?

I discovered another conundrum wrapped in a contradiction in the study of Western civilization. Arguably some of the most culturally, politically and scientifically advanced societies the world has ever known were also polytheistic. *Pagans.* It boggled my mind how such highly developed people could believe such silly superstitions: gods that took animal form and came down to copulate with women, celestial messengers with wings on their heels, multi-headed monsters, plus a panoply of outrageous adventures. *Mythology* our teachers called it. Fanciful tales told by simple, primitive people.

Somewhere between naiveté and curiosity I began to wonder, why were these stories considered fables and ours facts? Why were angels accepted without question, yet Pegasus and the flying god Mercury dismissed out of hand? Why was the flood of Gilgamesh any less plausible than that of Noah? Was it any more believable that the spirit of God could impregnate a virgin and have her give birth to himself than for Zeus to transform into a swan and have sex with Leda, causing her to lay two eggs that hatched into half-god, half-human babies? The more I thought about these things, the more questions I had. Trouble was, the answers I was getting always led to the same dead end: "Ours is right. Theirs is wrong." Frustration turned into suspicion. Either these teachers, ministers and even my parents didn't know the answers, or they were trying to hide something. It was beginning to sound like the old "Santa Claus delusion" all over again.

Having been raised in a rigidly Republican family, I was ill prepared for the liberal open-mindedness of the college experience. Still, I possessed an unquenchable—perhaps even desperate—thirst for knowledge of any kind. I found myself

3

drawn to anyone different from myself and the sanitized, white bread world in which I had grown up. I was captivated by the various ethnicities and ideologies represented on campus. Friendships formed. We hung out and talked about anything and everything, including the Big Three: politics, sex and religion.

I was stunned and appalled by some of the things I was hearing about my childhood faith. Christmas was in reality a Roman *pagan* holiday?! The entire birth-death-resurrection story of Jesus was nothing more than a rehashing of a much older *Egyptian* myth?! King David bought his wife with two hundred *severed foreskins?!* Could this be true? If it was, then perhaps I didn't know as much about the Bible as I thought. I felt embarrassingly ignorant. But more than that, I felt somehow betrayed. By my ministers. By my parents. Perhaps even by God himself. And so I decided to do my own research. I began reading the Bible for myself. Not just the sweet, "feel good" parts. Not just the familiar stories. I wanted to know *everything*. But I especially wanted to know what secrets lay hidden between those little pieces of yellow notebook paper.

Now, I would love to be able to say that I read the entire Bible in two weeks. But the truth is, it took nearly ten years. (Life has a funny way of altering your plans.) During that time I went in and out of being "religious". But the more I read, and the more people I could find to speak openly and objectively about the matter, the further "out" I went. I never discussed this with my mother. I guess I didn't want to disappoint her. Or maybe I couldn't bear to confront her with the realization that she had been deceiving me all these years. Then too, it was possible that she herself was unaware of what was really in that old book. I have met people, devout believers, who have gone their entire lives, sixty, seventy, eighty years, without ever knowing what their sacred writings really say. Like obedient sheep, they just keep going to church and listening to their ministers with rapt expressions, never questioning, never wondering, merely accepting. Blissful. Content. Subservient. Drinking their own kind of "Kool-Aid".

The years passed. I joined the workforce and made a life of my own. My views about society, morality and science were pretty well formed by then, and they were taking a decidedly different direction from what the mainstream church was preaching. Still, I was looking for something more, something that would bring my life into focus, center me in a cosmological way. Whatever that "something" was, I knew it wasn't God; at least, not the god I had discovered in the Bible. At one point I joined the Baha'i faith. (At least *they* believed in evolution, albeit a god-made evolution.) But eventually I had to admit to myself that I was living a lie, pretending that I was something, someone I wasn't. I simply did not believe. I could not *force* myself to believe. And once again I was alone, searching for that something that I *could* believe in.

The TV series *Cosmos*, narrated by Carl Sagan, did just that. Before the end of the first episode I was hooked. Dr. Sagan's "personal voyage" became *my* personal voyage. For the first time in my life I felt like I *could* fly to the stars in my own "starship of the imagination"! My curiosity had been fired like never before. Here at last was someone who was saying the things I was feeling. He inspired me, empowered me, made me realize that it was OK to be skeptical. It was OK to ask questions. And it was OK to challenge any and all preconceived ideas or ideologies. For the first time in my life, I knew how it felt to be a living part of the universe! It would be another decade or so before I had the courage to openly say I did not believe in a god, but I knew there would be no turning back to religion now.

So, why did I write this book? Why not just say, "Eh, to each his own, live and let live" and be done with it? Well, for the largest part of my life that is precisely what I did. Truth is, being an atheist or an agnostic in a dominant Christian culture is a lot like being a homosexual. "Coming out" can have some very dire consequences in regard to family, friends, employment and sometimes life itself. I personally was quite diffident until friends turned me on to books by fellow freethinkers: Sam Harris, Richard Dawkins, Christopher Hitchens. These were the groundbreakers, the voices of a new age. But there were still others: in the science realm, Bill Nye and Neil deGrasse Tyson; in the genre of irreverent comedy, Monty Python, George Carlin and Bill Maher. These were my kind of people!

But getting back to why I wrote this book. One thing I really despise is being lied to. I already mentioned the great Santa Claus deception. OK, I can forgive any parent that one. I mean, who wouldn't just melt at the sight of a child's eyes wide with wonder and delight on Christmas morning? The kind of lying I'm talking about is where greed, power and lust, plus all the other "deadly sins", are the motivators, and innocent, gullible, desperate, lonely people are the victims. As I got older it became clear to me that some of the biggest perpetrators of these crimes against humanity were to be found in religion. (Politics too falls into this category, but that's a subject for an entirely different kind of book.)

My generation witnessed the Jonestown, Waco Texas, Solar Temple and Heaven's Gate cult suicide massacres, as well as the crash-and-burn careers of such notorious televangelists as Jim Bakker, Terry Smith, Jimmy Swaggart, Oral Roberts, Bob Larson, Robert Tilton, Billy James Hargis, Ted Haggard, Juan McFarland... The list goes on and on. And while some of these may not have committed crimes of an outright felonious nature, *all* of them—and all the others like them—are guilty of perpetrating the greatest con game of all time: making millions of dollars while selling *nothing* (books, CDs, DVDs and assorted graven images notwithstanding). That hardly seems like a fair exchange. Some may claim that what they are selling is hope and comfort, a sense of belonging, even *love*. All right, but couldn't that also apply to the average prostitute? At least with the prostitute you would get a bit more "hands on" therapy. I suppose one person's crime is another person's public service. Kind of hard to tell them apart sometimes.

Hardcore apologists will strenuously argue that the aforementioned events and persons do *not* represent the true and fundamental teachings of the Bible. Perhaps. There are indeed many genuinely kind, loving, compassionate ministers of faith who use their pulpit-given powers to comfort those in need while maintaining their own personal integrity and humility. Even so, I'll wager the vast majority of these benevolent men and women of the ministry have not been forthcoming with *every* story or *every* peculiar passage contained in their sacred scriptures. Like my mother, they carefully select which portions they want their parishioners to hear, intentionally suppressing the rest. This in itself is a lie; a lie of *omission*.

But censoring the Bible is nothing new. For hundreds of years Catholic priests jealously guarded these ancient texts. In fact, there was a time in mankind's dark past when even possessing a Bible translation or any part thereof would get you burned at the stake. One has to wonder, just what were those priests so afraid of? What tawdry secrets were they trying to hide?

Some historians will contend that it was the rebellious actions of such men as Martin Luther, John Calvin and Henry VIII that brought about the eventual disintegration and gruesome brutality of the sixteenth century Catholic Church. I, however, suggest it began nearly one hundred years earlier with the invention of the printing press. The biggest threat to religion is not science or secularism or communism or atheism or even dirty dancing. The biggest threat to religion is *education*, specifically *literacy*. When people can read, they can see for themselves what despicable atrocities and sheer lunacy are contained in those tissue-thin pages.

A tongue-in-cheek response for the question, "How did you become an atheist?" goes, "I read the Bible." Speaking for myself, that's not exactly how it happened. The truth is, you don't have to read the Bible to become an atheist...but it helps. Still, my purpose in writing this book was not to "turn" people into atheists. I would simply like for them to read the Bible—*all of it*. Then they can decide for themselves if it really is the "holy" book they were led to believe.

Think of it this way: If you were told by your doctor that you had a serious condition and needed an operation to save your life, you wouldn't simply let him start slicing away at you. You'd want to know every detail about that condition and the operation to the nth degree, right? Furthermore, medical ethics require a doctor to disclose all the details of the procedure, the possible outcomes and potential dangers so that the patient can make a rational decision. This is called *informed consent*. Another example: You certainly wouldn't buy a used car based solely on the previous owner's word that it "runs great!" Yet people by the hundreds of millions buy into the claim that the Bible is the literal, unerring word of a loving god without ever reading the texts for themselves. Most of these people were indoctrinated as innocent and easily impressed children, as was I. (If adults can make you believe in Santa Claus, they can make you believe in anything.) My purpose here is to give people a choice; more specifically, to give them enough information to allow them to make their own choice by shining a very revealing light into some of the darker corners of biblical scripture.

In addition to lies, censorship and exploitation, I really hate it when some people—due to nothing more than their particular religiosity—feel they have the right, nay the obligation, to tell other people how to live their lives. Even worse, they use their theocratic clout to push through legislation designed to deprive certain others of their civil liberties, personal happiness and/or reproductive rights. It's one thing for a skeazy, spiritual snake oil salesman to start a mega church and con the foolish into voluntarily forking over their life savings; it's quite another for a religious bloc to force their political agendas upon the rest of society, agendas rooted in nothing more than ancient folktales and a colorful assortment of bigotry, misogyny and plain old fashioned batshit craziness.

As I mentioned before, I have always been deeply inquisitive. It was never enough for me that someone *said* a thing was a certain way; I wanted to know *why* it was that way. And so with that attitude, and a lot of unanswered questions, I began my research for this book. Like a detective trying to piece together a crime scene I dissected each story, looking for motives, creating psychological profiles of the main characters. But perhaps even more important, I used this forensic technique in trying to understand the *other* people, the so-called *enemies of God*, the ones he repeatedly commands his chosen people to destroy with "a great slaughter". Who were these people? Where did they come from? How did they think and feel? Why did the Hebrew god hate them so much? What had they done to deserve such unprecedented genocidal treatment?

And so, using logic, science, history, psychology (and a smattering of literary license) I began the task of recreating and retelling these stories. You will find that most of my reconstructions are told from the point of view of Yahweh's victims. In order to fully understand them and their situations, I gave them names and thoughts and emotions. They are no longer merely "the enemy". They are living, thinking, feeling, three-dimensional *human* beings. Presented in this format, the stories will allow you to see and know and *feel* for these "other people" in the Bible, the ones who are so casually and anonymously butchered at the behest of the *god of love*. Not only do they now have faces and personalities, they also have a *voice*, a voice which has never before been heard.

Some of these stories will be familiar to you, others not at all. They cover a wide range of topics and genres from the silly to the sadistic, erotic to repulsive. A few will be uncomfortable for you to read; others you will find downright preposterous. But remember, *they all come from the Bible.* Because the King James and New International Versions are the two most popular Bibles used by Evangelical Fundamentalists, I have drawn my evidence primarily from these sources. Book, chapter and verse notations are included in every story for easy reference. I encourage you to look them up and share them with your "believer" friends. The likely reaction you will get is, "That's *not* in the Bible!" Oh, but it most certainly *is.* The book you now hold in your hands is for people who want to know the truth in its entirety: ugly, asinine and uncensored.

The time for believing in Santa Claus and the Easter Bunny is over. It's time to put the Bible and similar works of fiction on the same dusty shelf with all the other mythologies, folk tales and superstitions. Knowledge, as they say, is power; and I hope to empower as many of my fellow freethinkers as possible to step forward with courage and resolve and make our voices heard. So here they are, the Bible Stories Mother Never Told Me...

...and the churches don't want you to hear.

God's "Other" Sons
As Found in the Book of Genesis
Chapter 6, Verses 1-2

Anyone who considers himself a Christian knows that Jesus was the "son of God". In fact, in John 3:16 of the King James Version Bible (KJV) we read that definitively famous passage, "For God so loved the world, that he gave his only begotten Son, that whosoever believeth in him should not perish, but have everlasting life." The New International Version (NIV) says essentially the same thing, but emphasizes that Jesus was God's *"one and only* Son". Jesus himself drove that point home in the Book of Revelation by stating, "I am the Alpha and Omega" (the "beginning and end").

Now, the subject of exactly *who* Jesus was—god, man, holy spirit, all of the above—and where he came from—egg-and-sperm, egg-and-spirit, or cosmic Silly Putty—have been the cause of much discussion, contention and division for centuries. But even this, like every other moral and ethical issue in the Bible, can be resolved "cafeteria style" by simply picking and choosing at your leisure from a deliciously contradictory assortment of quotes and interpretations. Whatever particular religious agenda you wish to subscribe to, you can find a scriptural passage to support your case. Still, at the end of the bickering and debating one unequivocal fact seems to remain: Jesus was the *one and only* begotten flesh-and-blood manifestation, i.e. Son of God. Period. End of discussion.

However... In the Book of Genesis, Chapter 6, Verses 1-2, we find a puzzling if not downright contradictory statement: "And it came to pass, when men began to multiply on the face of the earth, and daughters were born unto them, That the Sons of God saw the daughters of men that they were fair; and they took them wives of all which they chose."

"Holy matrimony!" I can just hear you shouting. "God had sonS?!" Apparently so; and while it never states how *many* sons he had, it nevertheless states the fact clearly, repeatedly and in the unequivocally *plural* sense.

But wait, it gets better. In Verse 4, when these women began cranking out offspring, we are told—and it must be true, because this is, after all, the *literal and unerring* word of God—

"There were giants in the earth in those days; and also after that, when the Sons of God came in unto the daughters of men, and they bear children to them, the same became mighty men which were of old, men of renown."

That's right, *giants*. The Sons of God came down from Heaven, had sex with Earth women and produced a race of giants. (Kind of sounds like the plot to a low-budget sci-fi movie.) The Bible calls these giants the "Nephilim". I'll talk more about them later.

Right now I would like to reconstruct the aforementioned storyline from that glorious moment when God the Almighty snapped his omnipotent fingers and created "Life, the Universe and Everything" (to quote from *The Hitchhiker's Guide to the Galaxy* by the brilliant British writer Douglas Adams). But first I think we need to ask ourselves, exactly *where* was God prior to creating "Life, the Universe and Everything"? Moreover, where were his "sons"? Since an offspring cannot logically exist before a parent, we must assume that God created (or *pro*-created) his sons before he set about the monumental task of constructing the material cosmos as we know it. But then again, attempting to use logic to comprehend scripture is like trying to solve a math problem by cracking your knuckles.

Still, we need to start somewhere, so let's pretend the omniscient, omnipresent "god essence" is floating around in utter nothingness. Empty, black, eternal, pre-existing nothingness. Since forever...and ever...and ever... That had to be awfully lonely, not to mention boring. It would be only natural for him to want some company. Now, most males in that situation, assuming they were all-powerful and could conjure anything in the blink of an eye, would create a smoking hot babe for celestial companionship. But not Yahweh. For some unknowable reason he completely bypassed the female factor of the procreative process and went right to begetting sons. (Kind of reminds me of a few TV shows from the 60s and 70s where it's just dad and the kids—usually sons—without a woman to upset their testosterone-based plotline.) Whatever his inscrutable reason or method, God became a parent—not once, but several times over. For the purpose of our story I'm going to say that God had seven sons because seven is *the* most "magical" number that appears in the Bible; and besides, that makes as much sense as anything else.

So there they were, God and his seven miraculously, spontaneously generated sons, just hanging out together in that immensely vast, empty, black void. What were they doing? What were they thinking? Did they ask themselves, "Where did I come from? What is my purpose?" or "What is the meaning of non-corporeal transcendental ethereal consciousness?" Further-more, being "sons" they by definition had to have *penises* (for how else could they have had sex with Earth women and beget offspring?) which brings my preamble full circle. So let us now try to imagine that omnipotently orgasmic moment when God decided that there was something missing in the celestial abyss and kick-started the whole creative process.

BANG!

"*Jesus Christ!* Did you hear that?"

Jesus shrugged. "Probably Father playing god again."

Biff stared at his little brother as if—and quite literally—for the first time. "You just shrugged."

Jesus shrugged again. "Yeah, so?"

"I mean, you *shrugged*. You've got *shoulders!*"

Jesus turned his head left then right. "Hey, yeah. What are shoulders?"

Biff thought hard for a moment. "I'm not sure. I just somehow know that that's what they're called."

Jesus glanced down. "I've also got arms, and hands, and legs, and feet..."

All the sons now began peering at themselves and each other, *seeing* each other for the very first time.

"We've *all* got them!" remarked Shangdi. Puzzled, he raised his questioning hands to his face, felt the odd protuberances that he perceived to be nose, lips and ears. "And—and I can *hear* you!"

The now noticeably dark-skinned Tukufu Mungu studied himself then exclaimed, "And we're all different colors too!"

Majid Abad, whose shade was somewhere between Tukufu Mungu's ebony and Biff's alabaster, made another observation. "And look at your faces. Your features are all quite different!"

They spent the next several celestial moments describing each other. In addition to his obviously lighter skin, Biff had round, blue eyes, flowing blond hair and a straight, triangular nose. Shangdi's skin was of a yellowish hue, his dark eyes slanted, his nose rather small and flat. Tukufu Mungu had tightly coiled black hair and broad nose and lips. Wakan Khili had reddish skin, long, black braids and high cheekbones. Akua Nui had bronze skin, a big smile and wide features framed by wavy brown locks.

Then there was Jesus. Try as they might they could not agree on exactly what he looked like. It was as if his appearance changed depending on who was looking at him. One thing they did agree on, he did have a peculiar glow about him.

Biff leaned close to Tukufu Mungu. "Looks like the Old Man was playing favorites with our little brother."

Tukufu Mungu chuckled. "I always sensed something was up with those two."

Majid Abad looked thoughtful. "Hey, I just realized something else—we have *names*."

"Names?"

"Yeah," Majid Abad nodded with his head part. "What's more..." He contemplated his name for a moment. "They all mean something. Mine means *God is the Exalted Eternal One*."

They all contemplated. "He's right," said Tukufu Mungu. "Mine means *Glorious is God*."

The others took turns reciting the meaning of their names. Akua Nui: *Greatest is God*. Shangdi: *God is Most High*. Wakan Khili: *The Awesome Spirit*.

Biff sniggered. "Isn't that just like Pops to bestow his mightier-than-thou moniker on the rest of us? *Pfft*, talk about an ego-tripper!"

There was a moment of silence, then all eyes of different shapes and colors turned toward Biff. "Well?" asked Majid Abad. "Tell us what *Biff* means?"

The tall, blond Son of God scratched his head and turned his blue eyes downward. "Um... That's not really my name. I kind of changed it."

"From what?" inquired Wakan Khili. "What does your real name mean?"

Biff pursed his lips. "*Rough Draft*."

A peal of laughter exploded from the six other sons. "*Rough Draft?*" cried Jesus. "Well, I guess that could explain a few things."

Biff could feel the hair on his newly embodied neck bristling. "OK, halo boy, and just what does *your* name mean?"

"*God Saves*," Jesus replied.

"*God Saves?* That's it?"

Wakan Khili's brow furrowed. "Saves *what?*"

Jesus smiled. "Saves the best for last, what else?"

The six other sons groaned. This entire experience of suddenly finding themselves incorporated into individual identities, shapes and colors took some getting used to. In fact, it seemed that everywhere they looked things were changing, solidifying, becoming...*dimensional*.

"I wonder what Pops is up to?" asked Shangdi.

Tukufu Mungu said, "I'll bet it had something to do with that big *bang*."

Akua Nui flipped the thick, wavy locks off his forehead. "I say we go talk to him, get some answers."

That sounded like a very good idea, and so they began walking through the strange nebulous of swirling shapes and colors that were even then coalescing around them. Not only had the Old Man created these fleshy capsules for them to move around in, he had also imbued the vessels with an array of sensual stimuli. There were sounds so pure and delightful, smells intoxicatingly fragrant, and the air that swelled their lungs...so sweet it could almost be tasted. Whatever was happening to them, whatever this substantial existence was called, they all agreed it was *good*.

Soon after they set out Tukufu Mungu felt something peculiar and glanced down. "What do you suppose this is for?" he remarked, pointing to the oddly shaped appendage dangling from his groin area.

They all paused and began to contemplate the things, first with mild curiosity, then with great vigor. And within moments they had their answer. "That was *definitely* good!" Biff exclaimed, panting and trying to compose himself. "We have *got* to thank Pops for *that* little perk!"

After a bit more contemplation, they decided to continue on. They finally found the Old Man at the very center of the great, swirling expanse. He—now appearing very much like them-selves—was seated in an ornately adorned golden throne perched atop an enormous dome of some sort. There were also several very strange looking creatures fluttering all around him. They had six wings apiece and seemed to be made of fire. They just kept circling around him in a frenetic swarm, all the while chanting, "Holy, holy, holy, holy, holy, holy, holy...!" Every now and then one of them would swoop in and snatch a piece of lint off his resplendent robes or quickly polish a gleaming jewel on the throne, always chanting the incessant, "Holy, holy, holy, holy, holy, holy, holy...!"

At his sons' approach the Old Man turned. "Well, it's about time you showed up," he remarked.

"Yeah, well, we kind of got distracted," said Biff, his gaze fixed upon the weird flying creatures which had now turned their attention upon the sons. The creatures began preening them, using their little tongues of fire to clean the sons' ears and various orifices. Biff shooed one of the overly attentive pests away from his hinter parts. "Just what *are* those things?"

"Seraphim," God replied with an air of divine smugness. "I

created them to keep this place tidy. I created a lot of things: seraphim, cherubim, angels."

"Why?"

"To do my bidding, of course. You know, *serve* me. I've been working my butt off for two days now. I needed some assistants."

Puzzled, Akua Nui turned to his brothers. "What's a *day?*"

God waved his right hand. The entire cosmos became bathed in illumination. "See that light?" He then waved his left hand. Just as suddenly, blackness engulfed the void. "See that dark? That's one day. Pretty good, eh? I've been working steady for two of those."

Biff glanced sideways at his brothers. "Uh, yeah. That must've taken a lot out of you."

A frown darkened the Old Man's countenance. "For your information, wise guy, I just created the whole damn universe. And that *includes* those bodies you've been so thoroughly enjoying."

"Every chance we get," snickered Wakan Khili.

The others snickered too. All except Jesus. "Well, *I* haven't!" he exclaimed.

God smiled. "I know you haven't. You're a good boy, Jesus."

Biff's lips curled into a sneer. "*You're a good boy, Jesus,*" he muttered. A chorus of tittering followed.

God breathed an exasperated sigh. "If you adolescents are finished, I want you to take a look down there." He pointed toward something below the great vaulted dome.

Tukufu Mungu shook his head. "All I see is a bunch of formless water."

"That's just half of the water," God told them. "After I built this dome on the second day I put the other half on top of it. It's a bit slippery, so watch your step."

"Why bother separating the water at all?" asked Shangdi.

"I dunno," God said with a shrug. "Seemed like the logical thing to do at the time. It was either that or build a bigger dome. Besides, I can always use it for something later on I suppose."

Biff folded his arms. "So, basically what we're looking at is a colossal cosmic puddle."

A grin spread across the Old Man's omnipotent lips. "Watch this!" He spread his arms wide—accidentally knocking one of the chanting seraphim into a flaming tailspin—and in a booming voice said, "Let the water under Heaven be gathered to one place, and let dry ground appear!" And as they all watched, there was a great heaving and shaking and suddenly rocky peaks began rising up out of the water, and soon an entire mass of dry land emerged right in the middle of it.

"Bit of an exhibitionist, isn't he?" quipped Majid Abad to the others.

"You're just jealous!" said Jesus.

Biff stroked his jaw. "OK, so now there's a bunch of lumpy dry stuff surrounded by wet stuff with a big dome of more wet stuff overhead."

"I'm not done yet," God replied, obviously annoyed. "Just shut up and watch."

And as they watched, the Old Man made a few more grandiose flourishes which caused the barren landscape to turn green all over.

"Looks like the whole thing's gone a bit moldy," said Akua Nui.

God breathed a weary sigh. "That's not mold, it's grass and trees and herbs. And for your information I think it's pretty damn good."

The Sons of God exchanged curious glances. "But what's it all for?" ventured Jesus.

The Old Man's mien softened. "I'll show you tomorrow, my son. Right now I've got to do that darkness thing again." He made a sweeping gesticulation with his arms. Everything beneath the dome turned black. "And now the light thing again." Another grand gesture, and everything beneath the dome was bathed in brightness.

Having witnessed all this, the sons leaned close to one another. "I think Pops has finally lost it big time," Wakan Khili whispered.

God rubbed his hands together. "This is where it's really going to get good," he remarked.

Biff muttered to his brothers, "Sure couldn't get any weirder."

With a snap of his almighty fingers, God conjured a yellow ball of fire, which he attached to the underside of the dome. Then he made a smaller, dimmer ball. "I'm calling this one the sun and the other one the moon," he told his bewildered offspring. "The sun will give off light during the day and the moon will give off light at night. This way I don't have to keep doing that *dark-and-light, dark-and-light* thing anymore."

"So, why didn't you just create *them* in the first place?" asked Tukufu Mungu.

God shrugged. "Creating a universe is kind of a learn-as-you-go process," he told them. "It's not an exact science. Hell, it's not *science* at all!"

"Not to split hairs," said Shangdi, staring at the dimmer light. "But I don't think the moon is actually giving *off* light. It looks like it's merely reflecting light from the sun."

The Old Man snorted. "Hey, my universe, my rules. Deal with it."

As they watched, God grabbed a handful of the fluttering seraphim and hurled them against the dome. They hit with a *splat* and stuck there, glowing and sputtering.

Biff cringed. "That seemed a bit harsh."

"Don't worry about them. I can always make more. Besides, I told them I'd make stars out of them when they were first created."

Majid Abad scratched his head. "I still don't see the point in all this."

"You will. Just watch." Leaning forward in his great throne, God stuck out his finger and made a swirling motion. "Wait for it... Wait for it..." And just like that, the sun began to slide down the side of the immense dome, slowly...slowly...slowly...until it had disappeared completely into the waters below. Now the dome-encapsulated Earth was dark except for the moon, which—despite Shangdi's observations—had indeed begun to give off a pale luminescence. "Told you so," the Old Man chuckled. And the seraphim-turned-stars twinkled overhead.

Smiling, God leaned back in his throne. "Pretty cool, huh?"

"But where did the sun go?" asked Jesus, his eyes wide with curiosity.

"Oh, it's still there, under the water," the Old Man reassured him. "Now, look there!"

And as they watched, the stars and moon continued to slip downward until they too were under the waters. But then, from the opposite side of the dome, the sun began to reappear, slowly...slowly...slowly climbing up the side of the great vaulted sky, once more bathing the green landscape in warm, yellow light.

God clucked to himself. "No doubt about it, boys. I am *good*."

"I still don't get it," Biff remarked. "The sun goes down, the sun comes up. That's it?"

"No, no, no!" The Old Man was obviously not pleased by the density of his sons. "It's the sun that makes all the plants grow. I call it *photosynthesis*. They can't survive without it."

"Well... Wouldn't it have made more sense to create the sun *before* you created the plants? I mean, if the plants were OK without the sun to begin with—"

"Look, I *told* you it wasn't a perfect science. Why the hell do you have to question everything I do? Have a little faith in your old man, huh?"

God stroked his long, white beard, which the remaining seraphim were busily grooming. "Let's see... What should I create today?"

By now Shangdi, Akua Nui, Majid Abad and Tukufu Mungu had lost interest and were amusing themselves on the other side of the universe. "Hey, watch this," said Akua Nui, grasping his oddly shaped lower appendage. "I can write my name in that nebula."

Majid Abad bent over and chuckled. "Stand back! I'm gonna create a *super nova!*"

The Old Man rubbed his beleaguered forehead. "Idiots."

Jesus peered down at the Earth. "Father, can you make the trees dance around?"

God smiled. "I can do more than that." And with a majestic wave of his hands he filled the waters with fish, both great and small, and he created flying things, some with feathers and some with huge, leathery wings and long, pointed beaks with rows of sharp teeth. Then he told them all to start multiplying and fill the waters and the land. And they all started jumping around and screeching and humping one another and spawning and laying eggs, and then the eggs started hatching, and those creatures got bigger, then *they* started jumping and screeching and humping and spawning and laying eggs until pretty soon there were millions of these things everywhere: jumping, screeching, humping, spawning, laying, hatching! Thankfully, just then the sun went down and everything turned dark.

The three sons exchanged dubious glances. "That was a bit unsettling," Biff remarked. Suddenly—

Thump! Thump, thump, thump! THUMP!

Wakan Khili stared down at the darkened Earth. "What's all that thumping?"

THUMP! Thump, thump, thump!

"Holy crap!" cried God. "It's the birds hitting the side of the dome! Guess I forgot about that. OK, uh... I'll create a magnetic field emanating from the middle of the Earth to ward them off."

A short while later the sun rose once more. Biff yawned and rubbed his eyes. "So, what's on today's ingenious agenda, Pops?"

"Well, I suppose if the waters are now filled with fish, and the skies are filled with birds, it would make sense to fill the Earth with something also."

"I've got an idea," Wakan Khili said. "Why not have some of the fish crawl up onto the land, and they could start breathing air, and grow feet and tails and fur, and they could change into all sorts of sizes and shapes and colors, and then some of them could learn to stand up, and—"

God stared for a moment, his brow furrowed with disbelief. "That is without a doubt the most *ridiculous* plan I've ever heard. Do you have any idea how long it would take for all that to happen?"

Wakan Khili hung his head. "Sorry. I just thought it would be kind of fun to watch. You know, give them a nudge and see how they managed to adapt and change."

"Now, why the hell would I want anything to change? When I make something, it's perfect. That's because *I'm* perfect!"

Jesus gazed up at his father with a beaming countenance. "You tell 'em, Father! Your will be done!"

God smiled and patted the lad's glowing, honey-colored locks. "Jesus, I swear you become more like me every day."

Turning away, Biff muttered, "I think I may vomit." He took Wakan Khili aside. "Hey, don't take it too hard," he whispered. "Don't forget, this is the same guy who created plants *before* a self-sustaining photosynthetic thermonuclear reactor was in place to keep them alive. And remember what happened to the birds? *Pfft!* Nothing very intelligent about *that* design."

God rolled up his great sleeves. "OK, back to business," he announced. He stretched out his arms once again, gave his fingers a flick, and the Earth spontaneously produced every living thing that would ever exist. And that wasn't just good, it was downright *awesome*.

Biff and Wakan Khili stared down at the trillions of fully formed creatures from shrews to zebras, civets and tyrannosaurs, mastodons, monkeys, dragons, raccoons, saber-tooth tigers, unicorns, buffaloes, kangaroos, cockatrices, plus an unimaginable assortment of insects and reptiles.

Biff shook his head in dismay. "No disrespect intended, Pops, but *what the hell* were you thinking? There are so many animals down there they can hardly turn around without stepping on one another."

"Well, maybe I did go a bit overboard on this one." The Old Man's heavy white brows came together in thought. "I guess I just won't tell *them* to be fruitful and multiply."

"But how will you feed them all?" Wakan Khili asked.

"I've got it!" Biff exclaimed. "See the ones with the big fangs and claws? They can catch and eat the others."

"*NO!*" God thundered. "*No* death! *No* killing! *No* eating of flesh! I made everyone of these things *perfect*. I made the entire

Earth *perfect*, and I want it to *stay* that way!"

"OK, OK, I get it," said Biff. "But they still have to be fed."

"Well... They can eat the grass and the trees and all the other green stuff."

Wakan Khili cocked an eyebrow. "Even the velociraptors, and the lions, and the crocodiles?"

"Yes, *all* of them. They will all eat plants. *Nothing* is to be killed. *Nothing* is to be eaten—*ever!*"

"What about sharks?" Biff asked. "Have you seen the *teeth* on those things?" He scoffed. "Well, of course you have—you *made* them, after all. How are they supposed to eat *grass*?"

The Old Man was becoming visibly perturbed. With an angry huff he crossed his arms in front of him and gave a quick blink. "There! I just created *kelp*. They can eat kelp. Are you happy now, smart ass?"

The four other sons returned right about then. Shangdi took a sniff and recoiled. "*Holy shit! Was is that stench?*"

"More of Pops' handiwork," Biff replied behind his cupped hand.

Majid Abad grasped one of the fluttering seraphim and pressed its feathered wings over his nose and mouth. "Well, you'd better do something about it soon. *Look!*"

And as they watched, the dome began to fill with a fetid gas. The temperature rose, and the polar icecaps began to melt.

"Look at that!" cried Jesus, pointing. "The oceans are rising! If it keeps up there won't be any dry land left!"

"All right, all right. Don't panic!" God told them. "I'll think of something. Say, how about if you boys go down there with some shovels and—"

"*No way!*" they shouted in unison. "Your mess, your problem!"

Teeth clenched in desperation, the Old Man glanced around. By no small coincidence all the seraphim, cherubim and angels had conveniently disappeared.

"Damn it! Fine, I'll just have to create somebody to take care of it."

"Better make it a *lot* of somebodies," Biff quipped.

After some divine decision making God sat upright. "I've got it! I'll create caretakers to clean up the place."

"Please, *God*, not more animals!" Tukufu Mungu groaned.

"No, no. They'll be more like...more like *us!* Yes, that's it. I'll create them in *our* image!" God rose from his throne and began pacing back and forth, sending ripples across the surface of the great dome. "Let's see... They've got to have hands like ours so they can use tools. You know, rakes, shovels, wheelbarrows. And strong backs for digging holes. Lots and lots of holes."

"Better not make them too smart," said Akua Nui.

"Why not?"

"Well, no pun intended, but that's some pretty *shitty* work you're expecting them to do. I mean, if they realize that's the only reason you put them on Earth—you know, to do your bidding—you're liable to have a mutiny on your hands."

"Yeah, you're right." God stroked his long, flowing beard in thought. "I've got it! I'll tell them that I created the Earth *for* them, and that everything there: the plants, the animals, the birds, the fish, it's all theirs to do with as they please—except they can't kill anything and eat it. Other than that, they will have complete dominion over the entire Earth. That ought to keep them happy."

Biff frowned. "So, it's just one big con to get them to clean up the mess *you* created?"

The Old Man breathed a weary sigh. "Do you *always* have to turn everything into a political statement?"

"I'm just saying, it doesn't sound like a very equitable arrangement. They do all the work, and what do they get in return? *Dominion?* Dominion over what—thirty-seven billion acres of raw sewage?"

God pressed his lips together hard. Biff did have a point, he supposed. "Very well. I'll give them the power to procreate. I'll create males and females, then I'll tell them to go fuck their brains out."

"Uh, yeah, but... Isn't the Earth a bit over populated *now* with all those other creatures milling around?"

The Old Man gazed down at the suspended liquid firmament that lapped gently around his feet. "Well, I guess I'll just have to deal with that problem at a later date."

He lowered himself once more into the lavishly adorned throne. Instantly, the seraphim returned and began preening, grooming, cleaning and polishing, all the while chanting, "Holy, holy, holy, holy, holy, holy, holy...!" in unison.

"All right, then," said God, rubbing his hands together. "Let's make some people." He peered at his seven sons, noting the differences in their appearance: eyes, noses, skin tones, hair colors and textures. *Well, no sense letting all that raw material go to waste.* And with the flip of an almighty wrist, he created a colorful panoply of human beings.

The sons gathered around, staring with delight at the assort-ment of two-legged creations that resembled themselves. "Nice going, Pops!" exclaimed Shangdi.

Akua Nui smiled broadly. "Hey, there's a whole bunch of them that look just like *me!*"

Indeed, there were groups of people that bore striking similarities to each of the seven sons in every respect.

Quite pleased with himself once again, God chuckled. "Can I cook, or can I cook?"

Just then Jesus came running up. "Father! The mastodon just stepped on the platypus! It isn't dead, but boy is it messed up!"

Exhausted, God laid his head upon a nimbus cloud pillow and closed his eyes. "I will be *so glad* when this day is over."

And it was so.

As the sun was making its slow ascent along the vaulted dome of the sky on the morning of the seventh day, the sons stared down with dismay at a troubling sight. The trillions of animals, which could eat only vegetation, had stripped every blade of grass and every fruit and every leaf from every plant on the entire surface of the Earth. Their shrieks and barks and howls and cries of hunger echoed throughout the great domed enclosure. And still the humans, the birds and the fish continued to procreate unabated.

"Pops is not going to like this," remarked Shangdi.

Akua Nui frowned. "Well, we have to tell him. We can't just let them suffer like that."

And so they made their way to the great, gleaming palace of gold and marble that God had created for himself. They crept into his resplendent bedchamber. Biff gave Jesus a nudge. "You go wake him up."

"Why me?" asked Jesus.

"Because he won't go all *wrath of God* on *your* ass."

So Jesus approached the slumbering figure. "Um, Father? Father, we need to talk to you. Something is happening down on Earth."

The Old Man gruffled and pulled the cirrus covers over his head. "Screw it, I'm taking the day off."

Wakan Khili took a step closer. "But it really is kind of important."

"Damn it, can't I even get one day of rest?" God propped himself up on his mighty elbows. "All right, just what is so blasted important?"

"It's the animals," said Biff. "They've eaten all the vegetation."

"And then there's the humans," added Shangdi.

"What about them?"

"Well, they're taking that *be fruitful and multiply* thing a bit too far. In fact, that's *all* they've been doing. They haven't even *begun* cleaning up all the piles of shit...and it's getting pretty deep in there."

God ran a weary hand over his eyes. "It seems to me that if the animals stop eating they will also stop shitting. Problem solved."

"But they're still hungry," remarked Akua Nui. "And it's only getting worse, seeing as the birds and the fish and the humans just keep multiplying, yet the food supply does not."

"Fine, fine! Here's what I'll do." God took a deep breath then held out his hand, fingers curled as if he were grasping a huge valve. He turned his wrist. "There. I created a mist over the land to water the plants, and I opened up some underground streams to wash all the shit into the oceans."

Biff frowned. "I don't think the fish are going to be very happy about that."

"Oh, fuck the fish! If they don't like it they can learn to live on land. Now, can I *please* get a little peace and quiet?" As the Sons of God were departing, the Old Man rolled over with a sigh. "I've really gotta get a caretaker for that mess down there. I'm getting too old for this crap."

❖   ❖   ❖

Biff poured himself another goblet of nectar before passing the jewel-encrusted pitcher to his brothers. "Now *this* is what I call Heaven." He stretched himself the full length of the silk-covered purple lounge. "You gotta hand it to Pops. When he creates a paradise he doesn't fool around."

Akua Nui took a handful of grapes and several slices of cheese from a platter perched atop the back of an attending cherub. The four-winged creature with the body of a lion and face of a human fluttered to the next brother. The poor thing looked as if it had been crudely fashioned together using spare parts from other animals.

Shangdi whispered to the others, "Just how drunk do you think Pops was when he created that thing?"

Wakan Khili dipped his fingers into the delectable ambrosia and chuckled. "No drunker than when he created the giraffe! I mean *seriously,* an eight-foot-long neck?"

Taking a deep draught of mead, Tukufu Mungu snickered. "You want to talk about necks? What's up with that brachiosaurus?"

They all had a good laugh over that one.

"If he's supposed to be *perfect*, and everything he creates is *perfect*," Majid Abad said. "How come he makes so many stupid mistakes?"

"Yeah, like putting all those hungry animals down there, then forgetting to make the plants grow," added Wakan Khili. "Not too smart, if you ask me."

Biff snickered. "And what about making whales breathe air out of the top of their heads, and giving them pelvic bones and hand bones, and then sticking them in the ocean?"

"And, and nipples on the *male* animals!" Akua Nui chortled, slapping his thigh. "How twisted is *that?*"

"Anyone notice those blind, naked, mole rats?" Shangdi asked. "Simply *pitiful!*"

"What about the satyrs?" remarked Majid Abad. "Half-man, half-goat. Who is that poor bastard supposed to have sex with?"

"You think that's bad?" said Tukufu Mungu. "What about putting an eight inch penis on the *female* hyenas?"

"No way! *Seriously?*" cried Wakan Khili. "So, how are they supposed to *do* it?"

"Well, when they want to mate, they kind of *suck it up inside.*"

"*No fucking way!*"

"That's not even the worst part," Tukufu Mungu added with a look of disgust. "During birth, the pups *literally* rip their way out!"

Groans of revulsion shuddered through the other sons.

"Half the pups die of suffocation before they're even delivered and twenty percent of the mothers. Those that survive are left with this ragged, torn, bloody—"

"*Enough! Enough!*" Biff cried, struggling to hold down the contents of his stomach. "Holy shit, Pops must've been feeling particularly misogynistic when he pulled that one out of his ass."

Everyone was in agreement that there was a serious *lack* of intelligence in the Old Man's design strategy.

Majid Abad's countenance turned somber as he tried to change the subject. "Really sad what happened to Adam and Eve."

"Yeah, they seemed like such a nice couple," Shangdi added.

Akua Nui nodded. "Kept the Garden real neat. Made sure the rivers kept flowing; never too much or too little water on the plants. Couldn't have asked for better caretakers."

Biff folded his arms behind his head, legs outstretched in full repose. Several fiery seraphim darted about, picking lint and bits of crumbs from his resplendent robes. "That whole *downfall* thing just doesn't make sense somehow."

"What do you mean?" asked Wakan Khili as he sucked warm, golden honey off his fingers.

"Well, if you think about it," Biff explained. "They weren't just perfect, they were *ultra*-perfect. What I mean is, the Old Man didn't just create them like he did all the others—*boink*, there they are. He fashioned them by hand to his own personal specs. And then using Adam's own rib to make Eve. He put some hardcore conscious thought into *that* little conjuring act."

Shangdi's almond-shaped eyes gazed askance at his brothers. "You could almost say they were like the children he never had."

The others chortled.

"But if that were the case, why throw them out like that?" asked Akua Nui. A second cherub waddled in with a tray of bread, milk and mead.

"Well, there *was* that fruit incident," replied Majid Abad, pouring first milk then honey into a goblet.

Biff took a bite out of an apple then hurled the remainder at the head of a circling seraph, missing. The dutiful creature quickly snatched up the discarded fruit and flittered away, chanting the incessant, "Holy, holy, holy, holy, holy, holy, holy...!"

"You really think it's about eating one lousy piece of fruit?" he asked.

Wakan Khili shrugged. "You know what a temper Pops has."

"Come on, we piss off the Old Man on a regular basis, and for a lot worse," remarked Biff, picking his teeth. "No, this was different. This was...*personal*."

"I'll admit," said Shangdi. "Cursing them and all their descendants for all eternity does seem a tad over-the-top."

"Not to mention filling the entire Earth with disease, famine, natural disasters and *death*," agreed Majid Abad. His nose wrinkled with disgust. "Have you *smelled* that place lately? Trust me, death smells a lot worse than shit!"

Wakan Khili's long, black braids swayed gently as he ate. "But I don't get it. If everything was so perfect just the way it was, why fuck it all up by cursing the entire world because two dumb kids ate a stupid piece of fruit? Why not simply take a switch to their butts and be done with it."

Biff's brow furrowed in thought. "That *would* be the easiest and the most logical. Unless..."

Akua Nui leaned forward. "Unless what?"

"Unless he actually *wanted* them to disobey and therefore ruin the whole place for *everybody*."

Shangdi gave his hand a dismissive flip. "That makes no sense at all. They were his most perfect creations."

"Yeah, but what if he made them a bit *too* perfect?" proffered Biff. He threw his legs over the side of the lounge and peered at each brother in turn. "Just why *did* the Old Man create them in the first place?"

Akua Nui shrugged matter-of-factly. "He needed a caretaker, somebody to be in charge of operations."

"Then why didn't he simply choose someone from the humans already there?"

Majid Abad's lips curled into a grin around the rim of his goblet as he sipped his milk and honey. "Because they're a bunch of idiots?"

Biff clapped his hands. "Right! They may have been *created* in our image, but mentally they're about as bright as those baboons. So, he made Adam and Eve special, made them more like...like *him!* And in order to oversee such a huge project, they would almost have to be..."

"*OMNISCIENT!*" they all cried in unison.

"Exactly! Now, suppose they started asking a lot of questions, started thinking...started *reasoning?*"

"Well, they'd soon figure out what a completely retarded situation they were living in," said Shangdi with a snort.

Majid Abad rolled his dark eyes. "And how fallible the Old Man is."

"And that the only reason they were created in the first place was to clean up *his mess*," added Wakan Khili.

"I think it goes even deeper than that," said Biff. "Remember how popular they were with the others?"

"*Adored* would be a better word," replied Akua Nui.

Biff cocked a blond eyebrow. "Or maybe...*worshipped?*"

"Of course!" cried Shangdi. "Adam and Eve *would've* seemed practically godlike to them. So, why put your faith in some unseeable, untouchable, unprovable entity when you can commune with living beings just like yourself?"

Biff shook his head. "I'll bet Pops' *jealousy meter* went off the chart when he saw what was happening."

"And you know how downright wrathful he gets," muttered Majid Abad.

"With his enormous ego, not to mention that galactic insecurity complex, *His Omnipotence* probably saw them as a threat," said Biff.

Wakan Khili nodded thoughtfully. "So, he had to get rid of them, but he had to make it look like an accident."

"He couldn't kill them outright or make it seem as if he were acting out of vengeance," Akua Nui added. "That wouldn't set well with the locals."

The sons were freely exchanging ideas now.

"No, he had to make it look like it was *their* fault; make it appear that *they* were the cause of mankind's downfall."

"So, he plants the *Forbidden Tree* and tells them that it contains all the knowledge of good and evil."

"Didn't he also tell them that if they ate from it they would die?"

"*Pfft*, how the hell were they supposed to know what *death* was when nothing down there had ever *died* before?"

"Chalk that up to another one of Pops' cosmic boners."

"Only problem is, they *didn't* eat the fruit. Not right away, that is."

"No, they had to be goaded into doing it."

"Word has it a talking snake convinced Eve to take the first bite."

"A talking snake, *seriously*? Of all the hundreds of billions of different animals down there, have you *ever* heard one talk?"

"Well, some of the birds can repeat simple phrases. And there's a gorilla that's pretty good at sign language."

"That's not the same. No, this thing was *sentient*. In fact... I'm betting it was one of those angels in disguise. You know how loyal they are to the Old Man."

"Like his own private militia. Even *I* watch what I say when I'm around those guys."

"OK, so the snake-angel talks Eve into taking the bite, she gets Adam to do likewise, and it's *lights out in Paradise*."

"Brilliant! So Adam and Eve get the blame for subjecting all of mankind to death, disease and various unspeakable horrors, and Pops comes out looking like the wounded father figure."

"But what about the poor animals? They didn't do anything wrong, so why torture them as well? I mean, ripping each other apart! It's *barbaric!*"

"Look, the Old Man was gonna have to invent death eventually, right? I mean, how long did he think the fish and the birds and the humans could go on *being fruitful and multiplying* before they filled that damn dome to the rafters? This way, he's able to fix the problem, put the smite down on Adam and Eve in the process, and get his master-of-the-universe mojo back. Win-win-win!"

"Still, rather than go through all the histrionics and hoopla, why not just fix everything with a simple *blink*. Shouldn't be too difficult for a being that is supposed to be all-knowing, all-wise and all-powerful."

"Or maybe it's just more fun to watch them suffer," remarked Biff. "You know, like pulling the wings off a seraph." One of the pesky flying creatures was just about to pluck a dab of ambrosia from Biff's collar, then made a sudden course correction.

"Well, Pops can certainly get his fill of that now," remarked Wakan Khili with a discomfited grimace. "I mean, have you actually *seen* a woman giving birth? That is seriously *messed up!*"

"Best of all," said Majid Abad, trying to shake that last image from his thoughts. "Now he has the *fear factor* working for him. If they step out of line, he smites them. If they lift a finger on his resting day—*smite!* If they try to worship anyone else—*smite!* If they don't love him unconditionally—*smite!*"

Biff wiped his mouth on the sleeve of his robe. A seraph swooped in to clean the garment. Biff reached out suddenly and flicked it with his finger, sending the creature into a flaming *holy, holy, holy, holy, holy, holy, holy...!* tailspin. "Yeah, kind of blows that *freewill* clause right out a black hole," he said.

Shangdi stretched his arms over his head and yawned. "I am sooooo bored. Anybody up for a game of *Asteroids?*"

"Naw," said Tukufu Mungu. "The last time we did that we wiped out an entire epoch. Pops is still fuming over that one."

A lascivious grin spread across Biff's exquisitely crafted countenance. "Hey, have any of you noticed those scrumptious Earth babes lately?"

Majid Abad nodded with a smile. "Yeah, pretty hot stuff. And not nearly as hairy as before." He turned to Biff. "Say, are you thinking...?"

"Whoa, dudes," cautioned Akua Nui, sitting upright. "You know how Pops feels about violating the *Prime Directive.*"

Biff leaned forward, hands resting upon his knees. "Hey, what he doesn't know... Besides, we'll go in disguise. Who's with me?"

Wakan Khili stood up and scratched his crotch. "Well, it sure beats laying around here playing *cream-the-cosmos.*"

And so the Sons of God decided to journey down to Earth for some supernatural sexual recreation with the daughters of mankind.

Now, in those days mankind had separated themselves into groups based on their physiological likeness to one another. They had also begun to travel far and wide in search of larger hunting grounds, the new concept of consuming animal flesh being a vast improvement over eating salad every day. But because of God's all-encompassing curse, the world was now a harsh place, filled with danger and catastrophe and sorrow and thorns. Pain and suffering and hardship of one kind or another were everywhere, and this pleased God, because after all, he had sent these troubles among them, cursed them all for the transgression of The Two.

Still, the humans persevered as best they could. They clung to one another for comfort and support. They established families, communities, villages and towns. They worked the land and domesticated livestock. They sang together in times of joy and commiserated with one another in moments of grief. In spite of all the misery and privations, they learned to rely on one another, find strength in their common need. And as their courage and self-reliance and love for one another grew, they turned away from the invisible, unspeaking, uncaring god whose only action had been to inflict upon them undeserved misery. The Sons of God saw all these things, and saw for themselves a perfect opportunity to have a little fun.

As they were making their way out of the palatial gardens an all-too-familiar voice caught their ears. "Where are you guys going?"

Biff came to a dead halt. "*Jesus Christ!*" he muttered under his breath. Forcing his annoyance into check, he turned to see the youngest son standing beneath the pink marble archway. "Hey, little bro!" he smiled through clenched teeth. "Didn't know you were there."

"Are you planning to go down to Earth?"

Biff glanced at the others. "What? Earth? That stink hole?"

"You know Father doesn't approve of that."

Shangdi stepped forward. "Uh, the Euphrates is backed up again, flooding the whole damn place. We thought we'd just go down and give it a shove."

"*All* of you?" asked Jesus, his suspicion obvious.

"Well... It *is* a pretty big river," said Tukufu Mungu, clumsily grasping for an answer.

Jesus' eyes narrowed. "If there *is* a problem I think Father should know about it."

The sons shot desperate glances at one another. As Jesus was turning to leave, Biff caught him by the shoulders. "OK, here's the deal," he told his youngest brother. "Pops' birthday is coming up, and we wanted to get him something really special."

"His birthday?" scoffed Jesus. "How can he have a birthday? He wasn't *born*. He's just always *been*."

Majid Abad took the cue. "Well, sure. And don't you think that's kind of sad? I mean, there he is, the creator of *everything*, and yet he's never had his own special day."

"That's right," Akua Nui added with a furtive wink at his brothers. "We wanted to get him the perfect gift. And what better place to look than the creation he's most proud of?"

Jesus pondered this for a moment. "How come you never told *me?*"

"I guess..." Biff thought hard. "I guess we didn't know if we could trust you to keep it a secret. Can we?"

A smile brightened Jesus' already effulgent countenance. "Sure! But I want to come too. I want to help pick out the present!"

The older sons collectively ground their teeth as they watched Jesus bound off toward the ethereal layer that separated the nebulous realm of Heaven from corporeal existence. "Man, this is *not* how I envisioned getting laid for the first time," grumbled Shangdi.

"How are we supposed to get jiggy with the Earth chicks with the kid hanging around?" Tukufu Mungu asked.

Biff scratched his head. "I'll think of something. He likes dinosaurs. Maybe I'll find him a damn triceratops to ride. That ought to keep the little bastard entertained for awhile."

And so they descended to Earth, each one in his own special way in order to impress the particular group of people that were created in his image.

With his golden locks falling about broad, alabaster shoulders, Biff summoned a great whirlwind of pure light to bear him earthward. Tukufu Mungu's ebony skin shone like exquisitely cut obsidian as he mounted the gem-covered chariot drawn by two magnificent lions. A fearsome looking dragon with emerald scales and ruby eyes became Shangdi's conveyance. Placing several colorful feathers in his long braids, Wakan Khili conjured for himself a winged stallion with a bold, spotted coat. Akua Nui made a rolling gesture with his arms, and a great cloud began to build like an enormous wave in the cosmos. Laughing with delight, he leapt onto a polished teak board and rode the wave down to Earth. From the very fabric of creation, Majid Abad wove a resplendent carpet with multi-colored tassels and shimmering gold coins. He took a seat in the middle of the carpet, folded his bronzed arms across his chest and arose with the celestial winds.

Jesus, complying with his Father's Noninterference Directive, donned an invisibility cloak and snuck down like a thief in the night.

And so the Sons of God descended to Earth, to every far-reaching corner of the great terrestrial plane where Mankind had spread. When the people beheld these fearsome yet magnificent beings coming out of the great sky dome they were filled with terror and threw themselves facedown upon the ground. The sons, thoroughly enjoying the prostrate reception accorded them, reassured the trembling populations that they came in peace. They dwelt among the humans and showed them many marvelous things like building irrigation canals, fashioning farming and carpentry tools, selectively breeding their livestock and rotating their crops. They taught them how to watch the heavens and predict the seasons. They taught them writing and counting and how to make and dye textiles and produce goods for trading with the others. But most important, they taught them how to improve their lives through some desperately needed sanitation. And they told them wonderful stories of heavenly realms and other worlds, most of which was total bullshit, but the humans really ate it up.

So grateful were the humans that they built beautiful shrines for the sons and filled the shrines with the most fragrant flowers and spices and offerings of every sort. They grew to love the sons of their god, adore them, even worship them. And the young women! Willingly, *eagerly* they came and made offerings of themselves to the handsome god-sons. With perfumed hair and honeyed lips they danced and sang and made music for the enjoyment of their celestial lords.

Reveling in the full, ripe, sensual bounty spread before them, the Sons of God partook with epicurean abandon. Their passions knew no bounds, their penises no bridle. They took as many women as they could. Took them *all*. Took them *often!* And when the fires of even *their* immortal lust had at last been quenched, they spirited away to the top of the highest mountain to commune with one another and reflect. "I think I could get used to this kind of lifestyle," said Biff, arms folded behind his head as he reclined against a lofty crag.

Smiling, Tukufu Mungu nodded. "Yeah, this *being worshipped* gig is awesome! No wonder Pops is so into it. I mean, just listen to them down there…"

They all gave ear to the mellifluous sounds rising up from every population on the great plane. "Praise be to the Son of God! He has shown us many wonders and eased our burdens!" chanted some, while others intoned, "A god we can see and hear and touch is better than one we cannot! For Yahweh is invisible and speaks to us not, yet he gives us pain and death and multiplies our sorrows."

Biff chuckled. "Can you imagine what the Old Man would say if he heard *that?*"

"He'd probably shit a constellation," remarked Shangdi.

31

"Well, it's his own damn fault," said Majid Abad, swirling his finger to create a lovely cloud pattern for the amusement of his people below. "If he weren't such a narcissistic, demanding hothead the humans might be a bit more inclined to throw a little love *his* way."

"*Love*?" Wakan Khili snorted. "Love for *what?* Sending death and disease and every sort of misery you can image upon them? Even *he* can't be so dense as to think they would return love for *that*. The only thing he's got going is the *fear factor*."

Akua Nui peered down at his shore-dwelling people as they struggled to master the technique of casting the fishing nets he had shown them how to weave. Smiling, he nudged a school of mackerel into their nets. "I think I'm beginning to understand this whole *children of God* thing," he told his brothers. "It really is kind of fun watching them learn and grow and try new things, giving them a little help along the way. Makes me feel all warm and paternal inside."

Pulling himself upright, Biff stretched. "Well, speaking of *children of God*, I think we better get topside before Pops discovers we're gone."

The words had not drifted far from his lips when there came a thunderous explosion that rocked the entire terrestrial plane. Shock waves reverberated throughout the firmament until it seemed the great vaulted dome itself might split in two! Massive tidal waves swept away entire communities from the coastal areas. Inland cities were crushed beneath landslides. Screaming in terror, the humans tried to find shelter. They ran to their shrines, but their gods were not there. Hands clasped in piteous supplication, they cried out for help.

The sons shot desperate glances at one another. They didn't have to ask what was happening. They *knew*.

"*Shit!*" remarked Biff. "Well, I guess it's time to face the music."

They found the Old Man seated in his jewel-encrusted golden throne, fingers curled like claws, tearing at the plush upholstery. His face was so red with rage that even his hair and beard were tinged pink. His eyes were molten fury. "What the *fuck* have you done?" he thundered.

The sons turned *en masse* toward Biff, the eldest. None too pleased at being designated the spokesman for the group, he took a hesitant step forward. "Hey, Pops... We were just having a little fun. No big deal."

"*No big deal?* You *know* my policy regarding interference!"

Just then Jesus peered around the back of the great throne. "I told them they shouldn't do it, Father," he said with a smirk. "They only went down there to have *s-e-x* with the Earth women."

Biff clenched his fists. "Why, you rotten little fink!"

Shangdi leaned toward Biff and whispered, "I thought you got rid of him."

Biff leaned back. "I *gave* him a herd of Iguanodons to play with. I didn't think the little bastard would actually *spy* on us."

"*Shut up!* All of you!" God commanded. He stood up and began to pace across the firmament. The weight of his angry steps created great peals of thunder below and caused the waters contained therein to heave in mighty tidal waves. He thrust his almighty finger earthward. "Do you see what you have done?"

The sons gazed downward. Akua Nui gave a meager shrug. "All we did was provide them a little technical support."

"Yeah, show them how to better utilize some natural resources," agreed Majid Abad.

Wakan Khili nodded. "We just wanted to help make their lives a bit easier."

God's eyes narrowed threateningly. "I didn't *want* their lives to be easier!" he growled. "I *wanted* them to know hardship and pain and suffering. I *wanted* them to know the penalty for *disobedience!*"

Having had enough of the Old Man's *mightier-than-thou* attitude, Biff squared his shoulders. "This isn't about obedience. This is about *control*. You gave them minds, you gave them hearts, you gave them souls, and you gave them freewill. And now that they're using them, you can't stand that they are relying on themselves and each other for their wellbeing and not on *you*."

"Nonsense!"

"But most of all," Biff continued. "You're pissed off because they put their faith in something they could actually *see* and *understand*; something that would *benefit* them, not torture and terrify them."

Emboldened by his brother's defiance, Wakan Khili stepped up. "You're just plain *jealous*."

"OK, fine. Call me jealous. I'm a jealous god," the Old Man shot back. "But this is still *my* universe, and I'll run it any way I see fit!"

Now Shangdi joined them. "Well, maybe if you hadn't been such a colossal dick about it, all those angels wouldn't have revolted against you!"

Biff snickered. "Sure doesn't say much about your managerial skills when a third of your employees walk out on you."

The Old Man's eyes turned to fiery slits. "And I suppose you think you could do a better job, hotshot?"

Biff folded his arms across his chest. "Yeah, I think I could."

"Think you could handle the responsibility of creating and orchestrating an entire cosmos?"

"Absolutely."

"OK then, Mr. Responsibility. Take a look down there at what you and your *responsible* brothers have done."

Their expressions turned puzzled, then shocked, then intrigued as they peered down at the strange, enormous creatures moving among the humans in the various populations of the Earth.

"What *are* those things?" asked Majid Abad as he stared at the giant beings.

"Nephilim," God replied with a barb of derision. "Your *offspring*."

"Our *what*—?"

God breathed a sanctimonious sigh. "You were all so damn preoccupied with polluting yourselves with women, you never even considered what the consequences of your actions might be."

Akua Nui rubbed a bronzed hand across his mouth. "Those are our…*children?*"

"Abominations!" growled God. "*Monsters* that possess qualities both human and godlike."

"*Godlike?*" queried Tukufu Mungu. "You mean, they have our powers?"

Brows knit in anger, the Old Man nodded. "Yes, but not for long." He held his arms widespread.

Biff rushed forward. "What are you going to do?"

"These evil things must be destroyed!"

The other sons rallied behind Biff. "You can't just kill them," cried Wakan Khili. "They're our children…your *grand*children! Surely you can see some part of yourself in them."

God glanced downward once more. All over the earthly plane the humans had rebuilt their shrines and temples in homage to the enormous offspring of their benevolent gods. They danced and sang songs of praise to the Nephilim. Their hearts were filled with love and rejoicing, but not in any heart could be found a remembrance of the vindictive god who had banished Adam and Eve and plagued all living things with myriad sorrows. They had forgotten. They had grown afar. They had found new gods, gods not only like themselves but *of* themselves. Under the tutelage of these gigantic man-gods the humans too were becoming godlike, with knowledge and wisdom that would soon enable them to unlock the secrets of the universe for themselves.

God's wrath waxed hot at the revelation. His jealousy was like the molten fire that spewed forth from the bowels of the celestial core. Clenching his fists until all of Creation trembled with his rage, he roared, "*Ungrateful bastards!* I'll show them who their one true god is. I'll *destroy* them! I'll destroy *everything*; every man, every woman, every child; *all of them*, including the beasts and birds and insects and the dinosaurs. I'm so sick of all this shit! I'm sorry I ever made that goddamned world!"

The Sons of God stared at one another, shocked and horrified. "He's lost his fucking mind!" murmured Biff.

"What can we do?" whispered Shangdi. "We can't just let him destroy the Earth—and our *children!*"

Majid Abad shook his head. "He's too powerful. He could destroy us too!"

"What if we combined our powers?" Akua Nui suggested. "Six against one."

Biff's gaze narrowed upon Jesus standing at the Old Man's right side. "Better make that six to one-and-a-half. You know that smarmy little twerp will side with Pops."

"I say we do it," whispered Tukufu Mungu. "Personally, I'd rather face oblivion than kowtow to a psychotic, baby-killing asshole like him."

It was agreed. To save their progeny, to save the people and the world they had come to cherish, they would wage an all-out offensive to overthrow the most powerful being in the cosmos. With a mighty roar of courage and conviction they rushed to stay the wrathful hand of God!

They lost, and in a flash were disintegrated.

With an air of supernal smugness, God lowered himself onto the resplendent throne. "If I told those dumbasses once, I told them a thousand times," he muttered. "I brought you into this universe and I can take you out."

Jesus came and stood at his right side. "Where did you send them, Father?"

"Under the Earth with the rest of those traitors. Let's see how they like a few millennia of total darkness."

"Are you gonna destroy the Earth now, Father?" Jesus asked with a little leap of anticipation.

"I sure am, Son. I just need to work out a few details first." God stroked his long, white beard. Several chanting seraphim swooped in to remove the loose hairs. "Let's see... If I kill everybody then there won't be anyone left to worship me and sing my praises and love me unconditionally. Then too, if I destroy the whole world I'll have to go through that damn process of re-creating everything. And of course there's the matter of *how* to do it. I need something big, something that will tell the humans, *you fuck with me again, you'll get even worse the next time!*"

Jesus climbed onto his father's almighty lap for a better view of the destruction. "I'll bet the *new* humans won't give you any trouble," he said, snuggling close.

God patted his son's honeyed locks. "Oh, eventually they will. In fact, the next batch will be even worse than the first ones."

Jesus peered up, puzzled. "So, why don't you just make them so they *can't* be bad or disobedient?"

"Oh, I could if I wanted to," replied God. "But in order for me to be certain that they really love me, I have to challenge their faith. That's why I allow pain and disease and suffering in general; so I know who the true believers are. And I gotta tell you, Son," God said with a chuckle. "Being worshipped is a hell of a rush."

"I want to be worshipped too, Father!" Jesus cried jubilantly.

God's heart swelled with parental pride as he gazed down at the radiant lad. "I think I might just be able to arrange that, Son."

As he contemplated mankind's utter destruction, God tapped his sandaled foot, causing great ripples in the liquid firmament that covered the sky dome. He thought for a moment then smiled. "I knew I'd find a use for this stuff one day."

ℬ . . . ℭ

Now, wasn't that just the silliest creation story you have ever read? And yet, if you have actually read the Bible you know that it contains *many* silly stories. The purpose of my own narrative is to examine the plausibility of God having sons. I used the creation scenario because logically the "sons" would have been sprung into being when Yahweh conjured up all the other heavenly host. And even though they are not mentioned until Chapter 6 of Genesis, they would have, nonetheless, been present to witness their "all-knowing, all-powerful" father's amazingly *illogical* and downright stupid engineering decisions.

When readers are confronted by the passage, "Let us make man in our image, after our likeness..." (King James Version of Genesis 1:26), the logical follow up question would have to be, who is the *"us"* and the *"our"* God is talking to? Justifiably confused and often embarrassed, some believers will say, "He was talking to Jesus," or "He was talking to the angels," or "That's just the way people talked in the old days." So in essence, they don't know either.

Now, when you ask them who the sons of God were, the majority will stare at you blankly for a moment then mutter, "God only had *one* son—Jesus." Show them the actual passage—pointing out that part about having sex with Earth women—and you'll hear crickets. The more learned among believers, the ones who have actually read the texts or heard the question before and have had time to prepare their defense, will boldly tell you, "It's a metaphor. The sons of God were the offspring of Seth," or "They are the fallen angels." The *one thing they will never admit* is that God did in fact have sons—*plural*. To do so would not only belie the uniqueness of their Christ persona, it would also cast the Bible god into the same mythological category as Zeus, Odin, Coronus, Osiris and Vishnu, all of whom were "alive" at the same time or even before the Bible stories were concocted (or *plagiarized*), and *all of whom* fathered sons—typically with Earth women—many times over! These gods, so much like ourselves in every way, really knew how to rock the cosmos, and they weren't afraid to show it! It is only the Hebrew god, Yahweh, who seems to find physical sexual intercourse so repugnant that he cannot force himself to *do it*, even in order to bring himself into the world as his own son, Jesus.

As I said, the creation story as described in Genesis is not only silly and illogical, it is *impossible* by every scientific principle we know to be true today. It's hard to imagine that there actually was a time when people believed the Earth was a flat plane surrounded by oceans, and that the sun, moon and stars were "stuck" to the underside of a gigantic dome that revolved around that earthly plane. I can just hear a young Bronze Age goat herding lad asking his father, "Why is the sky blue?" And his equally Bronze Age goat herding father would reply with certainty, "The sky is blue because water is blue, and up there is where God put the other half of the water when he divided it." Makes perfect sense...if you have the mental reasoning powers of a Bronze Age goat herder.

What I find particularly disturbing, however, is that even today in the 21st Century, there are *still* people who believe the Earth is flat, *and* that it is the center of the universe. This is no joke! They call themselves (what else?) *Flat Earthers* and *Geocentrists*. They even have websites. They hold meetings.

They publish books expounding their doctrines. They also sell coffee mugs and T-shirts. And they are as devout in their beliefs as any other religion-based, tax-exempt group of superstition peddlers. In fact, they can show you numerous passages *in the Bible* that very clearly support their *myth*-theology. Nut jobs, you say? Well, of course they are. But really, are the tenets of their faith any nuttier than those of people who continue to believe in a talking snake, a virgin birth, guardian angels, walking on water or a man living for three days inside a really big fish?

As I mentioned at the beginning, the biblical passage describing the sons of God and their horny exploits is brief and not very detailed. This is typical of the vast majority of passages in the Bible. They state a "fact" but give no sustentative evidence, no reason for a thing happening. That's because "faith" is supposed to fill in the gaps. Believers are cautioned not to think, just *believe*. Religion as a whole is built on the adage "Ignorance is Bliss". If human society had followed that rule literally, we would still be nothing more than bucolic Bronze Age goat herders.

I'm not going to dissect each and every completely ludicrous aspect of the creation story, tempting though it might be. Suffice to say that nearly every ridiculous, nonsensical and impossible thing that Yahweh does in my version can be backed up by passages from the Bible. (And I wasn't joking about the female hyenas with eight-inch penises!) I would, however, like to say a few words about the "Adam and Eve" myth.

One of the first fairy tales children are taught in Sunday School is that Adam and Eve were the first two people on Earth, and from them came all the other people. This brings up the ticklish and embarrassing problem of *whom* did Cain marry after he left home? The obvious answer is that he had to have taken one of his own sisters (even though no sisters are mentioned in the Book of Genesis until much later). This then would constitute a glaring case of sibling incest.

I have spoken with religious persons—Jehovah's Witnesses in particular—who affirm that, yes, Cain did indeed marry his own sister, and that it was not only necessary, because there *were* no other women to marry, it was also "safe" in the biological sense, since humans at that time were still so close to their "perfect, god-made state" there would be virtually no chance of genetic damage occurring. (I just love the way they use "science" when it benefits their argument.) And besides, that "commandment" about not marrying your blood kin didn't come about until several books later, therefore it doesn't count.

What astounds me is that these believers willingly swallow this holy baloney without question and certainly without even reading the book from which it comes. For if they *had* read Genesis they would see that the very first chapter clearly states that *man* (the New International Version Bible says man*kind*) was created on Day *Six*, after which a tired old Yahweh had to rest up for a day. Adam and Eve are not even mentioned until the *eighth* day. In fact, Genesis 2:2 states categorically, "And on the seventh day God ended his work which he had made; and he rested on the seventh day from all his work which he had made." It isn't until Genesis 2:7 that we read, "And the LORD God formed man of the dust of the ground, and breathed into his nostrils the breath of life; and man became a living soul." And it isn't until Verse 19 that the name "Adam" is even mentioned.

What this all boils down to is there were probably already hordes of humans running around, fornicating their brains out long before Adam and Eve showed up. So it stands to reason that Cain had quite a selection of ladies to choose from. Why so many "believers" continue to insist that Adam and Eve were the *first ever humans on Earth* is truly astonishing, especially when their own "infallible" book clearly states otherwise. But, such is the power of willful ignorance and some crafty *sleight-of-tongue* preaching.

The next great curiosity we encounter are the Nephilim, the offspring, the race of "giants" that were created when the sons of God had sex with Earth women. Here, as with nearly every other religious topic, you will find camps of believers who are stanchly and vehemently at theosophical odds with one another over what these words and passages mean. Again, some—those who claim the "sons of God" is a metaphor for the descendents of Seth—believe that "giants" too is a metaphorical reference, not to physical stature, but to *political* and/or *social* stature, e.g. a powerful human king might be called "a *giant* among men". Pretty boring and not very imaginative.

Then there are those who insist that the "sons" were fallen angels, demons who sought to muddy up the human gene pool by breeding a race of monsters filled with evil intentions. These believers don't necessarily stipulate a physical size, only that the Nephilim were some really badass dudes bent on turning the people away from Yahweh's benevolent wrath. (Side note: While the Christian Bible says amazingly little about the Nephilim and what they did, the Hebrew scriptures go into glorious and specific details about how the Nephilim would fornicate not only with human females, but with animals too, a process called *zoophilia*, creating all manner of weird, "impure" creatures like centaurs and satyrs. But what's even worse, those nasty Nephilim persuaded the *humans* to have sex with animals, and the animals of one species to have sex with animals of a different species, which even further screwed up God's "perfect plan".

One can only imagine the hideous monstrosities these matings would have caused: A giraffe with a hippo's head; a woman's torso with a fish's tail; a flying, fire-breathing chicken-snake hybrid, known in the Bible as a cockatrice; the entire Negro race, which—according to Seventh-day Adventist co-founder Ellen G. White—was a result of God's "pure white race" mating with monkeys and apes. *All this*, the believers state with unequivocal conviction, was the reason God decided to destroy the entire world with a flood. So there you have it. Perfectly logical in every way...except one: *IT IS COMPLETELY AND GENETICALLY FUCKING IMPOSSIBLE!*

What the Hebrew scriptures also say about the Nephilim is that they brought fire to the humans (just like the Greek god Prometheus) and taught them astronomy, agriculture, livestock management and other forms of "sorcery" that made them able to rely on themselves and each other and not on The Big Y. Well, if that's not a good reason to drown an entire planet, then I don't know what is.

Now, as to the actual size of the Nephilim. Here too you will find answers that run the theological gamut from the ridiculous to the *super* ridiculous. The Hebrew book of Enoch 7:11-12 says, "And the women conceiving brought forth giants, Whose stature was each three hundred cubits. These devoured all which the labor of men produced; until it became impossible to feed them." OK, let's see... A cubit is 18 inches; therefore, 300 cubits X 18 = 5400 inches or *450 FEET!!!* Now that is *one BIG giant!* It's no wonder the next two verses continue, "...When they turned themselves against men, in order to devour them; And began to injure birds, beasts, reptiles, and fishes, to eat their flesh one after another, and to drink their blood." With all those 450-foot-tall carnivorous giants lumbering about, you'd think the sensible thing for God to do would be to simply *let* them eat everything and everyone into extinction. Then, with nothing left to eat, they would have to eat each other until there was only one hungry giant left, and he would eventually starve...after gnawing off his own fingers, toes, legs, arms and various internal organs.

The Christian King James Version Bible recounts a much

more "realistic" stature of said giants. In the Book of Numbers (Chapter 13, Verse 33) we read that when the Hebrew spies returned to Moses after scoping out the land of Canaan for an upcoming unprovoked attack of bloody, genocidal conquest they said, "And there we saw the giants, the sons of Anak, which come of the giants: and we were in our own sight as grasshoppers, and so we were in their sight." So, the Hebrew spies are saying they were the size of grasshoppers compared to the giants. (I'm not going to break it out mathematically, but that makes the giants "only" about 182 feet tall!)

Some of you might have noticed the scriptural *faux pas* here: The Book of Numbers comes well *after* the Great Flood which wiped out every living thing on the planet. So, if the Nephilim too were wiped out, where did *these* giants come from? Believe it or not, there are people walking the Earth today who—with a straight face and in all sincerity—will tell you, "Well, since the giants were so tall, all they had to do was climb the highest mountain and wait out the flood." (I'm not even going to respond to that.)

The Jewish Midrash (a book that tries to add logic to the illogical) suggests that the last surviving Nephilim, King Og of Bashan, to be exact, snuck aboard Noah's Ark unseen and hid in a secret compartment until the flood was over. *REALLY?* A nearly two hundred-feet tall giant "snuck" aboard the Ark and managed to "hide" for the entire duration of the voyage? (I'm not going to respond to this either.) Another, far more sensible argument is that he simply clung to the outside of the hull for the duration of the flood, either 40 or 150 days, whichever contradictory verse you choose to believe.

Still another opinion has it that while Noah himself was as pure as the driven snow (despite those bouts of drunkenness and cursing), his wife and the wives of his sons were still carrying some of that corrupted Nephilim DNA. Ergo, when these women began popping out babies, that giant-producing genetic material would once more be released into the world. (Don't you think an "all-knowing" god would have seen that coming?)

Speaking of God, there is a very revealing "character flaw" that appears in the Hebrew Book of Jubilees 10:8-9. It reads, "When Mastema (Satan), the leader of the spirits, came, he said: 'Lord creator, leave some of them (the Nephilim's disembodied spirits) before me; let them listen to me and do everything that I tell them, because if none of them is left for me I shall not be able to exercise the authority of my will among mankind. For they are meant for destroying and misleading before my punishment because the evil of mankind is great.' Then he (God) said that a tenth of them should be left before him, while he would make nine parts descend to the place of judgment." (I added the parentheses for clarity.)

What this passage is telling us is that while God had the perfect opportunity to destroy Satan, his demon buddies and wickedness in general for all time, he *deliberately chose* to keep ten percent of the Nephilim's evil spirits alive for Satan to use against mankind. In other words, Satan—despite his rotten, loathsome, despicable malevolent nature—was nothing more than an agent, a *spy* working for Yahweh. It is clear, therefore, that God never had any intention of getting rid of evil. "Evil" was simply a tool he used to torture and torment the puny, imperfect mortals whose complete submission and worship he demanded under pain of an even worse—and eternal—punishment.

Like the "Flat Earth" folks I mentioned earlier, there are also tiny pockets of Bible-based pseudo-scientists who claim the Nephilim were quite real, and their bones have been discovered in various places across the planet. One such find made in the early 1800s turned out to be the remains of a mastodon. Others have proven to be glaring hoaxes. If you are interested in knowing more, there is plenty of this *dis*information available on the Internet or YouTube.

So obviously there are as many ways to interpret scripture as there are sects, cults and denominations (and there are over *40,000* Christian sects alone!) It's pretty clear by all the wildly varying opinions and outright infighting that *no one* has the definitive answer. Believing the Nephilim really were multi-storied giants who walked the Earth and ate people alive makes as much sense as believing in Paul Bunyan, Jack and the Beanstalk or any of the *thousands* of other folktales found the world over. Was Jesus the one-and-only "son" of God, or did he indeed have a family of sexually promiscuous siblings? The answer to both questions is, "Sure, why not?" The bottom line is, nobody can prove anything one way or the other, even *with* a Bible in hand.

Religion is an ever-changing smorgasbord where believers are free to pick and choose which myth-du-jour suits their spiritual appetite. Don't like what's on the menu? Just wait awhile; some *New Revelation* will be along shortly to tantalize the gullible. But really, with all the amazing marvels that exist in the physical, tangible world, why would anyone insist on feeding their intellect this ridiculous, nonsensical junk food?

Jephthah's Daughter
As Found in the Book of Judges
Chapter 11

Say the words "child abuse" and watch the emotional hackles go up. There is not a parent or compassionate human being on the planet that doesn't bristle with protective instinct at the thought of a child being harmed in any way. It is fundamental to our nature—and the nature of every living thing—to safeguard our offspring. Even so, in today's world there is a lot of heated debate over where to draw the line between discipline and abuse. Fifty years ago an ass-whooping with a belt or a smack in the mouth was considered perfectly acceptable by many parents. Teachers too had far more latitude in handing out corporal punishments. And often enough, when the chastised child got home with a note explaining his transgression, he would likely receive another dose of discipline from his old man. Here again we can thank "Bible wisdom" which gives us the famous line, "Spare the rod and spoil the child."

But I wasn't talking about discipline; I was talking about abuse: the flagrant, willful, even premeditated physical or emotional harming of a child. Now add to that the caveat, "in the name of religion", and the mind reels with grisly images of Satanic rituals and sexual mutilation. Surely the Bible—that most holy of holies—would not contain, much less condone, such atrocities. (Well, except for that male circumcision thing. But God told them to do it, so that one's OK, right?) The God of Love would never just come out and tell someone to hurt—or worse—murder their child. Oh, but then there's the *Abraham and Isaac* story, where God commanded Abraham to slaughter his one and only son as a sacrifice. But that story had a happy ending, so no harm done, psychological trauma to father and son notwithstanding. I guess what it boils down to is, one person's definition of abuse is another person's definition of obedience. This now is the story of a man who loved his daughter as much as he loved his god...almost.

Jephthah had a colorful if somewhat unfortunate start in life. His father was an adulterous scumbag who diddled a prostitute and got her pregnant, the resulting bastard child being Jephthah.

For some peculiar biblical reason his father took the boy into his home and raised him alongside his other sons. But the half-siblings (and no doubt the man's unnamed wife) despised Jephthah for his illegitimacy—and potential claim to their father's estate—and brutally tormented him to the point that he left home and went to live in the land of Tob.

Now, Tob was a pretty rough place, full of unsavory characters and criminal types. Fortunately for Jephthah, he was used to having the crap beaten out of him and managed to hold his own against the local riffraff. He gained quite a reputation for being a brawler, and before long he had his own gang of thugs and hooligans roaming about, terrorizing the countryside. (The Bible calls him a "mighty warrior".)

And so it came to pass that the Kingdom of Ammon attacked Israel in an effort to take back the lands the Israelites had stolen sometime earlier. Realizing they didn't stand much of a chance against the powerful Ammonite armies, the leaders of the various Israelite cities called out for someone to lead them. The elders of Gilead (Jephthah's original hometown) said they knew of just such a man. So they set out to find Jephthah, the "great warrior", and beg him to come help them fight against the Ammonites. "Come back with us," they pleaded. "Be our leader and help us defeat the Ammonites!"

Jephthah scoffed at them. "After the rotten way you treated me, laughing and calling me names, *now* you expect me to save your sorry hides?"

"Surely you're not still sore about that," they told him. "Look, if you come back we'll make you the ruler over all of us."

Jephthah stroked his bristled chin and thought. "The ruler over *all* of you? By the LORD you swear?"

"Yes, yes! As the LORD is our witness, whatever you wish! What we're trying to say is, Jephthah, with your sword so bright, won't you help us win this fight?"

The idea of being the supreme ruler over these people who had once treated him like donkey dung pleased Jephthah. And so he returned with the elders, and they made him ruler over all the people of Gilead. Reveling in his newfound good fortune, he took for himself a fine house in Mizpah and called for his family and slaves and livestock from the land of Tob.

The next thing Jephthah did as ruler was to send a message to the King of Ammon, telling him to stand down. The Ammonite king of course refused, and so Jephthah began preparing his armies for war. Before going into battle he made a vow to the LORD: "If you give the Ammonites into my hands, whatever comes out of the door of my house to meet me when I return in triumph will be the LORD's, and I will sacrifice it as a burnt offering." And the spirit of the LORD came upon him to seal the deal.

Then Jephthah led the armies of Israel against Ammon. Twenty towns he attacked, slaughtering the inhabitants and vanquishing them because the spirit of the LORD was with him, guiding him and supporting him.

Weary from battle but victorious, his donkeys laden with treasures, Jephthah returned to his home. His sword and dagger were still coated with the dried blood of his enemies as he trudged up the gently winding road that led to the fine house surrounded by rolling pastures and abundant orchards. The LORD had been good to him, he thought. Never had he known such grand accommodations in Tob. He recalled the small, dirt floor hovel, chickens and goats running in and out, shit everywhere! And that fat, worthless cow of a wife. A chieftain's daughter—*ha!* She was more of a liability than an asset. Not even pleasant to look at anymore. And what had she given him? Only *one child*, and a girl at that. Doubly worthless!

Jephthah's thoughts twisted inside his head. He could just imagine his selfish, greedy wife up there in that fine house with servants waiting on her hand and foot, feeding her like some sacrificial heifer. *Exactly like a sacrificial heifer*, he mused. After all these years he knew her quite well. She would be waiting for word of his arrival. Then, like a jackal set upon a wounded hare, she would lumber through the door, demanding her portion of the plunder. A chuckle rumbled deep in his throat. Yes, the LORD had indeed been good to him. Now there remained but one obligation to discharge: the sacred vow he had made to ensure his good fortune. He chuckled again, this time with delicious anticipation.

The door of the fine house opened and a figure rushed out. But wait—! It was not his wife nor one of her servants, not even the family dog. It was—*his daughter!*

"Father! Father! Welcome home!" the girl cried, playing happy music on her timbrel as she came dancing toward him.

At the sight of his daughter he dropped to his knees and tore his clothes to shreds. "How could you do this to me?" he howled. "I am devastated!"

She stopped and peered at him, shocked and confused. "W-what have I done, Father?"

Fingers curled like claws, he raked his nails across the dry, packed earth. "It wasn't supposed to be *you*. But now you have ruined everything!"

Tears slipped from her soft, sorrowful eyes. "I-I don't understand, Father. Why are you speaking to me this way?"

He struggled to compose himself. "I have made a vow to the LORD that I cannot break."

"A vow, Father?"

His clothes in tatters, he rose to his feet. "Yes. I promised the LORD that should he deliver the Ammonites into my hands, I would make a burnt offering of the first thing that came out of my house. I was hoping it would be your mother."

The girl wiped her tear-stained cheeks then nodded. "Well, if you gave your word, and the LORD has avenged you of your enemies, then you certainly must do to me that which you promised."

He blinked hard and stared at her. "Are you sure you understood what I just said?"

"Yes, Father. I am to be a burnt sacrifice to our loving and most generous LORD."

"I must say you're taking this awfully well," he remarked, scratching his head.

A little smile brightened her countenance. "All I ask is that you allow me two months so that I may wander around in the hills with my friends and bewail the fact that I will never get married or have sex and make babies."

"That's it?" he asked, nonplussed. "You're not planning to run off or anything?"

Smiling, she shook her head.

"Well, all right then, you may go." Bending closer to her, he whispered, "But let's not say anything about this to your mother. Especially the part about me wishing it had been *her*."

And so the girl and several of her friends went into the hills and remained there for two months to bewail the fact that she would never get married, have sex and make babies.

"So let me get this straight," said one of the girls seated upon a mossy boulder. "Your father is going to slaughter you like a goat and burn you on the sacrificial altar because he made a promise to the LORD?"

"That's right," replied the daughter, noshing on a latke.

A third girl popped a fig into her mouth. "Seems a bit excessive, if you ask me."

The daughter smeared a little more butter on her latke and shrugged. "A promise is a promise. Besides, it is the *LORD* we're talking about."

Another girl pressed her lips together in thought. "Doesn't

the Torah *forbid* human sacrifices?"

"That's right!" chimed in the first. "Leviticus 18:21 says, 'Do not give any of your children to be sacrificed to Molek, for you must not profane the name of your God. I am the LORD.'"

The daughter shook her head. "It says not to sacrifice children to *Molek*. It doesn't say not to sacrifice them to Yahweh."

"Still, it could be a loophole."

"But what about Deuteronomy 12:31?" queried another. "It clearly states that we should not worship the LORD in their way, because in worshipping their gods, they do all kinds of detestable things the LORD hates. They even burn their sons and daughters in the fires as sacrifices to their gods!"

Another girl raised her hand with enthusiasm. "Yes! And Deuteronomy 18:10—'Let no one be found among you who sacrifices their son or daughter in the fire, who practices divination or sorcery, interprets omens, practices witchcraft, blah, blah, blah... Anyone who does these things is detestable to the LORD.'"

"There! You see?" cried the first girl. "Your father *can't* sacrifice you. It would be against the Law!"

The daughter sat for a moment, peering at her friends. "You may have a point." Her thoughts brightened. "You know, I'll bet it's a test to prove my father's faith and loyalty!"

"Yes, of course!" the others agreed. "Like when the LORD told Abraham to sacrifice his only son, Isaac, on Mount Moriah to prove his faith."

"Then at the very last moment, the LORD sent an angel to stay Abraham's hand and provided him a ram to sacrifice instead!"

The daughter nodded. "The LORD does know how to build suspense." A smile warmed her features. "Yes, I see his divine purpose now. Oh, I'm so glad we had this talk!" And they all sang and danced in joy and great anticipation.

Meanwhile back at the fine house, Jephthah remained fraught with consternation. He hadn't told his fat wife about his vow to the LORD; he didn't have to. After rousing from her third nap of the day, she had fairly thrown herself upon the bags of treasures he brought. It had been a week before she even asked where her daughter was. "A sleepover with her friends," was all he told her, and that seemed to suffice.

Still reeling from the thought that he would have to slaughter his one and only child to make good on his vow to the LORD, he prayed in great earnest, listening for that still, small voice that would guide him. But when that voice came all it would say is,

"A deal's a deal. You know what you have to do."

At the end of the two month period the daughter returned. Jephthah had to admit he was pretty amazed by her good spirits and almost jovial resignation. "Well, I suppose we better get this over with," he told her.

While his fat wife was napping in the fine house Jephthah took his daughter to the sacrificial altar and told her to disrobe. She obeyed without complaint or modesty. He told her to lie down upon the altar and she did. Next he bound her wrists and ankles. His hands trembled, sweat stung his brow as he tightened the knots.

"Fear not, Father," she told him with that annoyingly complacent smile. "The LORD's will is just."

Grief and anger and guilt crashed through his mind. *Why had he made such a reckless vow? How could she be so damn accommodating?*

His hand was shaking so hard he could barely draw the ceremonial *chalef* from its scabbard. He placed the blade against her throat, held her forehead down with the other hand. *My LORD, I beg you! Please, tell me now to stay my hand!*

But the still, small voice inside his head said, *A deal's a deal.*

Tears blurred his vision. He blinked them away. One stroke of the *chalef*. It had to be done with one single, mighty stroke. His grip tightened. Heart aching with anguish, he took a deep breath, and…

Shock-confusion-agony flashed suddenly in the girl's eyes as the blade sliced through skin, muscle, tendons, arteries, esophagus and trachea. She gasped reflexively, inhaled her own blood through her severed windpipe and choked. A thick, red froth bubbled out of the gaping slash. Her muted lips formed a final word: *"Father?!"*

A cry of sorrow burst from Jephthah's lungs. Falling to his knees, he pressed the bloodied *chalef* against his own throat, ready to give the blade its final sacrifice. But then he remembered that committing suicide was a sin.

His chest heaving, eyes streaming tears, he pulled himself upright and gazed down at her. Movements numbed with grief but well practiced, he cut the ropes on her wrists and ankles, then began the process of preparing her for the fire. First, he slit her body open from ribcage to crotch. Then he removed her kidneys, careful to make sure the fat was still on them, and the long lobe of her liver. These he carefully washed with water and placed on the altar beside her. Next, he reached for the pail of embers. Still hot. He dumped the glowing coals onto the straw kindling below the altar grate. Within moments the fire was roaring all about her lifeless body.

Exhausted, barely able to stand, Jephthah stepped back and watched the flames consume her. His vow had been fulfilled, his faith proven. And the smell of the burning flesh was pleasing to the LORD.

℘ . . . ℜ

This story is so outrageously gruesome that after reading it I didn't know whether to write it as a tragedy or a comedy, so I opted for a little *humour noir*. The actual biblical account is brief, and all of the action takes place in a single chapter, most of which is a bunch of boring, convoluted narrative between Jephthah and the Ammonite king over who is rightfully entitled to the disputed lands. The details about Jephthah and his daughter are sparse and comprise a mere ten short verses. For this reason I had to embellish a bit in order to reconstruct the crime scene from the few fragments of evidence provided.

For instance, in the scriptural account there is no mention at all of Jephthah's wife. I added her as a nonperson character to make his "vow" seem more premeditated (and less stupid). I mean seriously, just who or what *did* he think would come out of the house first? A servant? A dog? A mongoose? Only certain types of "clean" animals were even *allowed* to be used for sacrificial purposes. Did he have these critters just running loose in his home? The whole thing sounds like a set up. He had to believe a *person* would come out. His intent, therefore, was *murder*.

Another feature that is so ridiculous that it's funny is the dialog/interaction between Jephthah and his daughter. It could be summed up thusly: "Jephthah came home and told his daughter that he would have to kill her to fulfill a promise to the LORD, and she said 'OK'." She doesn't argue; she doesn't break down sobbing; she doesn't try to flee; she just accepts her fate with an eerie kind of resignation. What makes this exchange even more repellent, and helps to define Jephthah's true character, is that he actually blames *her* for his lamentable plight by telling her *she* is the one who "brought him down" and "is one of them that troubles him" (depending on which translation you choose). We also find there is nothing to tell us what the daughter and her friends did or said during those two months in the hills (except that they "bewailed her virginity"). Equally important, we get no clue as to what Jephthah himself was doing in that timeframe. He obviously had God's ear, so did he beseech the LORD to forgive his debt or perhaps allow an alternative—

49

and proper—form of sacrifice? Maybe he did, and maybe his god of mercy told him, "A deal's a deal."

Finally, at the most climactic part of the story—the brutal, bloody sacrifice of his one and only child!—we get a paltry nine word denouement: "...and he did to her as he had vowed." My description may have been graphic, but that is precisely how the Bible says a ritual sacrifice is to be conducted. Leviticus Chapter 3 is all about how to kill and disembowel the hapless victim: "...the internal organs and all the fat that is connected to them, both kidneys with the fat on them near the loins, and the long lobe of the liver, which you will removed with the kidneys." The verse concludes by saying that the burning of said organs is "an aroma pleasing to the LORD". (Genesis 29:22 and Leviticus 1:9 also address these grisly protocols.) So you see, Jephthah couldn't simply do the old "kill it and grill it". According to Mosaic Law, he would have had to follow very strict and detailed "Kosher" guidelines which includes the near-severing of the head with a single, quick motion.

As with all the weird and outlandish stories in the Bible, the question must be asked, "Did this *actually* happen?" (Personally, I sincerely hope *not!*) But regardless of whether it is factual or metaphorical, the *bigger* question would have to be, what possible moral or spiritual lesson could be learned from this literary atrocity? Not surprisingly, that debate has been raging for thousands of years. You might even say this filicidal fairy tale has become the bastard child of the Bible. Jewish theologians don't want to take responsibility for it, and Christians will only acknowledge it under certain "modified" conditions. Let's examine the evidence from both sides of the argument.

First, keep in mind that it was the ancient Hebrews who wrote down the original biblical texts, therefore the steaming turd of accountability must fall into *their* laps. As I mentioned, they would prefer to distance themselves from this nasty little nightmare. First and foremost, Jewish theologians are adamant that human sacrifice is *strictly forbidden*. (I used the daughter's "friends" to point this out.) Second, Jews do *not* under any circumstances consider Jephthah one of their biblical heroes. They find his actions deplorable (as would any sane person). The theological position is that the Book of Judges in its standalone context represents a period of great moral disintegration among Israel; a kind of "anything goes" attitude. So in other words, there is no moral to the story itself. Rather, it—and several other equally despicable fables in Judges— demonstrate an obvious *lack* of morality on the part of the general populace. This in itself is a kind of preamble to justify Yahweh smiting the hell out of his wayward chosen people in the future.

Now, there are several very obvious problems with this story from a logistical point of view. If human sacrifice was forbidden, why didn't the daughter or her friends (or Jephthah's wife) speak up and point this out? Why didn't the obviously distraught Jephthah seek out the high priest to have the vow annulled as was permitted by law? Why wasn't Jephthah punished for murdering his daughter? But the biggest question of all is, why did God *allow* him to do it? Remember, "the spirit of the LORD came upon Jephthah", which means they had some kind of ectoplasmic ESP thing going. And since we know that God is omniscient, he *had* to know that the daughter would be the first thing to come out of the house, right? So, in one part of the Bible we hear old Yahweh laying down the law, commanding the people *not* to sacrifice their children as the pagans do, then suddenly he's just sitting there watching his main man Jephthah go *Texas Chainsaw Massacre* on an innocent little girl!

If you're puzzling over these questions and contradictions don't feel bad; you're in good company. As I mentioned, priests, rabbis and theologians of the highest order have been trying to make sense out of this grim, nonsensical tale for a very long time—and they *still* haven't reached a consensus! For our purposes it might help to compare and contrast some key points between this and two other "child sacrifice" stories.

Everyone is familiar with the marvelously sado-masochistic tale of Abraham and his son Isaac. Quick synopsis: God told Abraham to butcher and barbeque his one and only son as proof of his faith. At the last possible second, an angel grabbed Abe's hand, thus preventing the gruesome finale. There is another story with a filicidal theme found in 1 Samuel (14:43-45). King Saul decreed that prior to going into battle all the soldiers had to abstain from eating. The king's son, Jonathan, didn't hear the decree and ate some honey. When Saul learned of this he ordered that Jonathan be sacrificed to appease their bloodthirsty war god. But the other soldiers cried out in protest and thus Jonathan was spared.

The profiles of Isaac and Jonathan are quite similar. Both sons were born into aristocratic families: Isaac, because his old man was chosen by God personally to establish the Hebrew nation; Jonathan, because his dad was the first King of Israel. Both are the heirs apparent to their fathers' dynasties. And most importantly, both were saved in the nick of time. Now consider the daughter of Jephthah. Her father was a bastard and her grandmother a prostitute. Stranger still, she doesn't even have a name. (None of the women in this story do.) Could it be that the author thought her so unimportant, so disposable, that he didn't even bother to give her a name, much less a reason for living...or being *saved* as her male counterparts were? From a dramaturgical standpoint, not naming a character makes them seem "less real" and therefore the crime against them less horrific. In the long run, Jephthah wasn't really losing much by killing her, since she couldn't carry on his family name. God probably figured that too.

Some Jewish scholars suggest that God permitted the homicidal sacrifice to punish Jephthah for his lack of faith before going into battle; the reason being, if Jephthah had had true faith in the LORD, he never would have made that asinine vow in the first place. Others claim that God knew—because he *is* omniscient, remember—that Jephthah intended to kill his wife, so as punishment, he made Jephthah kill his own child instead. Now, God could have taken a big stick and beaten the holy shit out of Jephthah, but he chose instead to let an innocent girl be murdered, dismembered and burned.

Despite all the ambiguities and absurdities that comprise this repellent yarn, Jewish theologians are at least *mensch* enough to own it for what it is. Ask them if they think the story is true and that Jephthah really killed his daughter, far and away they will answer, "Yes, it's true. Jephthah killed his daughter. This was a crazy time in Israel. People did all sorts of *fercockteh* things back then."

When it comes to gerrymandering the facts to fit their religious agenda, nobody beats Evangelical Christians. For a group that believes the Bible scriptures are the actual, factual, indisputable and *literally true* Word of God, they sure seem to spend a lot of time and effort trying to change them. The story of Jephthah and his daughter is a prime example of this. I think we can all agree that if you are not sickened, disgusted and repulsed by this tale, you might be a very disturbed individual who should be seeking professional help. (A lot of Fundamentalists fall into this category. But I'll talk more about them later.) Evangelicals appear to have a bit more compassion for their fellow human beings, which is why they have reworked the sacred, "inerrant" wording to make it appear that the daughter didn't die after all. Instead, according to them, she lived out her life in virginal seclusion. (Just my opinion here, but if that's not a form of *death*, I don't know what is!)

Let's look at how they manage this feat of literary reincarnation. They begin by breaking down two key terms in the text: "vow" and "burnt offering". (In Hebrew these words are "*neder*" and "*olah*".) By using a technique called inductive reasoning, that is, starting with a predetermined hypothesis and then working backward, manipulating the facts to fit—and discarding the ones that don't—they have reached the conclusion that the daughter could not possibly have been killed. Here is how their reasoning goes.

Scenario A: Some ECs like to claim the "vow" had nothing to do with a *burnt* offering, but rather it was a redemption or giving of money to the LORD (a.k.a. the priests) in the name of a person you are "redeeming" to the LORD. (See Leviticus 27:1-8 for a financial breakdown of what a human life is worth.) It's kind of like donating to a charity in the name of your nephew. Your nephew gets the glory and you get the tax deduction. Supposedly Jephthah—really wanting to impress his cosmic bodyguard—was counting on a burly, adult male servant to come out the door first (burly, adult males having the highest redemption value at the Bank of Moses). But then his young, stupid, far-less-valuable, *female* child comes out—*Oiy!* It's no wonder poor Jephthah tore his clothes and blamed her for screwing up his plans. Instead of getting fifty shekels, the priests (I mean, "the LORD"—wink, wink) would only get a lousy *ten*, and Jephthah, as a consequence, would end up looking like a real *shnorer*.

That's an interesting scenario, all right. But it raises more questions than it answers. For instance, why would Jephthah get so upset because his discounted daughter came out first? You would think he'd be thrilled that he wouldn't have to cough up as much cash. Then again, if his heart was so set on making a good show of his generosity and gratitude, couldn't he simply have said to the priests, "Oh, heck. Here, have another forty shekels. *Shalom!*"? Ah, but there's that pesky other issue about the "burnt offering".

Scenario B: Still contending that the vow was a vow of consecration and not kindling, some Evangelical apologists have posited the notion that Jephthah's *neder* was made in public; therefore, numerous people heard it. During his long absence word of this pre-battle promise would naturally have gotten back to his family, including his daughter. So, either she was some kind of suicidal nut job, or she knew beforehand that being "it" had some kind of personal benefit. Here's how our friends from the Church of Perpetual Denial explain it: Jephthah's daughter was old enough (let's say 14) to see that being a married woman with a bunch of kids was a real drag. Since she was an only child, she was likely a lazy, selfish, spoiled brat who didn't want to share anything—especially her future inheritance—with anyone, not even a husband or children. However, if she were to be "consecrated" to the LORD, i.e. remain a vestal virgin for the remainder of her life, she could avoid the drudgery of wifedom and just hang around the tabernacle, being waited on by servants 24/7. *Sweet!* In other words, that crafty little self-serving wench had the whole thing planned from the start. And that bit about "bewailing her virginity" in the hills for two months with her friends? Well, that was just an act to throw her old man off the trail. By all Evangelical accounts they were probably laughing themselves silly and having one hell of a party. (Another oddball explanation claims that the daughter truly *was* sad about being a lifelong prisoner of her idiot father's vow, and that he built her a private chamber where she would live out her life, devoid of all human contact, save for her lady friends who would come around once a year to weep for their friend.)

Again, a very imaginative synopsis. **And completely ridiculous!** But I want to be fair here. First of all, there is *nothing anywhere* in *any Bible* I could find that says Jephthah made his vow to the LORD "in public". This is a classic example of pure fabrication on the part of Christian word-smithers. Here is exactly what he said per Judges 11:30-31 (NIV): "And Jephthah made a vow to the LORD: 'If you give the Ammonites into my hands, whatever comes out of the door of my house to meet me when I return in triumph from the Ammonites will be the LORD's, and I will sacrifice it as a burnt offering.'" This debunks the notion that the daughter had foreknowledge of her fate for good or bad.

Now let's talk about that other word: *olah*, the burnt offering. Those creative creationists really had to work overtime to twist this part of the story into something completely contradictory. They are quick to point out that technically, *olah* doesn't mean "burnt offering" at all; it means "that which ascends" or "goes up" (like smoke). And since the entire point of murdering innocent animals in a ghoulish fashion and then cremating their flesh, bones and entrails is to create "a pleasing aroma (that *goes up*) to the LORD", *olah* by default became synonymous with "burnt offering". And so, by using this transliterated logic, Evangelicals want you to believe that—rather than *burning* his daughter *up*—he *offered* her *up* to the LORD, figuratively speaking. To further punch "up" their argument, some will even claim that Jephthah made a two-part vow: 1) he would burn whatever came out of his house *if* the Law allowed it to be burned, or 2) if the Law disallowed burning it, he would consecrate it to God. That really clears the matter up, except for one tiny detail: *NOWHERE IN THE ENTIRE BIBLE DOES IT SAY ANYTHING OF THE SORT!* They can toss that word salad all they like, but it still comes out, "Jephthah made a vow to the LORD" and "I will sacrifice it as a burnt offering"—*PERIOD*.

This brings us to Scenario C: The Fundamentalist view, i.e. if the Bible says Jephthah killed and burned his daughter, then he killed and burned his daughter. End of discussion. As I mentioned earlier, Jews *do* believe this horrid event took place, but they do *not* condone the action. They view it as a symbol of a very lawless and even paganistic period in Mankind's history as evinced by the last line in the Book of Judges (21:25 KJV): "In those days there was no king in Israel, every man did that which was right in his own eyes."

As I said, true Christian Fundamentalists too believe the event took place just as the Bible says it did. The difference is, they not only *condone* Jephthah's actions, they see him as a shining example of a man whose love for his god was so powerful, no sacrifice was too great in order to prove his faith— up to and including the grisly murder of his only child. Frankly, I find these people downright *scary*. If they can believe—*blindly* believe—that their invisible "morality coach" is OK with a parent murdering his child to demonstrate his devotion and obedience (like Abraham was willing to do), then *what else* might they be willing to do?!

The New Testament Book of Hebrews, Chapter 11, extols the virtues of what early believers of the day considered to be the greatest heroes of the Old Testament; men revered for their courage, strength and—most important—their faith. Verse 11 goes so far as to declare, "The world was not worthy of them." In this group of biblical super mortals you will find Gideon, Barak, Samson, David, Samuel...and Jephthah. *Seriously?* The man who slaughtered and incinerated his daughter just to show his faith and titillate the Almighty's olfactory fancy? Some Fundies will argue that since Jephthah's own character was a bit sketchy (son of a prostitute, et al), it was necessary for God to permit the sacrifice in order to "cleanse" the man's spirit. So, it's all good.

We shouldn't be surprised that Christians are so embar- rassed by this dismally horrific tale that they would go to such lengths to change it. But is it really any worse than that other example of bloody human sacrifice that they revere as the very centerpiece of their faith? If the "Loving Father" could allow his *own* son to be tortured, mutilated and murdered in so grisly and painful a manner, it makes perfect sense that he could accept the death of some nameless, faceless, completely disposable daughter of a whore-spawn.

At the beginning of this chapter I mentioned child abuse and the many forms it can take. Without a doubt what Jephthah did to his daughter in the name of religion was an extreme example. Still, there are other *non-physical* forms of abuse that, while not lethal *per se*, can cause a lifetime of emotional and psychological suffering. For instance, filling children's heads with images of demons, Hell and eternal torture if they misbehave is a cruel and cowardly way to discipline offspring. But it doesn't stop with children. A TV commercial for the faith-spewing *Believer's Voice of Victory* features simpering co-host Gloria Copeland, her voice dripping smooth, Southern sanctimony as she tells the audience, "If you obey God, good things will happen." The alternative being, if you *don't* obey God, bad things will happen (a rather despicable way of blaming the victim). In other words, it's not about *doing* good or *being* good in order to receive good in return; it's about *obedience*: total, unconditional, unthinking, unwavering, absolute *obedience!* This thinly veiled threat of divine retribution is at the core of all faith-based brainwashing cam.

Psychological abuse, while highly effective and detrimental in its own right, carries with it a collateral damage by-product in the forms of fear, condemnation and outright hatred of people, cultures and ideologies outside the status quo. Persons of different skin tone or sexual orientation become easy targets. (And don't even get me started on those *atheists!*) Sanctioned discrimination, defined by religion and ignited by faith, takes on a quasi-noble quality. It subconsciously enables believers to bridge that tenuous gap between the sane and the insane. It also builds a wall between the "us" and "them". While "our" children remain sacred and precious, "their" children become the proverbial "nits that make lice".

In late December of 2014, a bright, attractive, yet deeply troubled 16 year old transgender person, who called herself "Leelah" Alcorn, chose to end her lifelong suffering by stepping in front of a speeding semi-truck. In an online suicide note she recounted that her very distraught, very religious mother had told her, "...it was a phase, that I would never truly be a girl, that God doesn't make mistakes, that I am wrong."

I can't even begin to imagine how much psychological pain it must take to drive a person to such a drastic extreme, yet we read about these kinds of tragedies all too frequently. And at the scene of nearly every crime is the same smoking gun: *Religion.* Contrary to what the pulpit pounders would have you believe, there is no "freewill" in the Bible. It's all about "DO AS I SAY OR I'LL KILL YOU!" (I can't help but picture Adolf Hitler screaming from his podium to the crowds assembled at Nuremburg. When you think about it, the Heavenly Führer isn't that much different.) Absolute faith. Absolute obedience. Take a pledge. Make a vow. Don't ask questions. Follow orders. Pull the trigger. Drop the bombs. Strap thirty sticks of dynamite around your waist and drive headlong into a loaded school bus. If the "still, small voice" tells you to do it and you want to prove your faith, do you really have a choice?

The Levite and His Concubine
As Found in the Book of Judges
Chapter 19, Verse 21 to Chapter 21, Verse 25

Of all the stories in this book, the tale of the Levite and his Concubine was by far the most difficult for me to write—and it will be the most difficult for you to read as well. I'll tell you right now, it does not have a happy ending. But then, few stories in the Bible do, especially if the characters happen to find themselves on the "wrathful" side of the Old Testament's main villain, Yahweh.

While there are numerous stories that glorify the wanton murder and general mistreatment of innocent peoples at the behest of the LORD, I have found none which exemplifies more clearly such complete and utter disregard, even contempt, for women as human beings than the parable of the Levite and his concubine. I can still recall my own revulsion and incredulity upon hearing of this vile tale for the first time. And I can recall the reactions of the many faint-hearted Christians to whom I have related its contents. Shocked, some of them stanchly denied that such a story really existed. To these theistic non-believers I gave the exact place in the Bible where it can be found, always with the request that after reading it they please tell me what "moral lesson" is to be learned from it. To date, not one of them has been able to come up with any kind of sensible answer. They will, however, give the all-too-familiar excuses such as, "God must have had a reason for doing it" or "We can't possibly know God's greater purpose." Actually, the answer is quite simple: *There is no moral lesson.* In fact, there is nothing "moral" at all in this gruesome narrative. It's just another reiteration that slaughter, rape and genocide are completely justifiable if your "god" says so. Yet differing from the numerous other sado-snuff pieces in the Bible, this particular fable contains a particularly grisly plot complication.

If you read the Bible account of this story you will discover that none of the characters has a name. This in itself is peculiar. Moreover, we really don't get to know anything about them. The "who, what, where, when, why and how" of character development is essentially nonexistent. Except for a very brief and desultory overview by the narrator these people are superficial at best. Dramaturgically speaking, this would be considered very poor writing indeed.

Now, in my estimation the concubine is by far the most fascinating character in the story. She is also the *pivotal* character, the catalyst for everything that happens later. So, if she was that important, why doesn't she even have a name? *Who was she*? What made her special? What were her thoughts and feelings and dreams? Did she have a boyfriend? Schoolmates? A pet? Did she like to sing or play a musical instrument? Did she possess remarkable storytelling, cooking or weaving skills? Since the Bible accounting gives us none of these details whatsoever, I took the liberty of imbuing her persona with human substance based on the social, cultural and economic environment from which she came. I began by giving her a name: Simha, which in Hebrew means "happiness." (You will see the irony of that later on.)

During the creative process I also found myself wondering, just how or why does one *become* a concubine? The biblical role of a concubine seems to be that of a "second class" wife; better in social status than a slave, but not as good as a "real" wife. All right, so why *couldn't* she be a "real" wife? The value of women in the Bible is on a par with that of the average farm animal. Drawing on that patriarchal philosophy and the Mosaic laws that were in place during this timeframe, I have crafted a scenario that helps to answer the aforementioned questions.

This particular Bible fable has numerous other gaps and unanswered questions that have left even professional theological scholars scratching their heads with confusion. Here then is my own version. Part I is purely a product of my imagination. It does not exist in the Bible. I created it solely for the purpose of establishing who Simha is and how she came to be a concubine. Part II, while embellished for dramatic effect, is fundamentally the biblical account that begins at Judges 19:21. As I mentioned earlier, this was NOT an easy or pleasant story to recreate. But remember, *it comes from the Bible*, the "Good Book," the "Infallible Word of God". To make my point, I have kept *very close* to the scriptural events themselves. Judge for yourselves if this "divinely inspired" story is something you would want your children to learn in Sunday School.

Part I

"Simha! Where are you, girl? Come here this instant!" The familiar male voice echoed amid the stone buildings. *Oi, vai iz mir*! She had dallied too long, and now it was nearly midday.

She quickly kissed the kitten's fuzzy head and tucked it back into the wicker basket with its wiggly siblings. "My father calls me," she said to the old weaver woman. "I'll ask him this evening if I may have one of the kittens. But I must go now. A pleasant day to you, *G'veret* Ashmalha. *Todah ve Shalom!*"

Clutching the lavender sash tightly at her waist so as not to lose the precious coins concealed within, she hurried through the congested streets past basket sellers and venders of dried meats. The many tantalizing aromas of the midday *aruchat* wafted past her nostrils, making her suddenly aware of her own hunger. Misgiving pinched her brow. *Abba will be hungry too, and I am not there to prepare his meal.*

Her sandals slapped hard against the dusty claypack until at last she reached the doorsill of her father's house. She pushed open the heavy wooden door and entered the dwelling. The warm, familiar smells of the morning's baked bread, leather dyes and livestock greeted her. Sunlight through the roof opening spilled straight downward, illuminating the interior. Her gaze darted about the small courtyard. To the far right, beneath the shade of a woven reed mat, several chickens scratched and pecked for bugs amid the straw bedding of the she-goat's pen. Along the adjacent wall was the long wooden table where *Abba* stored his leather crafting supplies. A half-finished saddle pouch awaited the final stitching. Her father was nowhere in sight. Probably on the roof where the lighting was better for tooling leather.

With a little sigh of relief, she descended the two interior steps and quickly made her way to the little kitchen area to the left. Bending down, she thrust her hand into the stone oven's open maw. Another sigh of relief. The embers were still warm. It would be easy to get the fire roaring again. She grasped a handful of straw and some wood from the nearby scuttle, chucked it inside the oven and began compressing the foot bellows. Within moments, the fire was crackling away.

"Simha!" Her father's voice came from overhead.

As she turned in the direction of the sound, she saw him descending the narrow wooden ladder. "I'm here, *Abba*. Dinner will be ready shortly."

He straightened his simple, cotton tunic and adjusted the brown sash that encircled his round belly. "A man could starve to death waiting for you, girl. So, what was it this time? A comely shepherd boy? Or perhaps a juggler from some far and mysterious land?"

Simha began slicing a round, flat loaf of bread. "No, not at all. *G'veret* Ashmalha's cat has some kittens. They're nearly old enough to wean, and—" She turned to her father with an imploring glance. "Oh, *Abba*, they're *so adorable*."

A heavy black eyebrow twitched upward. "Ah, yes. A kitten," he grumbled. "Just what we need, another mouth to feed."

She removed the lid from a bronze pot and reached inside for the cloth-wrapped ball of cheese. The sweet, pungent scent of the red wine vinegar stung her nose as she unwrapped the saturated cloth. "But a cat could feed itself on the mice and rats it catches."

A gruff laugh shook his belly. "We should be so wealthy that we could afford to have mice and rats in our home. If we *did* have mice and rats, we'd be eating them ourselves." He took a slice of bread and bit off a mouthful. "And speaking of *G'veret* Ashmalha," he said, chewing. "I trust she paid you for the harness repairs?"

"Oh, yes! I nearly forgot." Quickly she wiped her hands on a towel then slipped her fingers into the pocket concealed within her sash. She found the coins and handed them to her father. Pride swelled within her. "She said it was very fine work indeed."

The full lips curved upward in a smile. But as he peered down at the coins in his palm, his expression turned to one of concern.

"What is it, *Abba*? Isn't that the correct amount?"

He nodded slowly. "It's correct." His chest rose and fell. He appeared to be considering his words carefully before speaking. "Simha, we are not wealthy people. I have many debts—"

Clutching his wrist, her heart filled with apology, she gazed up at him. "*Abba*, I'm sorry. I don't need a kitten. It was selfish of me to ask such a thing."

His mien softened and he caressed the side of her face. "It isn't that." He motioned her to the plaster-covered brick bench that ran along the wall next to the oven then sat down beside her. "Simha... You are not a child any more. You are *Bat Mitzvah*, a Daughter of the Commandment. Do you know what this means?"

She dropped her gaze. "It means that I am now cursed with the monthly sickness."

Placing his finger beneath her chin, he gently lifted her face. "It means that you are now a woman. It means you need to start thinking and acting like a woman. It also means that you should be thinking about taking a husband."

Confusion tightened the skin across her brow. "I—I don't know how to do these things. I don't *feel* any different. How am I to know what is expected of me, *Abba*?"

Her bewilderment seemed reflected in his own eyes. He rubbed a dye-stained, calloused hand across his forehead. "Do you remember your mother?"

Simha nodded stiffly. "A little. She was pretty, wasn't she?"

A tired smile playing at his lips, he closed his eyes as if to savor some sweet memory. "Yes...very pretty." He breathed a heavy sigh as his thoughts returned to the present. "I am deeply sorry she could not have lived long enough to help you with these things. But now we must be practical. We must accept our lot and do what is best. And the truth, Simha, is..." He rose and walked a short distance from her, his gaze averted as he spoke. "I cannot afford to feed both of us. Therefore, I must find you a husband. This won't be easy. You have no dowry. What little *kethubah* your mother brought to our marriage, I was forced to sell long ago in order to pay our bills." He turned, but now his expression had changed, became like the look of a man appraising a new horse or the weave of a rug. "You're very much like your mother," he remarked, nodding. "You will grow into a beautiful woman. We must hope this will be enough to catch the eye of a suitor." He waved his hand toward the oven. "Finish preparing my dinner now. I'll need you to run an errand to *Adon* Zebulun later."

Revulsion shivered through her. Of all the merchants and tradesmen in Bethlehem Zebulun was the most repulsive. It wasn't his fault, she supposed. He was the hide dealer. And though his tannery was located at the far end of the city—and thankfully downwind—he nevertheless always carried with him the stench of rotting flesh and the fetid urine vats that he employed to cure the hides.

Simha gave the bellows several pumps then added more water to the steaming little cauldron suspended above the oven's iron grate. She knew her father was right, of course. The duties of a *Bat Mitzvah* were quite clear, even if the means of fulfilling them were not. Certainly the last thing she wanted was to be a burden to him. What other choice did she have then?

"So, tomorrow I'll start asking around about any eligible young men," he told her, slicing off a piece of cheese. Chewing thoughtfully, he looked her up and down. "From now on you must begin looking and acting more mature, more sensible. Wear your hair up, not in braids. And lengthen the hem on your *simla*. It isn't proper for a young woman to show so much of her legs."

She dipped some of the hot water out of the cauldron to make his tea. "But I will no longer be able to run," she murmured.

"Hmph, be more mindful of your time and you won't have to run."

After her father had finished his meal, she put the food away then went to the corner beneath the narrow window where her mending basket waited. This treasured basket and the simple tools it contained were the only mementos of the mother she could scarcely remember. *If only I could have known her, learned from her.* Simha removed the beautiful woven-grass lid and found the little goatskin pouch that contained her sewing implements. What she knew of the art had been learned by watching the other girls and their mothers. How happy they seemed, laughing together. How she longed to know the tenderness of those moments herself. Perhaps, one day, if she should be blessed with a daughter, she would teach her these things too.

"Simha!" *Abba's* gruff voice broke her reverie. "There's no time for that now. Here, take this money to *Adon* Zebulun. Tell him I'll have the rest soon." He handed her a small cloth bag. "Go now, and no more dawdling over kittens."

"Yes, *Abba.* I promise." Dipping her head in respect, she took the bag containing the precious coins and headed for the door.

Squinting against the brightness of the sun, she pulled the door shut behind her and started through the streets toward Zebulun's hide shop. Her father's admonishment rang through her ears as she walked, her sandals making scuffling sounds against the dry claypack. Yes, she must be more mindful and not dawdle. In truth, she was quite anxious to be finished with this errand as quickly as possible. It wasn't merely the smell of Zebulun's shop that repulsed her. There was something about the man himself, the way his eyes turned to slits between the puffy, dark lids when he peered at her, the thick lips curling upward as if in anticipation of a sale.

A shudder settled between her shoulder blades. She knew it was wrong to feel this way. The man couldn't help the way he looked or the type of work he did. And *Abba* would certainly not be pleased by her attitude. She had heard him several times remark that *Adon* Zebulun had extended him credit for his purchases when others would not. Drawing the hot, dry air deep into her lungs, she closed her eyes in brief prayer. *Forgive me, LORD, for my thoughtlessness, and bless the house of Adon Zebulun for his generosity. Amen.*

The blue and red striped awnings of Zebulun's shop came into view. Even from a distance, the sour stench of the freshly tanned hides permeated the air. Small wonder there were no food vendors in this part of town. One of the more affluent shopkeepers, the coppersmith next door, even paid two boys to stand outside his shop windows with large woven fans to waft the distasteful odor away from his establishment. With a resigned sigh, Simha removed the bag of coins from her sash and approached Zebulun's shop.

A lion pelt plus several foxes hung in one of the big windows; a cheetah and gazelle in the other. She entered through the open door and descended the two steps into the large showing room. Despite its size, it was still cramped and cluttered with rows of racks displaying hides and pelts of every shape, color and description, some with hair, some without.

A woman of notable wealth, as evinced by her exquisite wine-colored silk *tabard* and headscarf decorated with numerous tassels and shimmering gold coins, was discussing a zebra skin with Adon Zebulun. His thick lips curved upward as he told her the story of how he had obtained such a rare and exotic find. The woman at last nodded her approval, handed him several coins, then instructed her two servants to roll up the large skin. The woman cast a cursory glance at Simha in passing, her entire face seeming to glow from the glitter of her highly polished gold jewelry.

Simha politely averted her own gaze until the woman had left. She was alone now with the grinning shop owner. His puffy eyes turned to slits. "Ah, Simha. I trust you have brought the money your father owes me, yes?"

"Yes, *Adon*. Most of it anyway." She held the bag out at arm's length for him.

A scowl replaced the grin as he opened the drawstring and emptied the contents into his meaty palm. His eyes darted over the coins. "There are fifty shekels missing."

"I-I know, *Adon*. My father sends his apologies. Work has been very sparse—"

"And what of *my* work? *My* bills?" Closing his hand around the coins, he shook his fist. "I have been more than patient with him."

"Yes, yes, he knows that, *Adon*. He has said so many times, and he greatly appreciates your kindness." Oh, why did her father always send her to confront his creditors? Did he think they would not unleash their full wrath upon a girl? Still, it was so mortifying to have to stand and listen while they berated him.

Zebulun's anger seemed to wane. With an irritated sigh, he rubbed the back of his thick, leathery neck. "Water cannot be squeezed from a rock," he muttered and slipped the coins into his sash pocket. His eyes lingered upon her, narrowed. "I know what your father's problem is. He uses cheap tools."

Simha gave a meager shrug. "He can only use that which he can afford."

"My point exactly. Take my line of work." He puffed out his chest beneath the stained and foul-smelling tunic. "I have a special blade for every type of hide and every kind of animal. You can't skin a fox with the same knife you'd use on a bull."

"I-I suppose not."

"I've seen your father's tools. Not much variety. And they're very old. Shoddy tools produce shoddy work."

Anger stung the nape of her neck. "His customers are quite pleased with his work."

He waved his hand at her dismissively. "They're being polite, that's all. I hear the gossip. If there were another leather crafter in town, he'd be out of a job completely."

She clenched her teeth against the insult. What did this fat, smelly hide tanner know of true leather craft? *Abba* was an *artist*.

A grin twisted the corners of his thick lips. "But perhaps I can help," he remarked, tapping a finger against his chin. "I have some knives that I don't use anymore. They're old, but they're far superior to anything he has. I suppose I could part with a few of them."

Suspicious, she peered at him. "I'm certain my father could never afford—"

"Afford—ha! Of course he could never afford them. Consider it a loan, or...an investment on my part. With better tools he can produce better wares. And with better wares he can raise his prices. And with higher prices he'll finally be able to *pay his bills!*"

He was leaning quite close now, his odor enveloping her. Simha took a step back.

Zebulun straightened. "Come along then, I'll get them for you," he said, his tone a blend of impatience and boredom.

She hesitated a moment before following him down the rows of assorted hides, some draped across wooden racks, others laid in stacks, and some—like the lion and the zebra—with the head sections still attached, their flat, misshapen faces staring back at her with empty black holes where the eyes had been cut out.

He led her to a small room at the far end of the shop. Her breath caught sharply in her throat at the stench of a neglected chamber pot. The room was nearly dark save for what little light entered through the narrow slit of a window. A work bench stood against the wall. Upon this were several knives and tools of varying shapes and sizes, a sharpening stone and an oil lamp. A sleep mat and plaited goat hair quilt lay on the floor adjacent to the work bench.

Zebulun went to the work bench and selected a knife with a curving blade. Its keen metal edge glinted in the shaft of sunlight. "Now *this* is the kind of tool your father needs." He laid it across his open palm. "Come, see how well balanced it is."

The muscles along her spine stiffened. "I-I'm sure I would know nothing of such things, *Adon*."

His swollen eyelids narrowed. "A knife such as this has many uses," he said, holding the blade in front of him, turning it this way and that. "How old are you, girl?"

She had to force her jaw to move. "Thirteen. Almost."

"You are *Bat Mitzvah*? A woman?"

Simha nodded stiffly.

His gaze moved up and down her. "You do not cover your hair, so I presume you are not married. Are you betrothed then?"

"No, *Adon*."

"Not married. Not betrothed. A shame. You're very pretty."

As if moved by a will not her own, she took a step backward. Suddenly, with a speed she would not have thought him capable of, he lunged and grabbed the front of her tunic. She let out a startled cry and thrashed against him. "No! Let me *go!*"

Jerking her to him, he pressed the blade against her throat. "Do you know how many animals I have butchered with this knife?" he hissed through broken brown teeth. "It would take little effort to slit this delicate skin of *yours*."

Terror constricted her windpipe as she stared into his hideously contorted features. The vile smell of his nearness turned her stomach. She thought she would vomit, *prayed* she would vomit.

Without releasing his grip, he dragged her to his bed mat and forced her down, straddling her. "I'll teach you now what it is to be a woman."

Confused and terrified, Simha struck at him with her fists, tried to kick with her sandaled feet. She filled her lungs to scream, but before the sound could escape, his large, callused palm came down hard over her mouth. "If you make a sound, I will cut your throat!" He pressed the blade hard against the skin beneath her jaw. She gasped, afraid to move, afraid to *breathe!*

Still holding his hand firmly against her mouth, he laid the knife aside and fumbled with his clothing. He then began pulling, tearing at her tunic, forcing the garment over her hips. Driven by instinct and panic, she fought him. She raked his arms with her nails. "Be *still!*" he snarled. He repositioned his hand, covering her nose as well. *She couldn't breathe!*

He grasped her loincloth and yanked it free. She was fighting to breathe now, fighting to stay alive. His knee went between her thighs, forced them open. She managed to wrest her face free and gasped desperately for air. Then she saw it, the monstrosity between his legs, like a serpent—grotesque and *evil!* She didn't care about the knife, didn't care about dying. She started to scream—

He threw himself on top of her, crushing her, and pressed his mouth over hers. The rancid taste of his saliva, the thick, sour stench of his unwashed body overwhelmed her senses. He thrust his hand into her private place, groping, pawing. *What was happening? What was he doing?*

Then the agony! Ripping, searing agony, like her body was being torn apart. She screamed though no sound would come out, screamed until her throat was raw, screamed until her screams turned into muffled sobs of anguish and horror and pain. Tears flowed hot down her cheeks. *My LORD, my LORD! I pray thee, please help me!* His grunting was like that of a pig. He was killing her! His entire body went into a kind of convulsion and he stopped moving. She thought—hoped—he might be dead.

At last he lifted his repulsive bulk off of her. Simha scarcely noticed. Her body racked with an agony she could not have imagined, she turned on her side and drew her legs up close to her chest, sobbing and gasping.

Zebulun rose and adjusted his clothing. His shaggy brows came together in a scowl. "Stop weeping, you silly little fool. This is the way between men and women. Pick up your things and be gone now."

Shaking, barely able to control her movements, she collected her loincloth then pulled herself upright. Fear, shame, confusion burned through her, adding to the agony in her body as she eyed the beast who stood between her and the doorway. With no other avenue of escape, she crept closer.

Zebulun's thick lips pulled into a smile. "Tell your father he no longer owes me the fifty shekels. He'll understand why."

The instant he gave quarter she bolted past him, jabbing him in the belly in her haste, and dashed through the curtained doorway, out of the store, down the street. Tears blurred her vision as she ran. Sobbing, she gasped at the thin, hot air. People turned. She didn't care. She ran harder, ran until she thought her heart would burst.

When she reached the safety of home, she fell upon the door, shoved it open and nearly tumbled down the steps, exhausted.

"Simha!" *Abba* called from his workbench. "What have I told you about running?"

Fear and shame pounding like an iron mallet inside her, she quickly lowered her gaze and started for her room.

"Simha, wait." He rose from the bench and came toward her. His brow furrowed deeply as he stared at her. "What is this?" He touched the sleeve of her tunic, torn during the attack. A look of confusion and anger darkened his features. "What has happened?"

A sob choked her voice. She buried her face in her hands and wept.

He grasped her by the shoulders. "Who did this, Simha? Who was it?"

"It was Zebulun," she cried, shaking her head against the horror of the memory. "He—he pushed me down. He said it was the way between a man and a woman."

Her father's expression was a mask of roiling emotion. "He will pay for this," he exclaimed, clenching his fist until the knuckles blanched white. "As The Law of Moses demands, he will pay for this!"

She frowned, remembering something the beast had said to her. "Zebulun told me...he said you no longer owed him the fifty shekels, and you would understand why. What does that mean?"

His entire demeanor sagged beneath the weight of her words. "It means... It means he has used the tokens of your virginity to settle my debt." He shook his head slowly. "Fifty shekels. That is what the Law demands—*would* have demanded—he reimburse me for what he did. But now... Yes, the debt is settled, but I am left worse off than I was before."

"But how, *Abba*?"

He cupped the side of her face with his callused hand and sighed. "Because of this thing he has done, no man will have you for a wife now. You are defiled, unclean in the eyes of our people."

Tears sprang again to her eyes. "But they needn't know. We won't say anything."

He pressed his hands to his forehead. "Simha, you don't understand." Rubbing his brow, he paced the floor. "If your mother were alive she could explain these things. When a man lies with a woman for the first time, there is blood. This is the

Sacred Token that the LORD has provided, a proof for the husband so that he may know his wife is pure. Once lost, it cannot be restored. And should a woman be found by her husband not to be a virgin… The Law demands she be taken into the street and stoned to death. The LORD has so commanded it."

She wiped her face on the sleeve of her tunic. "I don't care if I cannot marry. I will *never* let a man touch me in that manner again!"

"Don't speak foolishness. But there is another way," her father said thoughtfully. "By The Law I can compel Zebulun himself to marry you. Because he took that which only a husband may take, he can be made to accept you as his wife. He can neither divorce you nor sell you as long as you live. Yes, this is what must be done. It is The Law."

Her mouth fell open in disbelief. "*Abba*, no! I would never marry that pig! I would *rather* be stoned to death!"

"Simha! This is not a matter for you to decide. You cannot live with me forever. Be thankful the LORD has provided this opportunity."

She clenched her teeth hard, the idea of it making her thoughts twist with revulsion. With an anguished cry, she turned and fled to her small room at the far end of the house. The horror and pain still pounding through her mind and body, she threw herself down onto her sleeping mat, clutched her pillow close and wept.

Part II

Enan gave the donkey's sweaty neck a pat then knelt to examine the torn leather strap that had secured the decorative and well-padded *numdah* to the Levite's animal. He shook his head. "I'm afraid it is beyond repair, Master."

The Levite adjusted his distinctively embroidered overcoat and sighed. "Bethlehem is not far," he said, gesturing toward the south. "I'm certain we can find a leather crafter there. Replace the strap on my *numdah* with your own and we shall be off."

Enan bowed his head. "As you wish, Master." He switched the straps then dutifully dropped down on his hands and knees in the hot sand so that the Levite could use him as a step to remount. He gritted his teeth, tried not to wince against the pain of the cane marks, scarcely three days old. It had been a justified beating, he knew. After all, to slip in blood while removing the sacrificial goat's entrails from the Altar was an inexcusable affront to the Temple. Had not the LORD burned men *alive* with fire for far lesser offences? Enan counted himself lucky indeed that a mere ten strokes of his master's staff was *all* he had received.

Lacking now a strap to secure his own donkey's humble back pads, Enan removed the blankets, tucked them under his arm and proceeded on foot to accompany his master to Bethlehem town. The coarse, hot sand burned his feet and chafed mercilessly between flesh and the sweat-moistened leather of his sandals. But he would bear it with dignity, bear it with the pride of knowing that he was the servant of a Levite, a man born of the house chosen by the LORD himself to protect and care for the most sacred of sacred places: The Holy Tabernacle.

Despite the searing heat radiating from both sand and sky, Enan felt a sensation like a chill tremor through his body. Pride was a mortal sin. But how could he *not* be proud? He too was a chosen one, in a manner of speaking. True, his blood was not pure; he was related to the Tribe of Levi only through the lineage of a distant female relative. Still, even as a child, his skills in mathematics and recitation had not gone unnoticed by the high priests.

A smile tugged at his dry, dusty lips as he trudged along beside his master's donkey. He could still recall the tears of joy in his mother's eyes, his father's squared shoulders the day the messenger had brought word that he, Enan, son of a simple pottery maker, had been chosen to become the personal attendant to one of the most respected and prestigious men in all the world! But, as his father had pointed out, there was more to it than the sublime honor of serving such a man. Among their other august duties, the Levite priests were also charged with collecting the *ma'aser*, the tithe, the "LORD's due". His father had once quipped that it was impossible to know just how much of the tithe actually reached the LORD once the high priests received the Great Bucket. Still, as a Levite's assistant, Enan would be entitled to at least a few drops from that bucket.

Sweat seeped down his back, stinging the still-fresh welts from his master's cane and causing his linen tunic to stick and pull against the smarting flesh. Ah yes, a lesson well-learned. He would be more careful next time. Yet even this misery was easily endured without complaint when compared to the joy of being able to give his parents the few extra shekels each month that were his allowance. His young heart swelled once more with pride, a deadly sin. He suspected the LORD would forgive him.

❖   ❖   ❖

"Simha! See who is at the door," her father cried from his leather tooling table near the light well in the ceiling. Late afternoon shadows were beginning to stretch across the earthen floor. Soon he would be calling for her to light his oil lamp so he could continue his work late into the night.

She slid the wooden bolt through the stocks then drew open the heavy door. "Yes?" She passed her gaze across the two strangers standing upon the stone verge at the top of the steps. Though both were dressed in traveling garb, it was evident by the fine quality of their white linen tunics and robes that these were no ordinary citizens. The elder in particular was a man of conspicuous importance. In his person there was nothing remarkable. He was rather short and plump with a goat-like nose and short, black beard, graying slightly at the edges. She estimated him to be in his late forties. Upon his head rested a conical *mitre*, the symbolic turban of a priest. Draped over this, and cascading over his shoulders and down his back almost to the ground, was an exquisitely decorated *tallit*. Every edge, hem and corner of his garments was embroidered with the most intricate embellishments she had ever seen. The woven sash he wore, wrapped several times around his middle parts then crossing over his chest, was a vivid blend of crimson, purple and blue. *And so we see how our tithings are being used*, she thought.

Simha peered next to the manservant. Although, *boy*-servant would be more accurate. The lad appeared scarcely older than herself, sixteen at most. He was dressed similarly to his master, but without the grandeur. His *tallit* was unadorned, so as to distinguish a person of his lesser station. Covering his head was a simple *tsaniph*, this held in place by a twist of linen fabric. A fringe of curly, reddish hair showed from beneath. His features were angular, his nose long and narrow. He was not of the full blood, she surmised; perhaps in part Egyptian. But most striking were his eyes: round and well-spaced, accented by long, auburn lashes. Their color was like that of a polished hazel nut, the late afternoon sun betraying a hint of green.

Without taking her eyes from the pair, she called back to her father, "It is a Levite priest...and his manservant."

"A Levite!" In his haste to rise, her father nearly upset his workbench. He rushed to the doorway. "What's the matter with you, girl? Bid them enter." Fairly throwing himself to the ground at the bottom of the steps, he knelt face down on the floor, hands pressed to his forehead as if to shield his eyes. "Welcome, *Tzaddik*. My home is honored by your presence."

The magnificent *tallit* flowing behind him, the Levite descended the steps. Pausing in front of her father, he reached down and lightly touched the prostrated man's head. "Arise, friend."

Simha had never before seen her father behave this way. He had welcomed into his home important persons before: Rabbis, dignitaries, and once an actual prince from the empire of Persia. All had been treated with cordialities befitting their station; yet foremost in her father's eyes, they were customers, a source of desperately needed income. Why now was he groveling before this priest, not even a high priest? It was as if he thought this Levite wielded the power of Yahweh himself. She sniffed. They certainly didn't *smell* any different from other men. Donkey sweat and the odors of travelers who had not seen a proper bath. But perhaps the answer lay closer to her father's heart. Perhaps he feared this Levite had come to collect some new tithe. *Oi, vai iz mir.* Another tax; that was the last thing they needed.

"I am Pesakh the Leather Crafter," her father told them, rising from the woven grass mat. "This is my daughter, Simha."

The Levite placed a hand over his heart. "I am Segan Asaph. And my servant, Enan."

As she had been trained to do from childhood, Simha fetched the ewer and basin with which to wash the strangers' feet. But scarcely had she filled the bronze vessel, when her father snatched the items from her and proceeded to perform the service himself.

With an air of utmost deference, he conducted them to the bench against the inner wall. He removed first the priest's slippers—seal skin they appeared to be—and gently lifted the man's feet onto the perforated bronze platform atop the basin. As he poured the water, reverently guiding it with his hand from ankle to toe, he asked, "Pray tell me, *Tzaddik*, how may I serve you this day?"

The Levite leaned back against the earthen wall. "The strap on my donkey's *numdah* is broken. I was told you can repair such things."

"Yes, yes, of course, *Tzaddik*! It will be an honor above honors."

Simha stood ready with towels. Her father took one and began drying the man's large yet remarkably delicate-looking feet. It was evident from their pale color and smooth skin that they had seen very little of the sun and littler still the toils of the ordinary traveler.

"Simha, fetch refreshments for our guests. Be quick, girl."

She laid the other towel across her father's shoulder then set about collecting the few remaining pieces of fruit, some nuts and a bit of leftover bread into a bowl. Perhaps when the priest saw what meager fare they possessed, he might be inclined to add a gratuity to her father's fee.

Her father was in the process of drying Enan's feet when she returned with the bowl. "I regret I do not have more to offer, *Tzaddik*," her father said.

The Levite's thick lips drew back in a smile. "Generosity comes from the heart, not necessarily the table, my friend."

Simha picked up the filled basin and dumped the water into the leather holding bucket by the door. *Perhaps the vegetables will grow faster and larger with water that has been used to wash a priest's sacred feet.* She then refilled the ewer from the large urn next to the oven so the guests could wash their hands. As she was pouring the water into the Levite's palms, she glanced up to see him peering at her. Quickly she averted her gaze. She hated it when men stared at her. Hated their smiles. Hated what thoughts must be playing in their heads.

"Your daughter is quite young," he remarked as he dabbed his hands dry on a fresh towel. "Yet she wears on her head the *tsa'if* of a woman in mourning."

Her father shook his head in a solemn gesture. "A widow, *Tzaddik*. Married only two years. Then scarcely three months ago— *Oi, vai iz mir*, such a tragedy!"

"Indeed, yes." The Levite turned his eyes upon her. "And how did your husband meet his fate, daughter?"

The skin at the back of her neck began to burn. She could still see it so clearly in her mind: Zebulun's great, disgusting bulk poised at the top of the ladder as he reached for a bundle of lambs' hides. The ladder teetered. "Hold it still!" he barked at her. She grabbed with all her might, but instead of trying to steady it, she gave it a shove. One of the legs snapped. Zebulun bellowed a curse as he toppled and fell. His fat body hit the earthen floor with a sickening thud. He writhed, not fully aware...*not fully dead*. Panic and desperation crashed like a lightning bolt through her mind. A voice screamed in her head, *Now is the moment—ACT!*

As he lay there in agony, struggling to rise, she grasped the heavy pounding mallet from the work table. Both hands wrapped tightly around the handle, knuckles aching, she raised the weapon over her head— *Two years* she had been his wife-by-force. *Two years* of the same horror as the day he ripped her body open. —The mallet crashed into his temple. Zebulun grunted, tried to strike her. She brought it down again. Blood spilled from his shattered eye socket. *Again!* The skin covering his cheekbone split like the peel of an orange, oozing bright crimson. The smells of blood and rotting animal carcasses filled her nostrils, ignited her rage. *Again!*

And then it was over. He moved no more. Breathed no more. Could hurt her no more.

She had sat there for a moment, her heart still thundering inside her chest, and tried to collect her thoughts. There was blood spattered everywhere. This would need to be cleaned up. Thankfully the shop was closed for the evening. She peered at the lifeless form, the pulverized side of his head. Taking a rag, she sopped up some of the blood then dabbed it against the corner of the table. "He was climbing a ladder when one of the legs broke. He fell and struck his head," she would tell the authorities.

After the cleansing had been completed, she retired to her room and laid down on the sleep mat. Alone. For the first time in two agonizing years, a free woman.

Simha brought her gaze level with that of the Levite. "He was climbing a ladder when one of the legs broke, *Tzaddik*," she replied without hesitation or qualm; the same answer she had given a thousand times before. "He fell and struck his head."

The young manservant, Enan, had finished washing his hands. "How dreadful for you."

She slid her gaze toward him. "Yes. Dreadful."

His eyes held hers for a moment. There was something different in the way he looked at her, softer, as if...

The Levite was talking again. "And have you any children?"

Her stomach knotted at the very thought. "I bore him no children, *Tzaddik*."

Enan was still looking at her, his expression one of sadness, or perhaps pity. "And yet another tragedy," he said.

She forced herself to look away. "There are far worse things to endure in this world."

The Levite took an apple and began to eat. "Enan, fetch the damaged *numdah*."

"Yes, Master." The lad sprang to his feet and gave a little bow before departing. He returned moments later with the lavishly adorned riding pad.

Her father examined the damage keenly. He would, Simha knew, frown and "tsk, tsk" and turn it this way and that, thus giving the appearance of it being a difficult job, all with the hope of impressing his customer with his skill and thereby getting a higher price. "Yes, yes. I can fix it. I can make it better than it was before," he said at last. That familiar play of concern clouded his countenance. "An exquisite *numdah* such as this deserves only the finest leather. Of course… Such leather is more expensive."

The Levite wiped his mouth with the back of his hand. "It must be befitting a servant of the LORD. Do what you think right, my friend."

Simha pressed her lips together hard as she began preparing the vegetables for the evening meal. *But of course, the LORD's servant must have only the finest, just as the LORD himself must have the finest of everything: our flocks, our harvest, our wares.* She recalled the teachings from the Sacred Torah. Even after the holy wars of conquest, the LORD was also allotted his share of the captured virgin girls. She had always wondered how this apportionment was *delivered*, though she suspected the high priests had their own ways of *offering* this sacrifice as well.

Her father called to her. "Simha, see to the donkeys."

"Enan, assist her," the Levite added.

She bowed her head as courtesy demanded then motioned to the lad. "Come. Our courtyard is to the left."

He untied the animals from the hitching post and led them along behind her. "I've never been to Bethlehem before," he remarked, glancing around. "It seems a very pleasant town."

Simha unhooked the gate that opened into the courtyard. Chickens cackled and scurried about. The she-goat bleated from her pen in expectation of a meal. "I've been to no other, so how would I know?"

He removed the donkeys' bridles and hung them on a peg near the manger. "Oh, I've seen many places. I've even sailed the Mediterranean in a great ship. My master is a very important man."

"So my father seems to think." Gathering her garments securely with one hand, she made her way up the ladder to the loft then threw down several heaps of dried grass. The donkeys rushed to eat. "He was practically *licking* your master's feet clean."

The lad chuckled. It was a pleasant sound. "People often have that reaction to a Levite priest."

She descended with care, her bare feet coming to rest upon the smooth, warm stone. "Perhaps that's because they're afraid of having yet another tax placed upon them."

"Oh, my master is not responsible for collecting the *Maaser Rishon*."

She scooped up some of the hay and carried it to the goat. "Yet I'll wager he receives his portion nonetheless."

"Only that which the LORD has deemed his due."

"Ah, but of course." She crossed the courtyard to the southern wall where the rainwater cistern stood. "And by what means does the LORD convey his wishes?" She mounted the two stone steps and slid the cover plate aside.

"Well, the LORD speaks directly to the high priest. He in turn tells the people what the LORD desires."

Grasping a small bucket, she retrieved water for the animals. "And has no one ever thought to question the accuracy of these *secret revelations?*"

The boy's jaw dropped. "To do so would be blasphemy," he replied, his voice nearly a whisper. "Besides, the high priest is infallible."

Infallible. Perfect. How many times had she heard those words? And were they not typically followed by *blasphemy* and *death*, like jackals that follow a wounded ibex? *Do not ask. Do not question. Obey the Laws—or you shall surely die!*

Enan stood in the middle of the courtyard, seeming ill at ease as she went about her chores. "Is there something I can do to help you?" he asked.

She peered at him. "Can you milk a goat?"

He gave a little shrug and smiled. "Well, I could certainly try."

Holding the bucket out to him, Simha opened the gate to the sheltered area where the she-goat was contentedly munching her feed. "There. Take care she doesn't kick you, now."

Concern played across his features. "Oh. They kick?"

Lifting an eyebrow, she quipped, "Wouldn't *you?*"

The youthful color in his smooth cheeks deepened. "I-I suppose I never considered it before."

Quite enjoying her game, she watched as he approached the small brown-and-white spotted animal and gave its shoulder a gentle pat. After a bit of contemplation, he squatted down at its flank and positioned the bucket beneath the engorged udder. He turned to Simha. "Like this?"

She nodded. "Now just start milking."

Tentatively, he reached for a teat and gave it a squeeze with no result. He tried the other side. "Why isn't anything happening?"

"You have to pinch off the teat at the top, like so." She held her hand up to demonstrate thumb and forefinger pressed together. "Then roll your other fingers together and downward."

He tried again, his movements awkward. "Like this?" But still without effect. He sat back with a sigh. "This certainly is more difficult than one would expect."

"You just need to pinch harder."

"Well, I certainly don't wish to hurt her."

A smile tugged at Simha's lips. "She'll let you know if you do."

"That's what I'm afraid of!" After several more attempts a small stream of milk trickled into the bucket. "Ah-ha!" he exclaimed triumphantly. "What do you think of that?"

Arms folded, she tipped her head to one side. "I think if you had only goat's milk for nourishment, you would starve."

Their laughter intermingled.

Simha entered the pen and knelt on the opposite side of the she-goat. "Here, let me show you." Reaching underneath the animal, she cradled his hand, maneuvering his fingers into position. A warmth from her touch radiated up his arm and through his being. Her hands were strong, yet remarkably soft and gentle. He had never before known such a sensation ...intoxicating and frightening at the same time.

"See?" she said. "Pinch the teat like this so the milk doesn't go back inside her udder. Then roll your fingers downward." The feel of her flesh upon his was exquisite. It took several tries, but then—! A copious stream of milk shot from the orifice.

"There! You did it," she cried.

He peered over the goat's back to see the young woman smiling at him. Her incredibly dark eyes had the luster of the sacred black onyx. Her teeth were as perfect as a string of carefully matched pearls. By all that was holy, she was beautiful! A heavy pounding filled his chest, and suddenly it was difficult to breathe. He glanced quickly away. "I'm afraid we'll never fill this bucket at the rate I'm going."

"Then we'll work together. Come, as I showed you."

She expertly manipulated the second teat while he struggled with the first. For every expression he produced, she produced four. The musky warm smell of the animal mingled with the sweetness of the hay was as delightful as any incense. He prayed this goat would never run dry, such was his joy at being in Simha's company.

"So, tell me," she said without disrupting her rhythm. "If your master is not a tax collector, what is the nature of his exalted duties?"

Pride swelled within him. "He and he alone is responsible for procuring the rare and precious *chilazon*."

She chuckled, the sound like music. "He collects *snails*?"

"The *chilazon* is not just a snail. It provides the many splendid colors for dying the high priests' sacred robes."

"Well, we certainly cannot have our priests dressed in less than the finest."

The barb of sarcasm in her tone puzzled and distressed him. He could certainly understand her misery, having lost her beloved husband but a few short months ago. Poor thing. She was like a wounded creature, lashing out from her pain. Still, he could not fathom her disdain for the priesthood.

"The necessity of their raiment is found in the Sacred Texts," he said in hopes of reassuring her. "It is prescribed by Mosaic Law, and therefore we must obey."

She paused and glared back at him, a darkness consuming her countenance. "Mosaic Law? The *Sacred* Law that commands that a woman found not to be a virgin on her wedding night be stoned to death by the men of her village? The same *Sacred* Law that prescribes death for a woman who is raped but does not—or *cannot*—cry out for help?" Her black eyes grew large and wild like those of the desert sand cat. "The *Sacred* Mosaic Law that forces a virgin into marriage *with the beast who raped her*? Are *these* the Sacred Texts by which you live your life and defend your venerable priesthood?"

Enan sat back, shocked and confused. "I—I was not aware... My studies have been limited to languages and commerce and caring for the Holy Tabernacle. I know very little about the Laws...and the ways...between men and women."

As suddenly as it had come, the fierceness left her eyes. She lowered her gaze and returned to her chore. "Most people are not aware of these Laws. They too have other duties and interests. They are content to allow the priests and the rabbis to interpret the Talmud and tell them what they need to know and how they should behave. But I have *lived* it. Laws made *by* men are laws made *for* men."

"But The Law was given to us by the LORD himself," he ventured. "For *all* of our people."

Her dark eyes narrowed slightly. "And yet it is *men* who are made in his image."

The silence that stretched between them was as dry and brittle as a viper's hide.

Enan paused to rub a cramp from his hand. "Do you have to do this every day?"

Reaching beneath the she-goat with both hands, Simha finished the chore. "I have to do this *twice* a day. Without kids to nurse from her, she would swell up and sicken, perhaps even die."

"It seems to me it would be much easier on the hands to leave the kids with her. Then you would also have meat for your table."

She sighed at his simplicity. "Meat is a luxury for the wealthy. The money my father made selling the kids purchased our winter supply of barley with a little left over for fresh dates and vegetables...the very dates and vegetables your master is currently enjoying."

"I'm sorry," he said, the soft hazel eyes downcast. "I wish there was something I could do."

The sincerity in his voice pierced her heart. "It's not your fault," she told him. "It is the LORD's will that we are where we are. Or so I'm told. Now, come. My father will be expecting his fresh milk."

With an effort, Simha lifted the bucket from beneath the goat, but before she could get far, Enan moved toward her. "Please, let me help you," he said, smiling.

The late afternoon light playing through the thatched awning ignited the amber-green hues in his eyes. His hands settled upon hers...soft...warm...strong. She wanted to protest, wanted to run, but her legs felt suddenly weak. The pounding of her heart was like a bird thrashing wildly to escape its cage. Gently...so very gently...he removed the handle from her grip. She tried to speak but could not find her voice. Confused and overwhelmed, she turned away and headed for the open doorway that connected courtyard to house.

The remainder of the evening seemed like something from a dream. Real, yet unreal; familiar and comforting, but also deeply disturbing. Throughout supper she found herself stealing glimpses of the young manservant. At those times when his gaze in turn caught hers, a sensation like liquid fire coursed through her body.

Repairing the damaged *numdah* strap had been simple enough for a man of her father's talents. Even so, he had insisted that the Levite stay the night so as to refresh himself and his animals before continuing their journey. He directed her to prepare sleeping quarters for the two men on the west side of the roof where the breeze was sweetest. How her hands trembled at the thought that Enan would be lying but a short distance from her. The fire filled her once more. Perhaps it would be better if she slept on the first level, away from him...away from the strange sensations. And then the grinding agony of knowing that tomorrow he would be gone, and she would never see him again. A sense of mourning settled around her.

After the guests had bid good evening and ascended the ladder to their sleeping area, Simha set about her evening chores. Her father brought over the empty wine cups.

"The Levite is a man of great importance and prestige," he remarked.

She gave a shrug as she dried the cups and set them aside. "To some, perhaps."

"I imagine his share of the *Maaser Rishon* is quite handsome."

"Of that I have no doubt. While ordinary people toil in the sun to scratch out their existence, he reaps a lion's share for pandering to a high priest's vanity."

"Take care, daughter," he snapped, wagging his finger. "Such talk is blasphemy!"

Scraping the remaining *leban* back into the crock, she smiled. "And if you have me stoned to death, who will grind the grain for your daily bread?"

"Yes, who indeed?" He popped a fig into his mouth, chewed thoughtfully. "Did you see the way he looked at you throughout supper?"

A sourness like vinegar filled her throat. "It made me shudder."

"He finds you appealing."

"Well, I cannot say the same for him."

"Fortunately, that matters not."

She peered over her shoulder at him. "What do you mean?"

Taking her by the shoulders, he turned her to face him. "Simha, I am not a young man anymore. My eyes are weak. My fingers do not obey me as they once did. The day will come soon when I can no longer earn a living, and then what is to become of me?"

Concern tightened her brow. "*Abba*, I will care for you as I always have, of course."

"Care alone is not enough, daughter. We must have income."

"But the hides and pelts I received from Zebulun's estate, we will sell them as we planned."

He shook his head, eyes filled with sadness and disappointment. "A few low-grade pelts will not bring much."

Indeed. Had it not been for Zebulun's jackal of a brother and various grasping creditors who came like vultures to the smell of a corpse, she might have received a much larger division.

She clasped his hand. "We'll find a way, *Abba*. I know we will."

"I already have, Simha." He turned his eyes from her.

"What are you saying?"

"Tomorrow when the Levite departs, you will go with him."

The words struck her like a slap. "You cannot be serious!"

"I have never been *more* serious."

"But... What would people think? I am still in mourning!"

He scoffed and waved his hand dismissively. "A dry eye is not a mournful eye. We both know the depth of your bereavement."

Her mind raced in desperation, trying to recall the teachings of the *Talmud*. "No, it is written: A priest cannot marry one who is not a virgin."

"Only a high priest requires the tokens of virginity. If you *were* still a virgin, I could ask a higher price for you. Tarnished though you are, he is still willing to take you, as his concubine." His eyes widened as they always did when contemplating a profit. "He offered me three hundred shekels for you, Simha. *Three hundred!* You should be flattered."

Frantic, she thought for a way to escape this dreaded prospect. She had studied The Laws, listened to the words and wisdom of the Elders. "I have been a *married woman*," she exclaimed with an air of triumph. "Therefore by our Laws you can no longer sell me into bondage!"

"No, I cannot sell you." He turned from her, apparently defeated. "But I can renounce you and throw you into the streets. Do you know what would become of you then? *Do you?*"

She gasped. "*Abba*, you *wouldn't!*"

Rubbing his brow, he lowered himself onto the stone bench. "Simha, these are difficult times. Had you been born a son to me, I could have taught you my trade. But as a female, your only value is to produce sons for a husband. Yet even this value is now greatly diminished since you have been with a man." He reached out and took her hand. "Simha, I have always done what was best for you. This I do now because it is the best for both of us. The Levite is a man of means. He can care for you far better than I. Even as his concubine, you will have fine clothes, a nice house and plenty to eat."

She pulled her hand away. "I don't care about those things!"

"Then care about *me*. Care about ways you might influence him to send me a humble pension in my old age." Rising, he turned away from her. "I will hear no more arguing. I have already accepted the money. I cannot go back on my word. Tomorrow you *will* go with him."

An anguished sob burst from her as she fled to the small, dark room that had been her sanctuary. The nightmare was beginning again. She could not bear the thought of that man—*any* man—even a *Levite*—putting his hands on her, forcing her to submit her body for his pleasure. Surely death would be preferable. Huddled in the corner upon her thin sleep mat, she wiped her face with the sleeve of her *halug* and peered up into the darkness at the ceiling. Yes, she would commit suicide. Even at the risk of losing her very soul. She would climb to the roof, scale the wall and hurl herself into the street. But she would have to wait until the two guests were fast asleep.

As she lay down to wait, an image drifted into her thoughts. *Enan.* Wretched sorrow ached through her whole being at the realization that never again would she see him. Never again would she gaze into his strangely beautiful eyes...never hear the music of his laughter...never feel the intoxicating touch of his hand...never...never...never...

Simha's back ached anew with every jarring step the donkey took as it picked its way across the dry, rocky terrain. The sky was pale with heat. The air smelled of dust and the sour scrubby weeds that dotted the surrounding hills. In the distance several vultures circled. She felt as lifeless as the sprawling desert around her. She cursed herself for falling asleep the night before. Her plan was ruined; her fate was sealed. She narrowed her gaze upon the figure riding ahead of her, his priestly white robes undulating with the movement of his mount. *Pity the poor beast that must bear such a load.*

Enan's voice caught her ear. "Are you getting tired?" he asked, holding the animal's lead as he walked beside her. "Would you like to rest for awhile?"

"Ask the donkey. He is the one who must carry the burden," she muttered without looking at him.

"Oh, he has carried far heavier things," Enan replied, giving the animal's sweaty neck a pat. "For him this is a mere stroll."

With an annoyed sigh, she rolled her eyes toward him. "Must you always be so cheerful?"

"I'm sorry. I'll try to be more dour." He drew his brows together in a heavy scowl and pursed his lower lip in an overtly comical fashion.

The urge to smile bubbled within her. She fought to subdue it and turned her attention back to the road ahead. "How much farther to Adullam?"

"Not far. We'll be there before the sun sets."

Dread crept through her joints at the thought of the impending night. If only she could slip away into the desert. The surrounding hills and canyons were filled with caves, some large enough to hide entire armies, it was said. If she could escape she could hide there. Of course, without food or water she would likely die. Even so, she would still be free.

Again, Enan's voice broke her reverie. "I know you miss your father," he said, his tone gentle with compassion. "I miss my parents also. I haven't seen them for several years. Nor my brothers and sisters, for that matter."

"Did your parents sell *you* into servitude?"

"No. It was a great honor to be chosen. As it is for you as well."

Honor? The irony burned through her thoughts. She pulled the *mitpachah* closer around her face to shield from the sun's glare. "I fail to understand this *honor* you speak of."

"Truly, it is! Consider, my master has traveled to many places. He has seen many women. He could have his pick, but he chose *you*. I know if I were a woman *I* would feel deeply honored."

"There is no *honor* in being treated like property. Or worse, like a common farm animal," she muttered, the taste of the words bitter in her mouth. She breathed a weary sigh and closed her eyes, tried to feel nothing but the movement of the donkey beneath her. "You're just a boy. What could you know of these things?"

"I know that if you were *my* wife, *I* would be the one deeply honored."

The words flowed over her like a cool breeze. She peered at him, startled, confused. Her eyes fastened upon his, large and round, filled with an exuberance for life, filled with joy...and... Why was he looking at her like that? *Why couldn't she turn away?* She hated and envied him his innocence. His nearness brought a different kind of pain, a burning, consuming, maddening thirst. And he was like a purling spring from which she would never drink.

The sound of her heart pounding in her ears, she forced herself to turn away. "What is the purpose of this journey?" she asked in a desperate attempt to be free from her own thoughts.

"We are bound for Ashkelon. Once there we will board a ship and sail the Mediterranean to ports where my master can procure the *chilazon*."

"How long will that take?"

"Three, maybe four months. Much depends on the weather."

"I have never been on a ship, neither have I seen the Mediterranean. I have only heard stories. There are great monsters that inhabit the sea, or so I am told. Is this true?"

"I too have heard such stories, though personally I have never seen any monsters. Oh! But there are such magnificent creatures nonetheless. And the smell of the sea and the feel of the spray in your face. And the merchants from so many different lands with their exotic spices and wares—!"

Caught up in his excitement, she peered at him.

A sheepish grin crept across his youthful features. "My apologies. I am being too cheerful again." He made the silly grimace once more. This time Simha could not contain her laughter.

He laid his hand upon the donkey's withers and leaned closer. "I know you are not here by choice, good lady," he murmured, his gaze so deep, his voice like summer honey. "But by my life, I swear I shall do everything in my power to make you as comfortable as possible."

Her eyes grew moist. A great heaviness filled her chest as if a sob might suddenly burst forth. If this purgatory of obligation was to be her destiny, there was some comfort at least in knowing that she would not have to face it alone. Simha breathed in the thin, dry air. More than anything now, she needed a friend. But then, she wondered...would the friendship of this delightful young man ease her misery or add to it?

❖   ❖   ❖

An oil lamp clutched in one hand, the innkeeper led the way up a narrow flight of stone steps to the second floor. He pulled aside the curtain partition to one of the rooms. "The finest lodgings I have to offer, *Tzaddik*," he said with a toothless grin. After setting the lamp in an alcove, he bowed to the Levite. "May you have a pleasant evening, *Tzaddik*." He cast a sidelong glance at Simha. His smile sent a shiver down her spine.

Enan set the packs in one corner then proceeded to unfurl the two bedrolls. The lamp's small, wavering flame cast his movements against the uneven contours of the wall. When he had finished, he turned to the Levite. "All is ready, Master. Is there anything else I can do?"

The Levite waved his had dismissively. "Nothing. You may leave us now."

"May you sleep well, Master."

Enan bowed, but as he turned his eyes caught Simha's gaze. Her heart fairly lodged in her throat. She wanted to cry out to him, "*Please, don't go!*"

He disappeared through the curtained partition.

Without looking at the figure standing next to her she murmured, "He will not be lodging with us?"

The Levite snorted. "Certainly not. He'll sleep in the stable with the animals."

She was alone now—with *him*—in the small room. Sweat stung her flesh like needles as he passed his eyes over her.

"Come here, girl," he said, beckoning with his hand. "Let me behold your hair."

She took a step backward, hands pressed against the sackcloth *tza'if* that covered her head. "No, you cannot! I-I am in mourning."

Seeming amused, he chuckled. "By my authority, I release you from your obligation. Besides, *I* am your husband and master now. You will show me whatever I wish to see." He stalked closer. "Now, let down your hair for me."

Her heart a hammer inside her chest, she continued to back away until the stone wall halted her retreat. Her breath caught sharply. She had studied well the Laws regarding women. There was little solace to be found. Yet still there was a chance.

"I am unclean!" she told him, struggling to keep the fear from her voice. "No man—not even a priest—may not touch a woman who has her monthly sickness."

The bearded jowls worked. He rushed forward, pinning her against the wall, his hands pulling at her clothing. She let out a startled scream as he thrust a hand beneath her garments and groped the area between her legs. With one meaty paw, he jerked her loincloth free and held it in front of her. "I see no evidence of your sickness," he sneered as he cast the garment aside. Grabbing her hard by the shoulders, he pulled her to him. His breath was hot and foul; his eyes afire with his despicable intent. "Enough of your trickery. It's time you gave me what I have paid so dearly for!"

He threw her down upon the thin sleep mat. Spurred by terror and instinct, she fought. His strength and weight overpowered her. She knew by Law she must give him that which was his manly right; she knew that he would have his way eventually, but still her anger and loathing drove her to resist like an animal tormented beyond the point of reason.

He wrested the *halug* over her thighs, ripping the material in the process. She felt the hated male part brush against her flesh. Rage and panic surged through her being. Without even thinking, she swung her fist and struck the thing full force.

The Levite let out a pain-stricken bellow and doubled over onto his side. Instantly, Simha scrambled to her feet and fled from the room. She couldn't believe what she had done. To remain now would surely mean death! With only a single small oil lamp flickering in the main room below to light her way, she stumbled down the narrow steps, fairly leaping from the last few, and hurried outside. Had anyone seen her? She didn't know; didn't care. She had to escape, and she knew where she had to go!

Once outside, she peered up and down the darkened street. The stable had to be close by. Instinctively she reached for the long *mitpachah* to conceal her face. *Vai iz mir*! In her haste she had forgotten it. Without even the smaller *tsa'if* to cover her hair, she could be flogged—or worse!

Holding close to the shadows, she located the stable and pushed open the large door. The smells of hay and manure washed over her. She caught the flicker of an oil lamp. In a far corner, currying the donkeys, stood the familiar image. "Enan!" she cried out and ran toward him.

"Simha!" In a sudden show of modesty, he dropped his gaze. "*G'veret*, I cannot see you this way!"

"Please, Enan, don't call me that." She laid her hands upon the firm, muscular shoulders concealed beneath his robes. "Look at me, *please*. I need your help!"

Reluctantly, as if he feared he might be struck blind, he lifted his gaze, noted the braids that encircled her head. "Simha," he said in a cautious whisper. "What are you doing here?"

"Oh, Enan. I have done a terrible thing! But I—I just couldn't bear the thought of him touching me."

He laid the currying brush on the stall railing. "What is it you have done?"

"I struck him...with my hand...in his secret parts. Do you know what this means? By Law, he can have my hand cut off!"

"No, no, Simha. He would never do such a thing."

Tears blurred her vision. "But he *can*. It is the *Law!*"

"I won't let that happen. I will speak to him. Come here." He folded her into his embrace. A warmth like nothing she had ever known filled every part of her. The sound of his heart was strong and reassuring.

"Why do I feel this way when I'm with you?" she whispered. "Why are you so different?"

"Simha..." He laid his cheek against her hair, the most forbidden of acts. And yet it felt so natural, so right. "The moment my eyes beheld you, it was as if I drew breath for the first time. If only..."

"If only what? Please, speak it!"

"By all that is holy, I dare not. But if only I could show you..." He pulled away only enough to peer down into her eyes. She tipped her face up toward his...closed her eyes. His lips, so soft, so warm pressed upon hers. A thousand emotions welled within her. She held him tighter...!

The stable door slammed shut with a crash that startled even the animals. "*Harlot!*" bellowed Segan Asaph. His face contorted with rage, he stormed across the straw-covered dirt floor. "So this is where I find you!"

Before Simha could react, Enan pushed her behind him. "No, Master. She did nothing wrong. It was I!"

"Silence, boy! I'll deal with this whore as she deserves."

Shoving Enan aside, the Levite grabbed a leather strap from its peg and began thrashing her. Simha screamed and held up her hands to protect herself from the vicious blows. The leather strap bit into her flesh.

Enan sprang to shield her. "Master, I beg you. Let me take the lashes for her instead!"

The Levite's lips drew back in a snarl. "Get out of my way!" He brought the strap down across Enan's face, opening a wide gash across his cheek. Simha screamed in horror at the sight of the blood streaming down those beautiful features.

Momentarily stunned, Enan staggered backward then recovered and threw himself at the Levite, grappling his arms. "Run, Simha!" he shouted. "*Run!*"

The sight of Bethlehem's towering stone walls made Enan's heart beat so loudly he feared his master riding next to him might surely hear the sound. Four long months it had been. Four months of agony, wondering what had become of her that night. Had she made it safely back to her home, or perished in the desert? The thought of such a creature, so young and beautiful, snuffed out like a candle flame made his insides ache with a renewed sorrow. And yet, to think of her yoked to Segan Asaph, to imagine him touching her, hurting her, consumed him with rage. Given that possibility, perhaps death in the desert would have been a more preferable fate. Enan cursed himself. It was sinful to feel this way. And still the thoughts and emotions and physical sensations burned within him. And the dreams... Oh, the dreams filled with forbidden passions! They were the cruelest torture of all.

He forced his mind toward other matters. It had been a highly successful journey. The *chilazon* were plentiful this year. His master had overseen their collection, choosing only those with perfect, flawless shells. He had recited the *berakhah* to sanctify their blood before it was extracted. Then only the finest, purest wools and linens were procured and placed into the dyeing vats. Enan glanced backward at the bulging pack strapped across his donkey's hindquarters. Yes, these sacred materials would indeed make excellent vestments for the Tabernacle priests.

Once inside the gated walls, his master reined his mount to

the right. Puzzled, Enan called out, "Master, the inn is the other way."

Segan Asaph snorted. "I have no money left to pay for lodging. We'll stay at the leather crafter's house. Certainly he owes me that much—and more."

Enan stared straight ahead as they made their way through the maze of narrow alleyways. "Do you... Do you suppose she is there?"

"If she is, I'll make her wish the jackals had devoured her carcass."

A fever rose within Enan, an anger that made his eyes burn in their sockets. He tightened his grip upon the reins until the leather bit into his flesh. Yet this was nothing compared to the lashing he had received in the stable the night he had been found with Simha. He had taken that beating without so much as a whimper, taken it with the desperate pleasure of knowing that *she* would not have to face his master's fury.

No longer able to contain his emotions, he turned to his master. "You have blamed her and cursed her for what she did. But did you ever consider *why* she behaved so? Did you ever consider what she had been through?" The words gushed forth like water from a broken cistern. He could not stop them, nor did he try. He had kept these thoughts and feelings pressed deep within himself far too long.

"Widowed at so young an age," he continued. "And not even permitted the respect of a proper mourning period. Then to be taken from her father's house by a complete stranger. Can you but try to imagine the depth of her fear and sorrow?" His face grew hot with anger. "How can you call yourself the servant of our LORD yet be so unsympathetic to the suffering of another of his children?"

Enan could not believe those words had actually come from his mouth. Segan Asaph appeared equally shocked and sat for several moments in silence. When he did at last speak, it was in a tone Enan had never before heard. "Perhaps... Perhaps I should have considered these things," Segan Asaph murmured. He breathed a deep, thoughtful sigh. "If we do find her at her father's house, I will speak tenderly to her. I will give her the time she needs. I do not wish a wife who fears and despises me."

It lightened Enan's heart to hear his master say these things. If Simha was indeed fated to be the wife of Segan Asaph, he could take some comfort at least in knowing that she would be cared for in a kindly manner. How he ached to be the one to care for her, if only as her servant. And yet he knew that to serve her best he must accept the painful truth. For her sake—and his—he must never let her know how he truly felt.

❖   ❖   ❖

She had spoken not a word, not to the Levite, not to her father, not even to Enan as he had helped her onto the donkey's back. There was nothing *to* say. It was done. The priest had come back for her, and her father had been more than delighted to hand her over to him. Her initial reaction upon seeing the robed figure was to cry out in dismay and collapse upon the earthen floor. It was Enan who had rushed to her side, lifting her up and speaking words of compassion and encouragement. Her own misery was suddenly forgotten by the sight of the hideous scar that now defaced those once beautiful features.

For five days her father had played the fawning host, plying his guest with the finest wine and meats that money could buy, all with the desperate hope, no doubt, that the Levite would pardon his troublesome daughter and take her off his hands once and for all. But more importantly, he did not want to give up his precious three hundred shekels.

And oh! What honeyed words had dripped from the Levite's lips. Promises of kindness and clement behavior. She had only to gaze upon the ugly seam across Enan's face to know the depths of such kindness and clemency.

The sun had already begun its descent when the men said their final farewells. Simha didn't ask where they were headed, neither did she care. In silence she prayed for strength and courage. There was no need to pray for deliverance. She knew it would not be forthcoming.

After awhile, Enan brought the donkey to a halt and pointed to the great walled city on a nearby hill. "Master, the day is almost gone. Should we not turn aside here and find lodging in Jebus?"

The Levite scowled. "No. The Jebusites are foreigners and not sons of Israel. I would sooner sleep with dogs. We'll keep going as far as Gibeah, which is of the tribe of Benjamin. We'll be welcome there."

Compliantly, Enan nodded and pulled on the animal's lead. In that brief moment his gaze caught that of Simha. Her heart cried out, and she remembered something he had said to her: *Where there is life, there is hope.* And she had murmured back to him, "Where there is hope, life can endure."

Oil lamps were being lit in the tiny windows throughout the city to stave off the encroaching darkness. Using Enan as his stepping block, the Levite dismounted and peered around

Gibeah's open square. "We'll wait here for hospitality," he said, seating himself on the low stone wall that surrounded the town's main cistern.

There were few passersby at this hour. Those that noticed the travelers gave but a fleeting glance and hurried on their way. Enan helped Simha to the ground then turned to his master. "I thought you said we would be welcome here?"

"Patience. I'm certain someone will be along shortly."

The darkness grew thicker, the night colder. The sound of raucous male laughter crackled in the distance. Simha pulled her *mitpachah* closer about her face, desperately wishing she could disappear from this place altogether.

Some moments later an old man entered the square, leading a pack donkey. By his dress he appeared to be a field laborer of some sort, perhaps a farmer returned from tending his crops. Pausing to adjust the long cloth bag slung over one shoulder, he studied the travelers. A smile came to his lips as he approached. "A Levite priest!" he remarked. He pressed his dirt-covered hands to his face in homage. "I am Dekel, the Farmer. Good sir, would you be from Shiloh then?"

The Levite returned his cordiality. "I am from the hill country of Ephraim, not far from Shiloh. We are on our way back there, but we are in need of lodging for the night."

The old man clapped his hands together. "I too am from Ephraim! I am here until the harvest. Please, come with me. I would be happy to give you hospitality. Come!"

The raucous male laughter grew louder, closer.

"Let us hurry," the old man said. "The streets are not safe after dark."

Dread enfolded Simha's heart. She stayed close, her body seeking Enan's comforting form as they followed their host through the maze of narrow, dimly lit alleys. The taste of fear was bitter like ash upon her tongue. Even the donkeys seemed to sense the urgency of their haste. They squealed and plunged from side to side, nearly trampling their human handlers.

At last the old man paused at a house with a high stone wall. "Tmira, open the gate!" he called.

There came the sound of iron grating upon iron and soon the big wooden door drew open. Dekel ushered his guests inside the courtyard and quickly closed and bolted the gate. "Welcome, my friends," he exclaimed jovially. He turned then to the young girl standing to one side. "This is my daughter, Tmira. Go now and make preparations for our guests," he told her.

What the rest of the townsfolk may have lacked in hospitality, the old man and his daughter more than made up for. Like two old friends, the Levite and Dekel talked and made merry. Enan sipped his wine and studied the two women. Tmira was little more than a child, yet she performed her duties with skill and swiftness. She seemed quite happy to have another female to talk to. Even Simha, despite her palpable sadness, appeared to be enjoying the girl's company. His gaze lingered upon Simha, the smooth curve of her face, each delicate movement like a line in a poem; her dark, penetrating eyes, filled with both pain and hope; and her lips...those exquisite lips...soft, red and full. His heart began to pound with the all-too-brief memory of their sweetness...

Segan Asaph cleared his throat gruffly. Jolted by the sound, Enan turned to see his master's dark glower trained menacingly upon him. The sensation was like that of a dagger thrust into his chest. Perspiration stinging his flesh, he quickly looked away.

The otherwise pleasant mood of the evening was shattered by a sudden pounding on the courtyard gate. "Hey, old man! We hear you got a Levite priest in there." The male voice was slurred from drink. "Bring him out to us so we can have a little fun!"

The Levite jumped to his feet, his expression frantic. "What is the meaning of this? Who are these men?"

"Worthless swine. Sons of Belial," the old man said. "They roam the streets, committing the most unspeakable atrocities."

"Better send him out, old man, or you'll get some of the same! My big, greasy cock isn't fussy about whose ass it opens up." The pounding grew louder, accompanied by drunken laughter. It sounded as if they might actually break the gate down.

Inside the little house the frightened inhabitants huddled together. Instinctively, Enan made his way to Simha's side. "Can nothing deter them?" he asked, glancing from Dekel to his master. "Food, money? We could offer them our donkeys and the goods they carry."

"*Never!*" Segan Asaph cried. He clenched his fists. "The sacred fabric will *never* be touched by heathen hands!"

"But Master, surely our lives are worth more than these things."

"It is not material things they desire," the old man said. "But perhaps there is a way to appease their carnal appetites." His gaze fell upon his young daughter clinging to Simha's side. "Tmira, come here."

Aghast, Enan stared at the old man. "What are you going to do? Surely, you can't—"

"Silence!" the Levite snapped. "This is a matter for men to decide. If this is what it takes, then so be it."

Enan could not believe what he was hearing. Surely the old man couldn't be serious. *This was his daughter!* It had to be a bluff. A ruse to buy some time.

Grasping the frightened girl by the wrist, the old man strode to the gate. "Hear me, I beg you! Here is my daughter. She is a virgin. Take her. Defile her in any way you like. But please do not commit such an abomination upon the man who is a guest in my house. He is a priest, a servant of our LORD!"

"It's *because* he's a priest that we want him," one of the assailants shouted back. "Everybody knows their purses and their assholes are the tightest things in all of Judea." A chorus of ribald laughter erupted from the brutes. They fell upon the gate once more, shaking it so hard that pulverized mortar began to fall from the weakening stone sockets. With one final assault the hinges gave way. Dekel and Tmira made it back inside the house only heartbeats before the attackers crashed through into the courtyard. The old man closed and bolted the door then stood back, his chest heaving. Immediately the marauders were at the threshold, pounding and hurling curses.

Sweat trickled down from beneath Segan Asaph's *mitre*. With a trembling hand he wiped his brow. Then his gaze fell upon Simha. "Perhaps if we increase the offer they will leave us in peace." He took a step toward her.

Eyes wide with horror, Enan rushed forward, interposing himself between Simha and the Levite. "*No!* I will not let you do this!"

"I've had enough of your insolence, boy!" Using his hands like battering rams, the Levite lunged, hitting Enan squarely in the chest and sending him over backward.

A rage like he had never known before ignited Enan's blood. He collected himself to spring upon Segan Asaph when—! Pain exploded at the back of his skull and he crumpled. Dazed, he looked up to see the old man standing above him, a stone grinding pestle clutched in one hand.

Simha screamed and rushed toward him. The priest caught her by the arm and jerked her away. "Dekel, bind him! Quickly, before he regains his senses," the Levite commanded.

The old man obeyed. In a semi-conscious stupor, Enan tried to fight. The ropes tightened around his arms, pinning them to his sides. Struggling against the bonds and the swirling darkness that threatened to engulf him, he could do nothing but watch.

The priest dragged Simha to the door. "Dekel, tell them they may have my concubine as well."

"Consider this!" the old man called out to the mob. "I have my virgin daughter and the priest's concubine. Please let me bring them out that you may humble and abuse them and do whatever pleases you. But do not commit your vile act against this man."

"*Give us the priest!*" came the reply. The battering at the door intensified, sending down a shower of dust from the loosening hinges.

Segan Asaph gnawed his thick lips as he contemplated the dire circumstances. "Tell them... Tell them that I will come out. But I need a moment to prepare myself."

"*Tzaddik*, you cannot!" the old man cried. "These are sodomites, the most loathsome of sinners!"

The Levite placed a hand on the old man's shoulder. "We must have faith in our LORD, my friend. Just as he spared Isaac from Abraham's knife, so he will provide for my salvation. Now, tell them I will come out, but first they must withdraw beyond the gate."

With reluctance, Dekel delivered the message. Dubious murmurings could be heard as the attackers gradually withdrew from the courtyard.

"They have gone, *Tzaddik*," the old man reported.

Still gripping Simha by the arm, the Levite peered through the small narrow window to one side. He then turned his attention to Simha. "And now, my lovely wife, it's time for you to pay for your infidelity."

Terror contorted Simha's features. She sobbed and shook her head in desperation. "But I've done nothing!"

Lips drawn back over clenched teeth, he gripped her hard and glared down at her. "Do you think me so blind that I cannot see the adultery in your heart? The lust you feel every time you look at *him?* You have played the harlot, now you will face the punishment of Yahweh."

"No, please! *No!*"

Simha's screams jolted Enan's senses. With excruciating effort, he pulled himself to his knees. "Master, I beg you—*please don't do this!*" In a rage of panic and desperation he thrashed against his bonds, tried to stand.

The Levite nodded to Dekel. "Open the door!"

An ugly smile spread across Segan Asaph's features as he leered down at Simha. "You'll be far more obedient once they have humbled you." With that, he threw her out into the courtyard.

Hardly had the door been shut and bolted when the assailants were upon her. Her screams shattered the night as they dragged her away.

"*Simha...! Simha...!*" Enan collapsed in anguish, his throat raw from crying her name.

❖   ❖   ❖

A sound roused him. So faint. Was it a dream? A terrible dream? He tried to move. Pain burned through every part of him. He realized then that his bonds had been removed.

The sound came again. Little more than a whimper.

Forcing his mind to full consciousness, he clambered to his feet and rushed to open the door. An anguished sob burst from his throat at the sight before him. In the dim light of dawn lay Simha, fingertips resting upon the threshold, naked, her white skin now covered with welts and bruises. Her long, black hair was unbound and matted with blood. Blood issued from every part of her.

Quickly, he removed his robes and covered her. She tried to reach for him. "Enan..."

He leaned close. "Do not try to speak," he whispered, his voice broken with sorrow.

"I must... I must say what is in my heart while it still beats." With a trembling hand, she caressed his cheek. "I love you, Enan. Until the day I saw you, I did not know the word had meaning. But now..." The once-lovely features contorted in agony. "For the first time in my life, I can taste its sweetness."

"Precious angel, I will always love you." Enfolding her gently in his arms, he pressed his lips to hers.

And she was gone.

Sorrow washed over him in great heaving sobs as he held her close. Time ceased to exist. Nothing mattered anymore.

He didn't know how long he had been there when he heard Segan Asaph's voice. "Well, it's about time she got back," the Levite remarked. He peered down at the motionless figure. "Come, Simha. Get up. We must be on our way." He gave her ribs a kick.

Ignited by rage, Enan sprang from her side and grasped the Levite's tunic with both hands, slamming him against the doorframe. "*She's dead, and you killed her!*"

Segan Asaph's eyes bulged. "Her life was a necessary sacrifice to prevent a far worse abomination from being committed."

"You threw her to them to protect yourself," Enan seethed. "You're nothing more than a murderer and a coward!"

"I have facilitated the LORD's will!" He knocked Enan's hands away and composed himself. "Woman was created to serve man. Suffice it to say she served a noble purpose. You may put her on my donkey, but be quick about it. We must be getting home."

Enan knelt beside the lifeless form, stroked her matted hair. "No. I will carry her."

"As you wish. But take care not to get any blood on the sacred fabrics."

❖ ❖ ❖

He saw nothing through his tears, felt nothing but the gentle weight of her slight body as he carried her into his master's house and placed her upon the linen sheet the Levite had made ready for her.

"I will prepare her," he told Enan.

Numbed with grief, Enan retired to his small chamber and laid down upon the sleep mat. His mind reeled with confusion. Love. Honor. Loyalty. Hate. He didn't know what he was feeling anymore.

Sometime later the Levite entered his room. "Come. She is ready. I will need your help," the priest said.

Enan followed him to the special room, the room where daily prayers were recited, ablutions performed and sacred offerings made. The delicate scent of incense wafted over him. But there was another odor. Something familiar. Something thick and heavy. Something that brought a tightness to the pit of his belly. The Levite drew aside the curtain. Enan entered.

Like a physical blow, revulsion assaulted his senses. His stomach rose up in his throat and he quickly turned away, but it was too late; the gruesome image was burned into his brain as if from an iron sear. Simha—what had once *been* Simha—lay strewn upon the linen-covered floor. Her head had been severed and placed to one side. Her arms and legs had been removed and further dismembered at elbows and knees. Even her breasts had been sliced from her torso and placed on either side!

Throes of nausea twisting his insides, Enan clutched the door post and sank to his knees. "What have you *done* to her?" he cried. "You *butchered* her! *Like an animal!*"

With eyes as cold and hard as granite, the Levite peered at him for a moment then calmly walked to his writing table and sat down. "I will compose twelve notes, one for each of the Tribes of Israel. I will tell them of the atrocity that was committed upon my wife. The men of Gibeah must be punished." He took up his quill. "Now, while I write the notes, you will wrap each of the twelve portions of her body in a piece of linen. Tomorrow I shall dispatch them with messengers. Hurry, boy, before she begins to stink."

℘ . . . ℂ

I warned you this wouldn't be an easy story to read. Nonetheless, it *is* in the Bible, and even without the graphic gore, it is still a reprehensible tale that demonstrates that the biblical view of women is equally reprehensible. The actual biblical account is surprisingly short (only twenty-seven verses). But the horrors don't end there.

After the Levite chops up his concubine and sends the pieces to the twelve tribes (the method of delivery is not mentioned, neither is the fate of the servant, who, in the Bible version, is nothing but a mindless, nameless lackey), a great cry of outrage goes up, and the collective tribes demand vengeance against Gibeah for this egregious offense. (Just to be clear, the offense is against the *Levite*, not the concubine.) Furthermore, when this distraught "holy man of God" is recounting his sad tale to the assembled tribal leaders, he conveniently leaves out the part where he threw her to the rapists in order to save himself.

The leaders then demand that the Benjamites, who control the territory where Gibeah lies, turn over the men responsible. When the tribe of Benjamin refuses, the other tribes launch an all-out war to exterminate their "brothers". Now, for those of you who have actually read the Bible, you know that Yahweh loves nothing better than a war of genocidal proportions, and this story does not disappoint in that respect.

Well, the fighting goes on for quite awhile with the Benjamites kicking some serious Hebrew ass. But then Yahweh, who apparently just couldn't make up his all-powerful mind which team to root for, decides to throw in with the collective tribes against the Bennies. Now the "great slaughter" gets serious, and the Benjamites: men, women, young and old, and of course, children (for what slaughter would be complete without children?) are wiped out to the last six hundred men. And just to make sure their revenge is complete, the attackers kill all the livestock, destroy the crops and provisions, and burn the cities. That's Bible vengeance, *Old School!*

When the eleven victorious tribes realize what they've done, they develop a sudden case of conscience and decide they simply cannot allow their Benjamite brothers to become extinct. Trouble is, all the Benjamite females have been killed, and the other tribes have sworn an oath not to give up any of their women to the Benjamites. (Don't ask me why. It's a "Bible thing".) To remedy this, they decide to launch another unprovoked attack on the neighboring province of Jabesh-

96

Gilead. But in truth the J-Gs had it coming, since they refused to send soldiers to be part of the "great slaughter" against the Benjamites in the first place. And so yet another bloody civil war ensues. The holy assembly tells its 12,000 soldiers to "put to the sword those living there, including the women and children. Kill every male and every woman who is not a virgin." (Chapter 21, Verses 10-11 NIV). Now, it is never specified just *how* the soldiers are to determine which females were virgins, but it was obviously too lurid to put in the Bible, a book that—ironically— glorifies the slaughter of little babies.

After the grisly chore is completed, they find among the captives four hundred virgin girls which are given as wives to the Benjamites. But wait! That leaves two hundred soldiers without wives. The problem is solved in true biblical fashion: Under cover of darkness, the Benjamites steal away to the happy, peaceful, unsuspecting town of Shiloh where a debutante ball is being held for all the young maidens. While the unsuspecting girls dance, the soldiers attack and kidnap two hundred of them as wives. (We can presume they were probably raped on the spot, since these are of course war-hardened, plundering soldiers, and we already know the status of females in the Bible god's eyes.)

While in the process of reconstructing the story of the Levite and his Concubine, I went to several religion-based websites to get their interpretations and explanations of why things happened and what was the "moral lesson" to be learned. The answers I found were every bit as despicable as the biblical account itself.

One such website is hosted by a gentleman named Richard Seel. Mr. Seel is the principal of a "virtual organization" called New Paradigm Consulting, whose members act as online facilitators to help companies, groups, even families deal with conflicts, changing roles and general responsibilities; by all appearances a rather commendable enterprise. From his bio, Mr. Seel himself appears to be a man of considerable education and accomplishment. He is also an ordained minister of the Church of England. In his own words he says, "My Christian faith offers a number of unique insights into organizations and change." Indeed it does.

The article he posted that caught my attention is an interpretation of our gruesome biblical tale. Verse by verse, detail by detail, he has dissected and analyzed the events, offering up his—Christian—opinion of why they took place. Of the gang-raping-to-death of the concubine he says, "The concubine's misdemeanor is uncertain. The Hebrew has *zanah* which is consistently translated as harlotry or adultery..." "However, [other Bible translations] have 'became angry with him'..." and "...'she was averse to him and did not return his affections, which led to quarrels and her eventual departure.'"

Mr. Seel, however, seems to fixate on the notion—though even by his own observations unproven—that she was indeed a harlot. He then cites for reference several other verses from the Old Testament that call for the *burning to death* of a woman believed to have committed harlotry. This would certainly explain how he could make the following, blood-chilling assertion: "Thus she may have 'deserved' to die according to law." And even more reprehensible, he adds, "The concubine's death was thus in a sense natural justice; the manner of it perhaps 'poetic justice'."

DESERVED TO DIE?! POETIC JUSTICE?! Religious apologists are notorious for being able to whitewash, dismiss and condone every execrable deed perpetrated in the name of their "loving god", but how could *anyone, anywhere* with even a shred of humanity or compassion proclaim that a woman—regardless of what she had done—*deserved* to be gang-raped to *death?* Sadly, Mr. Seel's analysis was only one of the many I found that echoed his sentiments and basically affirmed the age-old, bar room, good ol' boy attitude, "The bitch had it coming." If there is a "greater moral lesson" to be gleaned from this dreadful tale, I'm certain that champions of the religious right would have no problem affirming that it is far better for a woman to suffer such horrors and die in this fashion rather than to allow the homosexual act—consensual or otherwise—to take place.

As a woman, I was appalled by the ease with which these supposedly educated men (I found no women participants in these discussions) could so casually and with a coldly clinical callousness accept and, yes, condone such a vile act. In dissecting their rationale we must first remember that the religious mind is a mind that has been warped into believing that the Bible—with all its horrors—is the "word of God", either literally or inspirationally, and therefore *must be accepted* as having a "divine purpose". With this sort of brainwashing firmly established, the quest of believers is to twist this psychotic nonsense into something justifiable, even laudable, thereby giving credence to their weak assertion that "God has his hand in everything".

The subject of rape is particularly offensive to any civilized person. Unfortunately, even in today's "modern" society (I shall limit this term to my own American society) there are still persons—many of whom can claim some very impressive college credentials—who continue to believe that rape is a woman's fault and even "God's will".

In August of 2012, Todd Akin, the Republican senatorial candidate from Missouri, made the unbelievably insensitive, ignorant (and now internationally famous) "legitimate rape" comment, in which he claimed to know "for a fact" that women who become pregnant as a result of rape, haven't really been *raped* because in his own words, "If it's a *legitimate rape*, the female body has ways to try to shut that whole thing down." *Shut that whole thing down?* Not exactly what I would call the jargon of a person who has even the slightest clue about basic anatomy, much less the female reproductive system. But we must realize that the closest Mr. Akin ever came to receiving a degree in these specialties was a Master of Divinity from Covenant Theological Seminary, where, according to Wikipedia, "...he studied Greek, Hebrew and a socially conservative interpretation of the Christian scriptures." I rest my case.

In October of the same year, Richard Mourdock, a Republican from Indiana, made an even more outrageous and repugnant comment, declaring among other things, "...I came to realize life is that gift from God that I think even if life begins in that horrible situation of rape, that it is something that God intended to happen." *Really?* Your "god of love" *intends* for a woman—or little girl—to be raped and resultantly impregnated? Considering how many rapes occur worldwide, it's abundantly clear this omnipotent figment of the imagination has no intention of lifting an all-mighty finger to prevent them. Mr. Mourdock, a Fundamentalist Christian, added to his ludicrous blather by stating that pregnancies resulting from rape were still "a gift from God." Some gift, and some god that would put a woman through that kind of physical and emotional torture.

As I stated before, the station of women in the Bible—and in places where the Bible is revered for its "moral" and "judiciary" teachings—is nothing more than gender-based slavery. Women were created to serve men and fulfill domestic and sexual obligations—period. They are chattel, property to be bought and sold, killed if necessary, completely disposable. As I demonstrated in the story, rape is an offense against the victim's father or husband, *not* the victim herself.

But stupid, callous remarks about rape are not limited to right-wing politicians. About the same time the Akin/Mourdock comments hit the media fan, a story broke about a California

Superior Court judge, one Derek G. Johnson, who, in 2008, heard a case wherein a woman was stalked, harassed, threatened with death, held captive, forced to perform oral sex, and then raped by her former boyfriend. The rapist used a heated screwdriver and told the terrified woman he would disfigure her face and rip up her vagina if she didn't comply. The judge gave the rapist only six years, because the victim "didn't put up a fight". He supported his decision by saying, "I'm not a gynecologist, but I can tell you something: If someone doesn't want to have sexual intercourse, the body shuts down. The body will not permit that to happen unless a lot of damage is inflicted, and we heard nothing about that in this case." (I think I'll mention at this point that Derek G. Johnson received his B.S. degree—no pun intended—at Santa Clara University, a highly ranked—and highly Catholic—institution.)

The Honorable Judge Johnson's ruling follows the same path of perverse logic found in Deuteronomy 22:23-24 KJV. "If a damsel that is a virgin be betrothed unto an husband, and a man find her in the city, and lie with (rape) her; Then ye shall bring them both out unto the gate of that city, and ye shall stone them with stones that they die; the damsel, because she cried not, being in the city; and the man, because he hath humbled (vandalized) his neighbor's wife (property): so thou shalt put away evil from among you." (I added the words in parentheses for emphasis.)

OK, let's recap: The poor damsel is to be put to death because she didn't scream for help (possibly because she had a knife to her throat?) Whereas the rapist is put to death, *not* because of the rape *per se*, but because he damaged his neighbor's property, i.e. stole his betrothed's virginity, which "technically" doesn't belong to her; it belongs to her father until she is betrothed, then it belongs to her future husband. All this considered, I guess the California woman who was raped by her ex-boyfriend should just be thankful our Jesuit-trained Judge Johnson didn't condemn *her* to death because she "didn't put up a fight", but instead submitted to her attacker rather than have her eyes put out or her vagina ripped up by the heated screwdriver.

I suppose we should take some degree of comfort in knowing that the California Commission on Judicial Performance censured Judge Johnson for his "outdated, biased and insensitive views about sexual assault victims"—but not until *four years after the fact*. Even so, to my knowledge the Honorable Judge is still presiding in Orange County, California. The rapist, having paid his debt to society, was scheduled to be back on the streets in 2014. And as for the woman who endured the assault—first by the rapist, then by the judge—she is in her way a champion and a symbol of the unconscionable ignorance that continues to pervade, not just the lowest social denominators, but the highest levels of our political and legal systems as well.

After hearing patently anti-feminist comments like those from the men I've mentioned, it's hard to believe we're living in the 21st Century, CE—not 21st Century, *BCE* What all this demonstrates is that when a person's intellect is infected with the "religion virus", he is capable of excusing any type of horror—be it against an old blind man, a pregnant woman or even a child—if it is done in the name of their "loving god". One of my favorite quotes comes from Voltaire: "Those who can make you believe absurdities can make you commit atrocities."

Several times throughout my own adaptation of the biblical story, Simha, her father or the Levite make reference to "the Law". I intentionally crafted the plotline in this manner to demonstrate how cruel, heartless and even downright sadistic biblical laws were in regard to women. Every "Law" reference can be found in the Bible. The slow, torturous execution by stoning of a rape victim who does not cry out for help I have already mentioned. Here are where the others can be found:

(Deuteronomy 22:20-21 KJV) "But if this thing be true, and the tokens of virginity be not found for the damsel: Then they shall bring out the damsel to the door of her father's house, and the men of her city shall stone her with stones that she die: because she hath wrought folly in Israel, to play the whore in her father's house: so shalt thou put evil away from among you." Mind you, the reason she may have lost her virginity—whether through rape or incest—is of no consequence. According to the "Good Book", she must still die!

(Deuteronomy 22:28-29) "If a man find a damsel that is a virgin, which is not betrothed, and lay hold on her, and lie with (rape) her, and they be found; Then the man that lay with her shall give unto the damsel's father fifty shekels of silver, and she shall be his wife; because he hath humbled her, he may not put her away all his days." The girl who was raped has no say whatsoever in the deal.

(Deuteronomy 25:11-12) "When men strive together one with another, and the wife of the one draweth near for to deliver her husband out of the hand of him that smiteth him, and putteth forth her hand, and taketh him by the secrets: Then thou shalt cut off her hand, thine eye shall not pity her." Basically what this is saying is that if a couple of guys are duking it out, and the wife of one steps in to save her husband by grabbing the other guy by the balls, the *woman* shall have her hand chopped off—and you better not feel sorry for her! So, not only is a woman *not* allowed to defend herself; she's not even allowed to defend her husband (at least if it requires punching another man in the "secrets"). If she does, she will be subjected to a bloody, torturous form of punishment the likes of which no civilized, rational person could possibly condone.

(Exodus 21:7) "And if a man sell his daughter to be a maidservant, she shall not go out as the menservants do." This one is pretty cut and dried. Daughters—all females actually— are nothing more than property to be disposed of as the lord and master sees fit.

These are only a few of the truly despicable punishments meted out to women in particular. The Bible is reeking with many more. For a complete list, you need only Google "atrocities against women (or children) in the Bible". There are numerous websites devoted to spreading the ugly truth. Now, considering how many of our elected officials are—or claim to be— conservative, Fundamentalist Evangelicals, who believe the Bible is the *literal* word of a war-loving, woman-hating, invisible sky daddy, it was only a matter of time before some of them would slip up and reveal to the world the depths of their intellectual retardation.

Further proof of the Bible's misogynist manifesto is the way it frequently refers to "evil cities" as whores and harlots; obviously another slam against the female of our species. Ironically, one of the very few female heroes in the Bible is Rahab, the prostitute of Jericho (found in the book of Joshua). She becomes one of the "good guys" because she aides and abets some Hebrew spies who have snuck into the city to gather information which ultimately leads to the savage annihilation of her own people. (For her noble efforts, her family is spared.) The lesson here becomes, it's OK to be a whore, a liar and a traitor as long as you're doing it for good old Yahweh. (Brigham Young, the tyrannical leader of the early Utah-based Mormons, coined the phrase, "Lying for the Lord" as justification for breaking every civil and moral law known to mankind *if* it was done for the sake of furthering his cult's objectives.)

Now it's true, the comments made by Representatives Akin and Mourdock were quickly and roundly condemned by members of their own party, as well as the vast majority of Americans in general. But one has to wonder, was it the actual nature of the comments that stirred such outrage from the religious political sector, or the fact that these men were foolish enough to speak out loud what many others believed yet judiciously kept to themselves? As we witnessed in the 2012 elections, the comments cost both candidates their respective senatorial races and ultimately proved tantamount to committing career suicide. However, these two men were certainly not the only politicians to invoke their religious backgrounds as proof of their suitability to hold office and consequently make laws and policies to control how the rest of us conduct our private lives.

During the 2008 and 2012 presidential campaigns we heard several candidates spew platitudes about "getting back to *Bible Law!*" Obviously these people—like the frighteningly uninformed minions who cheered them on like a mob of seals in a tuna factory—don't have the vaguest clue what they would be unleashing upon society. For one thing, many of the Bible laws demand the death penalty for even the most minor of infractions (like tying a knot on the Sabbath). Another problem would be how to determine which "one true religion" we would be obliged to follow. Christians themselves can't seem to agree on whose godly-inspired book is the right one. And when they change the rules or the translations to suit their uniquely secular purposes, it makes it harder still.

Former half-term governor of Alaska and failed vice presidential candidate, Sarah Palin, a strong advocate of "Bible Law", predicted that Barack Obama, if elected president, would create "death panels" via his proposed Affordable Care Act as a way to get rid of medical undesirables. Now, since death is the most commonly prescribed punishment for breaking *any* of Yahweh's laws, it would be necessary under "Bible Law" to institute some form of sectarian "death panel" for meting out the wrathful Bible god's egregious justice. Can you imagine such a panel comprised of the likes of Sarah Palin, Pat Robertson, Fred Phelps and Jerry Falwell Jr., all sitting in sublime, sanctimonious judgment of the rest of us? In essence, the United States Constitution and the Bill of Rights would ultimately be gutted, shredded and burned by these "political Christians".

But there is another double-edged consequence of "getting back to Bible Law" that these Fundamentalist windbags obviously haven't considered. First of all, there wouldn't be any more women in politics, that's for sure. Those mouthy, painted, strutting Jezebels would get their faces scrubbed, their heads shaved, manicured fingernails cut back to the quick and told to go home, make babies and "keep silent!" Secondly, their "rebellious children" would find themselves on the receiving end of some serious Old Testament whoop-ass. For instance, the foul-mouthed, sexually promiscuous and unwed mother, Bristol Palin; the underage booze guzzling, pot smoking Bush twins Barbara and Jenna (the latter having gained notoriety for removing her panties in public and flashing the "family namesake" for photographers); Mary Cheney, lesbian daughter of former vice president Dick Cheney, just to name a few.

According to "Bible Law", they would be dragged into the streets and stoned to death—or burned alive—for their per-verted behaviors and shameless displays of harlotry. For as the Bible repeatedly states, only in this way can we "put away evil from among us." It seems only fair that the politicians who embrace the Bible as their divine source of justice and morality should be the first ones to make grisly examples of their own children as proof of their sincerity.

Obviously, it doesn't take a student of law or philosophy to see how asinine and impractical—not to mention downright sadistic—it would be to impose a religion-based legal system upon society, *especially* a society founded on the self-defining principles of liberty and freedom of choice. Actually, under "Bible Law" there would be no freedom or liberty of any kind. There would be only a narrowly interpreted, brutally enforced adherence to a monotheistic dogma born of ignorance, superstition and xenophobic intolerance. We need only read a magazine or watch a TV news program about the Middle East to see firsthand the savage effects of theocratic dictatorships, especially upon women. The fact that these are Islamic dictatorships is irrelevant; for Judaism, Christianity and Islam all come from the same blood-drenched work of genocidal fairytales: the "Holy" Bible. We may condemn fanatical Muslims for their barbaric Sharia Law, but remember, Sharia Law *is* Bible Law.

And for those Christians who insist on claiming that Jesus changed the "Law", I offer this passage from Matthew 5:17-19. And Jesus said, "Think not that I am come to destroy the Law, or the Prophets: I am not come to destroy, but to fulfill. For verily I say unto you, till heaven and earth pass, one jot or one tittle shall in no wise pass from the Law, till all be fulfilled. Whosoever therefore shall break one of these least commandments, and shall teach men so, he shall be called the least in the kingdom of heaven: but whosoever shall do and teach them, the same shall be called great in the kingdom of heaven." Christian apologists will argue that Jesus himself was the "fulfillment", and therefore his very presence changed the Law. They forget—or perhaps they desperately choose to ignore—the fact that Jesus was *not* "of the House of David", as the prophecy stipulates. Joseph, husband of Mary, was of the House of David, but Joseph had *nothing* to do with the conception of Jesus—*right?*

As I mentioned, we need only turn on the TV to see what atrocities people of "faith" are capable of inflicting upon others. And let us not forget that odious period of history known as the Dark Ages, when Christianity did in fact rule most of Europe. Here again it was women, a.k.a. "witches", who particularly felt the wrath of religious persecution. Thankfully, secular enlightenment coupled with scientific discoveries have driven the purveyors of superstitious terrorism back into a shadowy corner of Western society. But do not think for a moment they are content to remain there. The lust for power and the consuming desire to control others, once tasted, is an addiction that can neither be kicked nor quenched. Add to this a mentality warped by the belief that there is an all-powerful, vengeful, chauvinistic, Mafia Don-type father figure lurking in ether-space, sending telepathic messages to his "chosen people", and you have a recipe for a modern-day political jihad. The actual burning of people at the stake and stoning disobedient children might be a thing of the barbaric past, but right now in the United States there is an uneasy reawakening of the same hate-fired ignorance and bigotry that underscores nearly every "Law" the Bible hands down, and which has fueled centuries of heinous crimes against humanity. If not in literal terms, then certainly in legislative terms, we could be looking at the rise of our own *Christian Taliban.*

The Holy Hemorrhoids
(A Farce of the Arse)
As Found in 1 Samuel
Chapters 4-6

After a story as grisly and depressing as The Levite and His Concubine, I thought it necessary to brighten the mood with a little biblical levity. "*What?*" I hear you ask. "Levity in the *Bible*?" While it's true the Old Testament is geared more toward inspiring fear, horror and guilt rather than laughter, every now and then we do come across a delightful little gem of a tale that can't help but make us giggle at its sheer absurdity. Here then is a story that proves Yahweh is not only jealous and vindictive, he also has a devilishly keen sense of humor. And I ask you, what could be funnier—and more effective—than to punish your enemies with a plague of hemorrhoids?

The King James Version Bible calls them "emerods". More modern versions of the narrative, e.g. the New International Version, refer to them as "tumors". Obviously the writers of these later editions were embarrassed by their own silly scriptures—as well they should be—and therefore felt the need to diminish the term to make it sound less "icky". But here's the rub: Chapter 5, Verse 9 of good old King James clearly states that the emerods were "in their *secret parts*". Besides, if you go to any dictionary and look up "emerods" you will find hemorrhoids or piles, but *not* tumors. This is just one more lame attempt by religious apologists to censor what they know to be not only laughable but downright ridiculous. So, how did the scriptural censors address Chapter 5, Verse 9? Simple. They deleted it entirely. How convenient, if not borderline heretical.

As I've mentioned before, I have chosen to draw primarily from the 1611 King James Version because it is the one most often championed by Evangelical Fundamentalists as being the "unerring, incontrovertible Word of God". And so, if the KJV calls for hemorrhoids, then HEMORRHOIDS it is!

When I first learned of this story my own reaction was, "You have *got* to be kidding me! God gave them *hemorrhoids?* Wow, talk about being *anal!*" Obviously, this is a story that can neither be taken nor told with *any* degree of seriousness. The only fitting genre in which to relate it, therefore, would be a farce, as my subtitle suggests. Now, when it comes to "classical farce" no one does it better, drier or more poignant than the British. And when sheer lunacy and silly-ass nonsense is called for—as this biblical panto clearly demands—what better Muses to inspire me through the creative process than the cast of *Monty Python's Flying Circus*! That said, I hereby dedicate this slightly naughty narrative to the brilliantly warped minds of John Cleese, Eric Idle, Michael Palin, Terry Jones, Terry Gilliam, and Graham Chapman.

It all began with the classic and seemingly never-ending rivalry between the Israelites and the Philistines; a traditional tale of "us" (the good guys) versus "them" (the bad guys). These two belligerent forces fought a total of thirteen battles throughout the two Samuelian sagas, the final box score being Israelites 10, Philistines 2. The fourth battle of the series actually ended without a win by either side, as the Israelites, upon seeing the size of the Philistine army ran for cover and hid until the danger had passed. (And remember, the Philistines had "giants" in their ranks; some of those leftover Nephilim, no doubt.)

It is impossible to know exactly what the Israelites had against the Philistines and vice versa. The Christian Bible takes us back to the time of Abraham and the Philistine king, Abimelech, and a dispute over a livestock well. Abraham claimed the well belonged to his people because he had dug it. Abimelech claimed it belonged to *his* people because the Israelites were essentially squatters on Philistine land. (Many Jewish Bible scholars discredit this account altogether as a mere Christian fairytale with no historical or archeological basis whatsoever. But that's an entirely different feud.)

You might recall that there was another to-do when Abraham and his wife, Sarah, were traveling in Philistine territory. King Abimelech received word of Sarah's extraordinary beauty (despite the fact that she was *90 years old!*) and wished to see her. Fearing that the king would kill him and lay claim to Sarah if he knew she was his wife, Abraham—another one of those "righteous men of God"—in order to protect his own life, lied and told the king that she was his sister. The ploy backfired, and Abimelech, delighted by the discovery, took Sarah to be his wife anyway.

Now Abraham really was in a pickle. He had saved his own selfish skin by lying, yet he lost Sarah all the same. He feared, if he were to 'fess-up at this point, Abimelech might kill him out of anger at the deception. (It must be stressed that Abimelech, king of the "barbaric" Philistine tribes, had acted with the utmost courtesy and generosity toward his guests. And even after learning of their rude deception, he offered gifts and safe passage.) Our hero, Abraham, never did summon the courage to tell the truth. Instead, God himself had to speak to Abimelech in a dream (but only after causing all the Philistine women to become barren until the king returned Sarah to her coward of a husband). When the king asked Abraham why he had lied and said Sarah was his sister, Abe told him that "technically" she *was* his sister, as they shared the same father but not the same mother. So once again we see that as long as you're one of Yahweh's "chosen people" it's perfectly all right to lie, cheat, steal or even commit "half" incest.

In a nutshell, the Israelite/Philistine conflict could be summed up thus: The Philistines had land; the Israelites wanted land. And as anyone who has actually read the Old Testament knows, the main theme is mostly about the Israelites wandering about or being driven from place to place and eventually waging one bloody, genocidal war after another for the sole purpose of depriving other people of *their* land. Now, when one considers the situation in the Middle East today, one has to ask, has anything really changed?

But our story begins over a thousand years further down the highly subjective biblical timeline, circa 1100 BCE, when the Israelites are camped out in the land of Canaan. The Bible book's namesake, Samuel, is a prophet and the last of the traditional judges, a.k.a. lawgiver, a.k.a. mouthpiece of God. The whole point of the Samuel series is to show the social and political movement of the fragmented, tribal Israelite people away from their dependency upon one guy, i.e. a prophet with self-proclaimed powers of divination, and toward the more tangible, visible and empirical rule of a human king.

Bronze Age biblical pseudo-historians bewail this transition as one more lamentable case of mankind turning away from its god and his immutable, inscrutable laws in favor of a world filled with fleshy familiarity. Freethinking sociologists, on the other hand, would view this fable as metaphorical evidence of a people's cultural and psychological turning point, an emergence from the shadows of superstitious domination coupled with a desire to become a united nation, governed by a corporeal ruler made of the same mortal stuff as themselves; a ruler who can "feel their pain", so to speak, and converse with them on a personal level. Too soon for true secular independence perhaps, but a nascent recognition that getting your laws and directives from some crazy-eyed coot who talks to an invisible floating head and cooks with his own excrement (actually, that was Ezekiel) just might not be the smartest thing to do.

It was during the first battle of the series that the problems began. The Israelites started the fight, acting on the word of their main man, Samuel, who of course took his marching orders directly from the Big Kahuna in the sky. However, by the seventh inning the Phillies were winning quite handily, having already killed 4,000 men without even breaking a sweat.

Back on the sidelines of Team Israel, the elders were scratching their heads and asking, "Why did the LORD bring defeat upon us today before the Philistines? Especially when it was all his idea in the first place."

And that's when the Israelites, realizing they were about to take a serious drubbing, decided to bring in their heaviest hitter: God Almighty himself. Well, this is a little hard to do when your god doesn't have a face or a body or any other physical attribute with which to strike terror in the hearts of your enemies, so they did the next best thing. They sent messengers to Shiloh, asking the high priests to bring out God's home-away-from-Heaven: the Ark of the Covenant, the magical gilded packing crate that supposedly contained the second draft of the Ten Commandments and served as a supernatural radio transmitter between Yahweh and his earthbound talking heads. Surely the sight alone of this magnificent god-in-a-box would cause their enemies to flee in abject terror!

We join the action at halftime. Bloodied, demoralized and perhaps a bit hungry too, the Israelites have limped back to their home base at Ebenezer to lick their wounds, have a nosh and a grog, and wonder why their all-powerful god has allowed them to suffer such a beastly shellacking. And then, from the distant hills, a cloud of dust and the sound of trumpets as the sacred caravan approaches!

"Look there! It comes!" shouted a great chorus of exuberant Israelite voices in joyful unison. "The Ark of God is coming! Now we shall have victory over our enemies, for no army can withstand the mighty force of our LORD! We shall kill them with a great slaughter as we did the Aradites; and the Midianites; and the entire populations of Jericho and Ai; and also the twenty kingdoms that are too numerous to mention right now; and the Anakim; and the Canaanites and Perizzites; and all the inhabitants of Jerusalem and half a dozen kingdoms around Hebron, Zephath and Bethel; and a bunch of Mesopotamians; and the Moabites; and some other Philistines; and the

Canaanites again; and the entire army of Sisera; and the Amalekites; and the Midianites again, even though we slaughtered all their men 250 years ago; and all the inhabitants of the twenty Ammonite cities; and forty-two thousand of our own brothers, the Ephraimites, because they wouldn't help us slaughter the Ammonites, and that really pissed us off, so there; and then we had to have this civil war with our other brothers, the Benjamites, because they wouldn't hand over the guys who raped to death the Levite's concubine from the other story, so as punishment, we slaughtered all their women and children and babies, but then that's nothing new for us, and anyway, if God tells you to do it, it must be OK!"

And the sound of this mighty cry was so great that the entire earth shook! Even in Aphek, where the Philistine army was camped, the reverberations caused every soldier to look up and ask, "What the fuck?"

The Philistine general sent scouts to see what all the fuss was about. When the scouts returned, they carried grievous news: "The Israelites have brought their magical god box into their camp!"

"Magical god box?" inquired one soldier. "Bligh me, you mean their god lives inside a ruddy box?"

"How big of a box?" asked another.

The scout thought for a moment. "Oh, I'd say roughly two and a half cubits long and about one and a half cubits, yea by yea." He spread his arms for emphasis.

A lance bearer rubbed his whiskered jaw. "Would that be an Egyptian cubit or a metric cubit?"

"Well, um... I don't rightly know. I didn't really get a good look at it. They keep it covered in a blanket."

"Oh yeah, that's good thinking," said a soldier. "The starlings are downright nasty this time of year." Several soldiers nodded their helmeted heads in agreement. "Why, just last week I took me new chariot out for a spin; parked it under that big cedar tree in me front yard. Two hours later the dirty little gits had covered the whole thing with shit."

"Bloody plague of the little buggers, I'd call it." More nods and murmurings of agreement.

"Nights are a bit chilly too. Could be they don't want their god catching a cold, eh?"

"No, no, can't have that."

"Still, it can't be much of a god if it lives in a tiny little box like that, right?"

One of the archers made a comical face. "Maybe he sits all

scrunched up in there, and when somebody opens the lid he *jumps* out and shouts, "*Booga-booga!*"

A wave of ribald laughter rippled through the encampment.

"Size matters not!" came a gravelly voice from the ranks. It was Adoy, the Philistine water carrier and mascot. "Judge *me* by my size, do you?"

An awkward silence fell upon the group as they scuffled their sandals and averted their collective gazes from the diminutive member. "Well, yeah. We do, actually," said a warrior. "Nothing personal, mate. It's just that, we have this image to uphold, right? I mean, race of giants and all."

Adoy's toad-like eyes narrowed upon the warrior, whose name just happened to be Goliath. "Then heard you have *not* how the god of the Israelites, plagues against the Egyptians brought, and slew he did the first born male of every household, hmmm?"

One of the foot soldiers turned and whispered to the man beside him, "Does he always talk that way?"

"Yeah, but don't pay him no mind. It's a glandular thing. He's aces as a water carrier though."

Another cut in, "But he *is* right about the plagues and the killing of the first born males in Egypt, y'know."

When the rest of the Philistine army heard this, they all cried in unison—because that's the way people talked in those days—"Woe unto us, for a god is come into the Israelite camp, and there hath not been such a thing heretofore...except for that time awhile back when the Israelite prophet Joshua used the bloody thing to destroy the city of Jericho, not that anyone's counting." And with tears in their eyes, they continued to wail, still in unison, "Who shall deliver us out of the hand of these mighty gods? These are the gods that smote the Egyptians with all the plagues in the wilderness!"

The Philistine general, having had enough of their unison wailing and collective blubbering, gave them an inspiring pep talk and essentially told them to suck it up, grow a pair, and start acting like Philistines, which they did, then returned to the battlefield and proceeded to beat the ever-lovin' matzos out of the Israelites once more, this time slaughtering thirty thousand foot soldiers. Then, to add insult to injury, they captured the magical god box and carried it off to their stronghold at Ashdod.

The surviving Israelites now, having taken to hiding in their tents like frightened school girls, were needless to say a bit perplexed, not to mention downright disappointed that their precious Ark had not exactly lived up to expectations. Now they really began to wail and make a righteous spectacle of themselves. In the town of Shiloh, where the Ark keepers lived, the lamenting was especially vociferous. An old, fat, blind ex-prophet named Eli, who started out being Samuel's spiritual tutor until he pissed off God and turned to the Dark Side, had been sitting in a chair on top of a wall waiting to hear the battle scores. When a messenger told him what had happened, Eli got so upset he accidentally threw himself over backward, toppled off the wall and broke his neck. Some townsfolk wondered why an old, fat, blind guy was sitting in a chair on a wall in the first place, so they chalked it up to God's inscrutable revenge.

Meanwhile, the Philistines were reveling in their victory. Now that they had the Israelites' magical god box, they had to decide where to put it. The priests concluded, logically, that it should go in the temple next to the altar of their own fish-man god, Dagon.

"A teensy bit to the left...a bit farther... Right there—perfect!" The head priest smiled and waved to the movers. "Thanks, fellas!"

After the movers had gone, the priests stood back to admire this latest acquisition. The head priest smiled and clasped his hands in front of him. "Oh my, yes. That really does tie the whole room together. Don't you agree?"

"Well, to be perfectly honest, I think it's a tad gaudy," remarked the second priest. "I mean, I just *adore* the little cherubs, don't get me wrong. But all that gold bric-a-brac...tack-*E*! Good heavens, even the Persians show more restraint."

Arms folded across his exquisitely embroidered bosom, the third priest nodded. "You would think that a people who are forever wandering about in the wilderness, constantly complaining of being cold and tired and hungry and thirsty would learn how to better invest their assets."

"Yes, quite, absolutely," they all agreed. And with that they departed with a priestly flourish.

The following morning when the priests came into the temple, they discovered a dreadful sight: The big, heavy statue of their god, Dagon, had fallen over and was lying face down next to the Ark. Horrified, they called upon a few of those Philistine giants to help put him back on his pedestal. "Thanks again, fellas! Sorry to be such a nuisance," called the head priest as they were leaving. He turned to the other priests and whispered, "Did you see the calves on Goliath?"

The second priest pressed a hand upon his thumping heart. "*Did* I! And what about those biceps? You could've knocked me over with a pebble."

"Well, he certainly has *my* vote for Philistine of the Year," tittered the third.

The head priest gazed at the now righted statue of their fish-man god and drummed his fingers together speculatively. "So... what *do* you suppose it was that caused Dagon to fall over?"

The other two exchanged nervous glances.

"Vandals?"

"Gust of wind?"

"Earth tremors caused by Israelites wailing in mass unison?"

Then they all peered at the glistening, gold-plated Israelite god box still sitting exactly where they had placed it the day before.

"Do you think...?"

"Is it possible...?"

The third priest gasped. "Are you suggesting that their god *crawled* out of the box and tipped Dagon over?"

A collective shudder ran through the three. They huddled close to one another. "Perhaps someone should look inside," said the head priest.

The second priest nodded. "Yes, someone with the *most* authority."

The head priest frowned. "Or someone with the *least* seniority."

"Surely you can't mean *me*," cried the third priest. "I have thirteen children!"

The second priest rolled his eyes. Oh, puh-*lease*! You have thirteen *cats*."

"And they are as precious to me as any child," the third replied with a huff.

After considering the situation carefully, the head priest made a sage decision. "Perhaps it would be best to simply ignore the whole thing." And so they did.

On the morning of the second day the three priests entered the temple to find an even more dreadful sight. As before, the statue of Dagon lay face down upon the floor beside the Ark, but this time his head and hands had been broken off until nothing was left but a very unattractive fishy stump. Upon seeing this, the three priests screamed aloud in terrified unison.

"It *must* be the god of Israel!" cried the priest with the least seniority but with a lovely soprano voice. "He has risen from his magical golden box and smited Dagon!"

"Smote," said the head priest.

"What's that?"

"Smote. I believe it's smote. 'He has risen from his magical golden box and *smote* Dagon.'"

The second priest looked thoughtful for a moment then shook his head. "No, actually I think it should be *smitten*. 'He has *smitten* Dagon.'"

"Are you sure about that?"

"Quite sure. 'I smite. I smote. I have smitten.' It's being used in the past perfect tense, you see, with the auxiliary verb *has*, ergo 'has smitten.'"

The third priest nodded. "I think he's right. It should be smitten. Oops, silly me."

Hardly had they concluded this grammatical meeting of the minds when the air became filled with a cacophony of pain-filled screams. The priests scurried outside to see that the entire city had been smitten with some manner of grievous calamity. Bodies lay strewn here and there, many dead, many more twisting and writhing before eventually dying. Children and babies too were not spared an agonizing death, but then, the god of Israel was known not to discriminate when it came to smiting. Within moments the entire population of Ashdod, with the exception of a few hundred men, was dead.

Hands clasped in horror, the priests looked around at the scene of carnage. "Dagon, save us!" they cried in unison. But Dagon could not help them because he was, after all, nothing but a mere stump of his former self.

And then something else began to happen. The men who had been left alive began to squirm in great discomfort. The priests too felt it; a burning itch deep in their secret parts. "What manner of curse *is* this?" cried the lesser priest, whose lovely soprano voice had become a piercing screech.

The head priest tore away his outer robes and plunged his fingers into the crevasse between his secret-part cheeks, digging furiously, hoping to find relief. But the painful, burning itch only intensified. "Never have I known such agony—except that one time during High Mass when we all got really drunk..."

"How can we make it stop?"

"To the fountains! Perchance we can quench our misery there!"

But when they got to the fountains in the center of town, they discovered that every man similarly afflicted had had the same idea. Fights broke out for a chance to squat in the cooling waters, yet try as they might, no relief was to be found. Not surprisingly, no one was at all concerned any longer with the thousands of dead bodies lying about.

"It is a scourge from the god of Israel!" some wailed.

"He has set upon us a plague of *emerods!*"

The giant, Goliath, ran mincingly by. "Fe, fi, fo, fum. I've got a fire down deep in me bum!"

Someone pointed a smelly finger. "Look there—the priests! *They* should have done something!"

The head priest stared at the angry, itchy mob, which was growing angrier and itchier by the second. "Don't blame *us*. We're not the ones who brought that wretched box here. And besides, we're just as afflicted as the rest of you." With that, he turned around and hoisted his tunic up over his backside to reveal his secret parts. "*See?*" he said, bending over.

Gasps and groans of revulsion reverberated through the crowd.

"Gawd, look at the size of those things!" someone cried.

"Uhg! It's like a big cluster of bloodshot grapes!"

"By the gods, are we all going to look like that?"

"This itching and burning in my secret parts is *maddening!*"

"You're still our spiritual leaders!" a townsman shouted as he tried to position himself over a bucket of water. "We pay your salaries, so *do something!*"

"Yes, *do* something!" they all began to shout. In unison.

As the miserable swelling and pain in their own secret parts grew worse, the priests quickly conferred amongst themselves. At last the head priest turned to the crowd. "We must get rid of the magical Israelite god box. We must send it away immediately."

"But send it where? Who will take it once word of this calamity gets out?"

The head priest pondered this for a moment. "We must act quickly before the news is spread. We'll send it to our sister city, Gath." He whispered aside to his two companions, "Ever since they won that goat's head soccer championship last year they've been positively insufferable. Methinks a little dose of humility would do them good."

And so despite the itching and the burning and the painful swelling from the curse of emerods in their secret parts, the men of Ashdod loaded the troublesome Ark onto an oxcart and sent it away to the Philistine city of Gath where the same damn thing happened all over again. Only this time, along with the indiscriminate smiting of its citizenry and the scourge of painful emerods in their secret parts, the city was besieged by a plague of mice that ate everything in sight. Here too the local priests came up with the brilliant idea of sending the accursed Israelite god box to the next Philistine city of Ekron. (Can you guess what happened next?)

Now, the priests in Ekron weren't nearly as stupid or vindictive as those in Ashdod and Gath. Rather than send the extravagant Israelite god-in-the-box to yet another Philistine city and cause those people grievous injury as well, they concocted another plan. The head priest of Ekron called for a conclave between the five Philistine city-states to decide what could be done to remedy their mutual problem. Since Ashdod, Gath and now Ekron were already besieged and quite literally up to their collective asses in emerods, mice and the stench of rotting corpses, it was decided that the conclave would be held either in Ashkelon or Gaza.

"Oh please, not Gaza," the second priest opined. "That place is an in-breeders meat market."

"He's right about that," the third priest agreed. "I heard that the king passed a new law in Gaza: When a couple gets divorced, they're still legally *brother and sister.*"

The three erupted in laughter.

Holding his sides, the second priest added, "Hey, what do you have when you put thirty-two Gazans in the same room?" He paused for effect. "A full set of *teeth!*"

Barely able to contain himself, the head priest cried, "Stop it! Stop it...! Oh bugger, I think I'm starting to bleed again." Trying to recover his composure, he wiped his eyes. "Right then, Ashkelon it is." He continued to chuckle despite the aggravation in his secret parts. "I rather fancy a few days on the Mediterranean, perhaps a long soak in some warm salt water." He grimaced as he pressed his fingers deep into the source of his misery. "Bloody hell, if these things grow much larger, I'm afraid they'll get wrapped around a chariot axle."

And so the word was spread, calling the priests from the five Philistine city-states to gather in the balmy and affluent seaport city of Ashkelon to confer on the matter.

Now, the Ashkelonian priests were not exactly thrilled with having their polished marble temple descended upon by this assemblage of dusty, itchy, smelly inlanders, but what could they do? They had heard about the horrific plagues that had befallen their kinsmen, and not wishing the same fate for themselves, decided that it would indeed be in their own best interests to assist in the matter.

From a wide balcony overlooking the sea, they peered down their patrician noses into the meticulously adorned courtyard at the varied collection of fellow holy men. "A rather motley assortment, wouldn't you say?" remarked the first in his resplendent robes of peacock blue with gold tassel trim.

The second priest sniffed as if detecting an unpleasant odor. "Indubitably; the type that gives 'Philistine' a bad name."

The third breathed a heavy sigh. "They brought this entire problem upon themselves, you know. Why they did not dispose of the monstrosity at the first sign of trouble is beyond me. But to keep it for *seven months!*"

"Well, I suppose we should be grateful they didn't bring the infernal thing *with* them," said the second priest.

The priests from Gaza stood off to one side of the courtyard, muttering amongst themselves.

"Just look at 'em with their hoity-toity fancy robes," remarked the highest priest, giving his own desert-camo patterned robe a swish. "Well, they don't look so high-and-mighty now, do they?"

The second priest snorted. "Yeah, when they're in trouble *then* they call us."

"Did they really think we'd believe that donkey shit about our invitation to their king's birthday party gettin' 'lost in the mail'?" said the third as he wiped the henna chew from the corner of his mouth.

"They're just jealous, y'know," sneered the second. "All of Philistia knows Gaza has the best strip mines, strip malls and strip clubs in the entire Mediterranean. They don't call it 'The Gaza Strip' fer nothin'."

The highest Gazan priest scratched his whiskered jaw. "Y'know, this little emerod affair might just give us the leverage we need to push for secession. I mean, with nearly everyone in Ashdod, Gath and Ekron *dead* and the rest runnin' around either scratchin', scootin' or soakin', who could stop us?"

The third priest smiled at the notion. "Yeah... Finally, our own country."

"A new country's gotta have a new name," said the second priest. "How about Gazania?"

The other two priests looked thoughtful.

"A bit girly, don't y'think?" remarked the third.

"And I reckon you gotta better idea?"

"Well, we're still Philistines, y'know. And we do have a certain image to uphold: race of giants, strike fear in the hearts of our enemies and whatnot. I think we should work with that."

"He's right, y'know," said the head priest.

"OK, how does Gazastine sound?"

"Gazastine..." The head priest mulled the word over. "Yep, I think you're on the right track. And we can call ourselves the

Gazastinians! I'll run it by King Palles the minute we get back."

The third priest hocked a loogey into a potted palm. "Shoot, with *his* ego we'll probably wind up bein' called the '*Palles-tinians*'."

After a round of refreshments, the Ashkelonian head priest called the gathering to order. "All right then. We all know why we are here. We must find a way to undo the curse—or curses—that have been placed upon our brother Philistines by the god of the Israelites."

The Gazan second priest grabbed a handful of shrimp from an ornate silver tray and began thumb-chucking them into his mouth. "Seems pretty straightforward to me," he said as he chewed. "Just get ridda the dang thing."

The Ekronian priests took a collective step backward so as to avoid any wayward spew from the Gazan priest's slack-jawed masticating. "We considered getting 'ridda' it, but that tactic didn't help the Ashdodians nor Gathians any," replied the Ekronian head priest. "Besides, if we damage the Israelite's magical box in any way, it's likely to piss off their all-mighty god even further."

The Ashkelonian head priest held up his hand. "I believe the logical course of action would be to return the god box to its rightful owners as soon as possible."

"Do you think that alone would be enough?" asked the Gathian head priest, who, up to this point, hadn't said much of anything. "After all, a god with the power to inflict so much carnage and suffering upon innocent women and children probably won't be appeased by the mere return of his property. We'll have to do more if we are to rid ourselves of this dreadful plague of mice and emerods."

They all nodded and murmured in agreement.

The Ashkelonian priest agreed as he wiped a bit of half-chewed shrimp from his exquisite peacock-colored robe. "What do you suggest then?"

The head priest of Ekron stepped forward, for the Gazan had finally swallowed. "Perhaps we should send along some sort of guilt offering to seal the deal."

The Gazan priests exchanged puzzled looks. "You mean a *bribe*?"

"More like a kind of material apology."

"A very, very sincere apology," added an Ashdodian priest as he squirmed this way and that on a fleece-covered ottoman in the desperate hope of finding relief from the maddening itch that burned in his secret parts.

"But what manner of guilt offering should this be?" asked the third Ashkelonian priest. "It should be something worthy of the status of such a powerful god."

The Gazan second priest reached up and dug around his few remaining teeth to extract a piece of shrimp shell. He inspected it briefly then flicked it over his shoulder. "What's so dang special 'bout this holy tote box anyway? I mean, what's it even look like?"

The priests of Ashdod, Gath and Ekron took turns describing the magnificently beautiful Ark with its gold plated sides, and ornately crafted solid gold molding all around, and solid gold carrying rings, and gold plated carrying staves, and the solid gold lid, and the solid gold cherubs.

The head priest of Ashkelon stroked his chin thoughtfully. "It would appear that this Israelite god is quite fond of gold."

And so it was decided that the guilt offering should be made of solid gold, because everybody loves gold, even gods, and especially the mortals who represent those gods. Now, as to the actual form the offering should take... The priests conferred once more, all of them talking so that it was difficult to follow who was saying what.

The Ekronian priest stopped scratching and wiped his fingers on a nearby curtain. "We should make it in the shape of the things that are afflicting us, so that the Israelite god will know that *we* know that he is the cause of our great suffering."

"That's good. We'll make a gold mouse to represent the plague of mice!"

"A mouse? A single, bloody, gold *mouse?* That hardly seems like much of an apology."

"Well, all right then—*five* gold mice, one for each city state. That should get our message across."

"Er, beg pardon," said a Gathian priest, who was standing with the fluted edge of a marble column wedged firmly between his secret parts. "But what about this *other* affliction? How are we going to address *that*?"

The Ashkelonian priests recoiled in disgust at the sight of the emerod-stricken holy men using their resplendent sacred temple for a rectal scratching post.

Beads of sweat trickled down the Ashdodian priest's forehead as he tried desperately to press himself deeper into the fleece-covered ottoman with a twisting motion. "He's right, you know," he groaned. "We can't exactly ignore it."

"Right then, I suppose we have to address it. But just how do you propose we do it? I mean, I haven't the foggiest idea what *it* even looks like."

"We'll need a model."

"A model?"

"Yeah. Someone with a proper set that we can use for a design."

"Maybe we don't need a model. Maybe each of us could just, you know, give 'em a squeeze, compare notes, and mock something up."

"Right, mate. And do think a god powerful enough to cause all this mess is going to be fooled by a *mock up*?"

"He's right, you know. If we go at this thing half-assed—no pun intended—this god is liable to do something much worse!"

"He's already killed nearly every woman and child in our cities and most of the men and smote the rest with emerods. Hard to believe it could *get* much worse."

"I agree. We've got to do it first rate. Therefore, we have to find someone with a set that's worthy of replication. That way, the guilt offering comes off as truly sincere, like we're saying, 'Here you go, god of Israel. We get it. You're Number One. Really, really sorry about taking your magical box.'"

They all agreed that this was the most logical course of action.

"Right then, any ideas how we're going to find out who's got the biggest cluster?"

Their eyes darted about the room with nervous non-commitment.

"Oh, come on, lads. We're all in the same boat here. And besides, how else is there to do it?"

"We'll need a judge," a Gathian priest ventured timidly.

They all peered at the three Ashkelonian priests. "Oh, no!" the head priest exclaimed. "We allowed you to use our temple for your little...gathering. That's as far as we intend to go."

Obviously enjoying their fellow Philistines' predicament, the Gazan priests began to snicker. "How 'bout gettin' one of them ASS-dod fellers to help out?" the first priest chortled.

The second joined in. "Yeah, I hear they're experts at workin' *behind* the scenes."

"Hey, you know what they call emerods in ASS-dod?" snorted the third. "*Speed bumps!*"

The three Ashdodian priests stood with hands on hips, glaring. "Seriously?" remarked the head priest, shaking his head. "That's the best you can come up with—infantile name-calling?"

"They can't help it," added the second Ashdodian priest. "It's a product of their infantile mentality. They are lucky though.

With all those wonderful strip malls, they can go shopping for a present for their mother, their sister and their girlfriend and only need to buy *one gift.*"

The third Ashdodian priest smiled to his companions. "And they will *never* be smitten with emerods, because the gods made them all such *perfect assholes!*"

Everyone was doubled over with laughter now, except the Gazans, who stood looking rather puzzled. "I don't get it," said their head priest. "How can you have three women but only buy one gift?"

The room erupted in hilarity once more.

Clapping his hands, the head priest of Ashkelon brought the group back to order. "We have to focus, people. Since the priests of Ashdod, Gath and Ekron have the most...intimate...knowledge of the situation, I propose that they orchestrate the...uh...fact finding."

The head priest of Ekron took the fore. "All right, then, lads. I think the fairest way to do this is democratically."

"Oh, goody—*Greek style!*" tittered the third Ashdodian priest.

"Each city's representatives will evaluate the other two. Points will be awarded for size, shape, texture and overall artistic presentation. When everyone's had a chance to judge and be judged, we'll tally the scores and choose whose emerods will serve as the model for our guilt offering. Please remember, we're looking for the most symbolic example of godly smiting and indiscriminate vindictiveness on the part of a deity."

The nine priests withdrew to a private chamber for the judging of their emerods. It was a solemn and purpose-driven undertaking, punctuated by groans of disgust and a considerable amount of retching. At one point a rather nearsighted priest from Gath got a bit too close to his subject with a candle and inadvertently performed the first-ever emerod cauterization.

After a grueling hour of proctological evaluations, the head priest of Ekron, looking a bit pale, emerged from the chamber. "Well, I think we've got our model," he said, wiping a bead of sweat from his forehead. "Turns out *I'm* the lucky bloke."

One of the Gazans nudged the other and whispered, "I wager the whole dang thing was rigged."

And so the royal sculptor was summoned to create the guilt offerings: five solid gold mice and five solid gold emerods to represent the five Philistine city-states.

"Hold still!" the squint-eyed sculptor snapped as he drew his metal calipers together on the head priest's afflicted parts.

Teeth clenched, the priest gripped the frame of the chair he was bent over. "Bloody hell! Be careful with those things!"

"Hey, you want this accurate or don't you?" The sculptor flipped the priest's robes higher up over his backside for a better view. "Besides, it ain't like *you* got the worst part of this job, mate."

Once completed the guilt offerings were laid in a fine cedar box which was carried home by the Ekronian priests and placed next to the accursed Ark.

"All right then, now what do we do with it?" asked the second priest.

They all thought very hard on the matter, trying to come up with the most sensible and logical course of action; one that stood the best chance of assuring their deliverance from their dire afflictions.

"I've got it!" cried the third priest. "OK, here's what we do. We put the magical god box on an oxcart with the guilt offerings beside it. Then, we find two cows that have just given birth and are heavy with milk, but we don't let their calves nurse. Instead we lock up the calves."

The second priest frowned. "They'll go bonkers screaming for their mums."

"And likely tear down the barn in the process," added the head priest.

The third priest continued, "Then, we'll hitch the cows to the cart. But these have to be cows that have never been harnessed before!"

The two other priests exchanged worried glances. "That's it then, he's gone off his donkey."

"Completely barmy."

"No, no, listen!" the third priest persisted. "Once we get them hitched, we send them off down the road, let them go wherever they want."

"Straight off a cliff, I'm thinking," chortled the second priest.

"And our only chance for salvation along with it," the head priest remarked with a shake of his head. "I'm *not* hanging my clusters out again for some jolly wanker to pinch and jab!"

Now notably frustrated, the third priest pressed on. "Don't you see? If the cows run willy nilly then we'll know our problems are merely happenstance, a fluke, not the result of divine retribution at all. But..." He paused for emphasis, his eyes wide with enthusiasm. "If they calmly head straight for the Israelite city of Bethshemesh without hesitation or waver, then we'll know proof-positive that it was the god of Israel who smote us with these grievous afflictions."

"I thought we had pretty much already concluded that."

The two other priests stood for a moment in solemn contemplation. Then the head priest shrugged. "Well, that makes perfect sense to me."

"Me too," agreed the second. "Flawlessly logical in every detail. Let's get to it at once!"

So that's exactly what they did. And just as the third priest had predicted, the cows set off toward Bethshemesh, mooing gently as they went, turning neither right nor left until they came to a stop near a big rock beside a wheat field. And when the Israelites working in the field saw the Ark coming they rejoiced (no doubt in unison) and did what any civilized religious people would do: They smashed the cart and piled the wood in a heap, then slit the throats of the cows and threw their carcasses on top for a burnt offering to their LORD. Next, the Levite priests removed the Ark and the box containing the guilt offerings—yes, in *that* order—and placed them on the big rock.

The Philistines meanwhile gazed on from a safe distance. "Bloody good trick that," commented the second priest. "I mean, smashing the cart to splinters, burning the cows on top of it, *then* removing the magical god box."

The head priest scratched his head. "I guess that's the great thing about miracles; don't require too much thinking, right? And speaking of which..." A smile shone from his heretofore incommodious features. "I do believe I'm feeling a bit better in my secret parts!"

The third priest beamed. "Come to think of it, so am I!"

The second priest clapped his hands triumphantly. "All right then, who's up for a sitz bath in the sacred ceremonial font? I'll bring the lavender-scented olive oil!"

And they all laughed in unison, because everything turned out well...in the end.

℘ . . . ℭ

There now, wasn't that a delightful little tale? With a happy ending for all. Well, it *would* have been if we could leave it at that. Trouble is, old Yahweh just can't seem to stop smiting people. And when he isn't smiting his enemies, he's smiting his own people. If we read a bit further (1 Samuel 6:19 KJV) we see that "...he smote the men of Bethshemesh, because they had looked into the ark of the LORD, even he smote of the people fifty thousand and threescore and ten men: and the people lamented, because the LORD had smitten many of the people with a great slaughter." Good grief—*50,070 men*, his own adoring people—

snuffed out simply for looking inside the pretty gold box?!

But wait, maybe it isn't as bad as all that. If we read from the New International Version of the Bible we find, "But God struck down some of the men of Beth Shemesh, putting seventy of them to death because they had looked into the ark of the LORD. The people mourned because of the heavy blow the LORD had dealt them." This time only *70* men were murdered in an angry, vindictive pissy fit by the god of perfect love. *Wow*, that's some difference! But it does make me feel a lot better. Still, doesn't it strike you as strange that the two different versions of the "same" Bible story could have such a *drastically dissimilar* body count? I mean, I could certainly see it being off by a couple of hundred or so—but 50 *THOUSAND*?

There are a few other dissimilarities between the two versions. In the NIV offering the two pestilences are "rats and tumors"; whereas in the KJV it's "mice and emerods in their secret parts". This is just more proof that the Bible—in *all* its many versions—is nothing more than a silly, nonsensical, downright idiotic fabrication concocted by *mortal men* with very poor communication skills and even worse math skills. As for the discrepancy between "70" men slaughtered vs. "50,070", this is obviously a pathetic attempt by the NIV word-smithers to "soften" old Yahweh and make him seem less of a galactic-sized homicidal maniac, which he still is, no matter how you reduce it.

I also find it quite odd (one might say completely *absurd*) that the Philistines themselves—despite having the Ark in their possession for *seven months*—didn't take a peek inside at the very beginning, which would certainly be the logical thing for a bunch of plundering, barbaric conquerors to do. I mean, wouldn't *you*? But then again, if they *had*, our story would be a lot shorter and not nearly as amusing. So I guess we'll just have to chalk that up to one of those many "Bible mysteries" that never get addressed.

And if you're wondering what on earth became of the magical, mysterious Ark of the Covenant...you'll have to rent *Raiders of the Lost Ark* to find out, because one work of "fantasy fiction" is just as good as any other!

Elisha and the Bears
As Found in the Book of 2 Kings
Chapter 2: Verses 23-25

There is much being said in the news these days about trying to stem the rise of bullying in schools. Bullying happens at all age levels and can assume many forms from verbal taunts to outright physical attacks. It can cause severe and lifelong consequences, including driving certain hapless individuals to commit suicide or even murder. This is a story about bullying and how the prophet, Elisha, deals with the problem—"*God style*".

As with all my literary reconstructions, I first try to get to know my main characters, who they are, what they want in life, where they come from and why they behave as they do. In police circles this is a task known as "profiling". It is a forensic tool used to understand the workings of a criminal mind with the ultimate goal being to capture said criminal. I consider every one of these Bible tales to be in its own way a crime scene; actually, a crime scene within a crime scene, for the "victims" are not only the literary constructs on paper, they are also the readers (or *listeners*), who have, throughout history, been forced through psychological bullying and even physical torture to accept and believe that these fairytales really happened.

Let's take a moment to examine the character of Elisha. All the Western religions regard him as a great prophet (though not all of them can agree on where he came from or what he did *per se*). Nevertheless, he is overall credited with performing a multitude of miracles, including parting the waters of the River Jordan, curing diseases and raising the dead. But then, this is pretty standard fare for a prophet. (On a side note: It's kind of funny how Christians point to the "miracles" of Jesus as proof that he is "The Promised One", "Son of God", etc., yet nothing he did was particularly special or unique in any way, and that *includes* getting born to a virgin, which had already "happened" over thirty times in various other pagan religions, sometimes thousands of years before *he* was supposedly born!)

Actually, the whole business of being a "prophet" seems to carry with it a laundry list of preternatural prerequisites. It's like in Olympic figure skating: You *must* execute certain basic moves if you even want to get on the board. I think being able to call yourself a "prophet" must be a lot like that. I mean, if you can't perform a simple parting of the waters, conjuring manna out of thin air or healing a blind guy, you better go back to school.

OK, so what makes Elisha special? In my opinion—not a damn thing; at least, not as a prophet. However, as a villain he ranks right up there with Eric Harris and Dylan Klebold (Columbine High School Massacre, April 20, 1999) and Adam Lanza (Sandy Hook Elementary School Massacre, December 14, 2012). Please believe me, even though I do at times use satire and humor to punctuate and elucidate the utter absurdity of these stories, I am *in no way* making light of these two very real and very heartbreaking events that took place in the United States. My point is exactly this: While the world mourned in grief-stricken shock at hearing the news of these (and numerous other) atrocities perpetrated upon children, the vast majority of that same world prayed to a god who is himself a coldblooded mass-murder of the most innocent and helpless of victims— *children*. This then is another story that proves unequivocally that the biblical "god of love" is anything *but*.

Getting back to the character of Elisha, according to the Bible he was pretty much a nobody from nowhere; the son of a farmer, probably in his late teens, unmarried, no doubt a virgin (that seems to be another prerequisite for prophets, since everyone knows that having sex makes you dirty and evil). Then one day while he was out plowing the communal field with a bunch of other guys, he was confronted by the *prophète du jour*, Elijah. Elijah told the young Elisha that he had been chosen to be the next great prophet to God's chosen people. Elisha was so overjoyed that he immediately killed his oxen, hacked them up and threw them in a pot. Then he smashed the plow, threw that into the pot as well and boiled the whole mess into some sort of ox-and-plow-going-away stew for his friends and family. (I wonder how his father viewed the boy's killing of two perfectly good oxen and destroying the family's plow.) This is the first hint we get of his questionable mental stability.

For the next eight years Elisha kept a low profile, earning his keep as Elijah's "Boy Friday" and learning the ways of the Force. It is only toward the end of old Elijah's life that things really get hopping, drama-wise. Now, since Elijah was responsible for molding the lad's spiritual character and strengthening his moral backbone in preparation for such a weighty respon- sibility, I think it important to explore a bit of Elijah's psychological composition as well.

Around the 9th Century BCE, the Kingdom of Israel was being ruled by Omri, a monarch known for his liberal views, particularly his tolerance toward other religions, something old Yahweh simply *cannot* abide. King Omri even went so far as to allow Canaanites, Sumerians and Phoenicians to construct temples for worshipping their own gods in his kingdom. (Apparently he found the laws of Moses too repressive, even downright barbaric, like the ones about burning to death accused harlots, and stoning to death disobedient children or girls without hymens, stuff like that.) He even achieved a great level of domestic security by arranging for his son, Ahab (not the guy with the whale fetish, but another Ahab) to marry the Phoenician princess, Jezebel (yes, *that* Jezebel), who also happened to be a high priestess of the god, Baal. Throughout King Omri's reign, and later that of his son, Israel experienced economic prosperity and cultural enrichment. Everyone was happy. Everyone, that is, except the priests and prophets of *Yahweh the Enforcer*, who no doubt saw their iron-fisted control eroding away due to the influx of personal, intellectual and spiritual freedoms.

It was during the reign of King Ahab that Elijah really made his mark in the Bible. (FYI: In Hebrew, "Elijah" means "My God Is Yahweh!". This is not merely a name, it is also a mission statement.) Elijah could best be described as an arrogant, pushy, obnoxious, sanctimonious, pompous ass. He made it his life's goal to uproot and destroy anything and anyone who refused to worship The Big Y. He prophesied droughts and famines against the people who had chosen to practice freedom of religion. Then, after performing the miracle of conjuring magical fire from Heaven to light his sacrificial pyre, he whipped the believers into a murderous frenzy, which resulted in the wholesale slaughter of hundreds of Baal's priests and followers. Jezebel was so upset by this that she swore to kill Elijah. And who could blame her? Many of the dead were no doubt her friends and family members. (How typical of biblical authors that *she* should be demonized simply because she chose to worship a different god. Yet Elijah, who orchestrated the slaughter of *hundreds of innocent people*, is extolled as one of the greatest prophets of all time.)

With a death sentence hanging over his head, Elijah did what any biblical hero would do after instigating mass murder for the sake of his own religious bigotry—he ran away and went into hiding. Near the point of death from hunger and thirst, he began whining for God to end his life. Instead, God spoke to him in that "still, small voice" inside his head, (probably the same "voice" that has told countless other psychopaths throughout history to commit unspeakable horrors, frequently in the name of God) and sent him on yet another mission. During that time frame he encountered Elisha, prophesied the grisly death of Jezebel and burned to death with more "magical fire" one hundred soldiers who had been sent out to apprehend him.

Just a note before we move on: Now, it's true that Ahab and Jezebel were not exactly sterling citizens by any means (if you can believe anything the Bible says about them). But I promise you this, no matter what crimes or machinations they may have committed, *NOTHING* they did even came close in terms of causing more agony and human suffering to what Elijah himself did. Furthermore, the Bible is in fact *packed* with glorious tales praising the virtues and heroics of God's chosen minions, whose actions bear a striking similarity to the most execrable criminals history has ever known. But then again, if the "still, small voice" tells you to do it...

Perhaps the most remembered story about Elijah involves his death. He didn't really "die" in the traditional sense. He was sucked up alive in a tornado, accompanied by a flaming chariot and flaming horses...as if being sucked up by a tornado wasn't a dramatic enough exit for him.

Upon hearing that his beloved master was soon to be taken away, Elisha, grief-stricken, refused to leave Elijah's side. To console his loyal lackey Elijah asked him what gift he might like as a memento. Elisha wiped his eyes, took a shaky breath and replied, "I want *DOUBLE* your magic powers, old man!" OK, maybe he didn't quite say it that way, but that is precisely what he asked for, to have twice the miracle-making power that Elijah had had. And thus we get another revealing glimpse into Elisha's true character. Though this was a mighty tall order (not to mention patently selfish), Elijah granted the request. And then, as the tornado swirled him away, Elijah dropped his magician's cloak, which the greedy Elisha quickly snatched up and cackled to himself, "*My precious!*" Again, the Bible fable doesn't say he said that, but in a moment you will understand why I threw it in. Now, as anyone who has ever seen a movie about an ordinary guy who suddenly gets superhero powers knows... (say it with me) "*With great power comes great responsibility.*"

I began this article by talking about bullying. When we hear the term we typically think of children being naughty and teasing one of their classmates. Modern disciplinary convention recommends that the two parties sit down and talk things out, share feelings, find common ground, and try to resolve problems in a mutually respectful manner without the need for name calling and *certainly* not violence. Religious apologists will have you believe that mankind's morality and ethics come from the Bible. Fair enough. Let's see how the great prophet, Elisha— a man with *twice* the god-given power of his superlatively divine predecessor—deals with a simple case of bullying.

Immediately after Elijah had made his grandiose departure, the doubly-endowed Elisha began testing his new powers. At the River Jordan he parted the waters as his mentor had done and walked across the dry riverbed to the awe-struck thrill of fifty onlookers. A few days later he purified the tainted well-spring of Jericho by throwing salt on it. In less than a week he had begun to make quite a name for himself. This must have been a colossal ego trip for this one-time simple farm boy, to be able to summon the power of God Almighty Himself with a few voice commands. If power is indeed the most potent aphro-disiac, this guy must've been sporting wood like a Sequoia!

After "healing" the waters he headed to Bethel (perhaps to "heal" some fallen women). As he was approaching the city, forty-two little children came running toward him. Now, the sight of a bald head must have been a rare sight in those days, and apparently Elisha had quite a shiner, because the little children began laughing and mocking him for it. So there he was, the Mighty Prophet of Yahweh, presumably the most powerful man on earth, a man who could part rivers, heal the sick, raise the dead, inflict leprosy, cause famine and drought, restore the land to plenty, smite the entire Syrian army with blindness, *unsmite* the entire Syrian army *from* blindness, cause an axe head to float, cause an oil pot to never run out, *ad infinitum*, and yet he was stymied and infuriated by a few dozen giggling little children. Let us now recreate the scene with all the drama-turgical evidence in place. And...*action!*

The day was warm and pleasant as the children frolicked through the fields at the edge of the big forest, picking wildflowers and singing songs. Yashi, a bright-eyed lad of seven, spotted a man walking along the road to Bethel. Now, it was not at all unusual to see people walking the road, but this man seemed different. For one thing, his head was completely bald and uncovered. Even little Yashi knew that the hot sun would burn skin left so unprotected. "Look there!" he called to his play-mates. "See the bald man without a *salmah* to cover his head!"

Six-year-old Janna stopped picking flowers and glanced up.

"Does he not know his skin will turn red and blister?" she queried.

The word spread quickly among the forty-two little ones, and soon they were all gathered together, peering at the strange traveler who drew nearer to them. "See how his head shines!" giggled one of the littlest boys. Then they all began to giggle, for the man's bald head did indeed shine like a highly polished muskmelon.

"I have heard the elders speak of a baldheaded man who walks alone and works wonders," said a little girl with long black braids. "They say he has very great powers."

"And a magic cloak!"

"It must be the new prophet, Elisha!"

"They say he was with Elijah when the LORD carried him away to Heaven in a whirlwind!"

Tomar, a precocious boy of twelve, stepped forward. "Yes, I too have heard the stories. But did anyone actually *see* this miraculous thing take place?"

The children exchanged puzzled glances. One little girl shrugged. "Why would they say it if it wasn't true?"

Tomar narrowed his eyes in thought. "Maybe Elisha made the whole thing up. Maybe he *killed* Elijah and stole his magic cloak."

"Oh, Tomar, you're always making up stories to frighten the little ones!"

"That's right," agreed another child. "Besides, fifty men said they saw Elijah part the Jordan by slapping it with his magic cloak so he and Elisha could cross on dry land."

A second boy, the same age as Tomar, nodded. "Fifty men saw Elijah, but they didn't see what *happened* to Elijah once he and Elisha got to the other side. They only saw Elisha come back *alone* after he too struck the water with the magic cloak."

"Emon is right," Tomar agreed, giving his friend a wink. "And if he *did* kill Elijah, he must've hidden his body well, because the fifty men who went out looking never found it. So maybe this Elisha is a *false prophet*. A false prophet *and* a murderer!"

"Or maybe he is a *demon*," Emon said, thoroughly enjoying the game at this point. "He probably conjured the fiery whirlwind to *consume* Elijah so there would be no trace of him left—and he might do the same to all of us as well!" He spread his arms wide and lunged at several youngsters. Most of them scampered off, laughing, but a few of the littlest ones began to cry.

"Do not fear," Tomar reassured them, now feeling a bit guilty. "Emon and I will protect you."

"But how can you protect us from a demon?" asked one little girl, her rosy cheeks streaked with tears.

Tomar wiped her face with his sleeve. "Did you not know? Demons lose all their power when they hear laughter."

"They do?" she sniffed.

"That's right," agreed Emon. "Look, when he draws near we'll put him to a test, and if he tries to use his demon powers, we'll all begin to laugh and he will *vanish* in a puff of smoke!"

All the children were comforted by this, and they agreed it was a very good idea.

❖   ❖   ❖

Elisha's thoughts were full with the glory of the LORD, his spirit engorged, as he made his way up the dusty road toward the town of Bethel. The magnificent cloak billowing around his body like a living thing to remind him of the great powers he possessed, he paused on a knoll at the edge of a great forest and peered out at the rolling countryside. He closed his eyes in solemn prayer. *My LORD, creator of all things, I am thy most humble servant. I ask only strength enough to do your bidding and make your glory known.*

And God heard, and God answered him in that still, small voice, *Elisha, know always that I am here, and I am watching over you. With every beat of your heart and every breath that you take, I am with you. Whatever you desire, however great or small, ask of it in my name and it shall be done.*

Elisha was greatly comforted to know that the LORD was with him, guiding him, protecting him. He could feel God's power pulsating through every part of him, *twice* the power possessed by his former master. But now *he* was the master, the Prophet of Yahweh. The feeling continued to swell within him, growing seemingly stronger by the hour. Intoxicating, exhilarating, burning like a fire. There was nothing he could not do; no enemy he could not vanquish. *Let the heathens come. Let them challenge the might of our living god. Then by the vehemence his wrath will they know that he is the one true god!*

The sun blazed hot against his bare scalp, yet he refused to use the *salmah*, refused to let anything come between him and his god. The pain was his testament, his show of humility and subjugation before the LORD.

A sound caught his ears. It came from the nearby underbrush. An animal perhaps? He had no fear of animals. The LORD was with him. It came again, but this time accompanied by whispers. "Whoever you are, show yourselves!" he commanded.

A rock landed several feet behind him. He whirled. This time he heard giggling. "Are you such cowards that you cannot face a lone man?"

A boy of perhaps twelve stepped into view. "I am Tomar. I am no coward. I will face you."

Elisha's eyes narrowed upon the lad. "You think it amusing to accost travelers? Perhaps my *shebet* will teach you some manners." Elisha raised his walking stick to strike the boy.

"*No!* Don't hit him!" A little girl with long, dark braids rushed from behind some bushes. "He only wanted to see if you were a demon." Several more children appeared now.

"A *demon*?" Elisha ground his teeth and held the *shebet* high over his head. "Do you not know who I am? I am the Chosen One! I am the profit of Yahweh!"

He lunged to take hold of her when a second youth sprang forward and pulled her aside. "Your bald head is *red* like that of a demon," the boy said.

Fury burned through Elisha's veins. "Impudent little whelp!" He swung at the boy with his *shebet*, lost his footing on the rocky ground and fell. All the children began laughing now.

"If you really are a prophet, then go up into the clouds like Elijah did," the first boy challenged.

"Yes, go up, bald head," one of the other children chimed in.

"Go up, bald head! Go up, bald head!" they all began to chant.

Elisha's eyes were hot with rage as he pulled himself to his feet. *Do you see how they mock me, my LORD?*

I see.

They have no respect for your messenger.

I know.

They must be punished!

Whatever you wish, ask it in my name and it shall be so.

His heart, his mind, his body and his soul coursing with anger, Elisha drew a deep breath and raised the *shebet* aloft. "In the name of God, I curse you all! Let his vengeance be upon you!"

There came a guttural roar from the forest, and a moment later two large she-bears burst into the clearing. The children screamed at the sight of the ferocious creatures and tried to run, but they could not escape. The bears were swift and powerful. They overcame the children, tearing tender flesh with fangs and claws. High-pitched screams of terror and agony shattered the air. The children sobbed and cried for their parents but to no avail, for the power of God was in the bears. With bloody saliva dripping from their jaws, the beasts continued to kill and disembowel their helpless prey until all forty-two children lay dead.

And when it was over, Elisha gazed down at the clearing, now awash in blood and littered with the mutilated bodies of the little children. *God's will be done*, he thought to himself with a nod of satisfaction, then casually went on his way.

ॐ . . . ॐ

I have no idea what purpose this sick tale serves. I have no idea what "moral" lesson is to be learned from it. Is it supposed to be a warning to children not to make fun of people? "You better be good or God will send bears to rip *you* up too!" Isn't that in itself a form of psychological bullying? And let's not forget the "loving god's" ultimate commandment: "Love me or I'll torture you for all eternity!"

If we were to carry this story even further to the point where the worried parents go out looking for their children, can you imagine their horror upon finding this grisly scene of carnage? Their grief would be indescribable! Would these shattered parents then fall down on their knees and pray to Yahweh for consolation?

The Bible is very clear that God was fully aware of the situation, and that he sent the ravenous bears to maul and "tare" the children at the request of his devoted sycophant, Elisha. So, if this "all-mighty, all-knowing, all-loving" deity could simply sit back dispassionately, apathetically, even approvingly and allow little children to be torn to pieces by wild animals, it makes perfect sense that he was doing the same when the children of Columbine and Sandy Hook were gunned down in cold blood. But let's not forget one crucial element: The children in the biblical account *deserved* what they got for making fun of poor old Elisha's bald head. Therefore, God was well within his rights as Supreme Creator-in-Chief to inflict this gruesome form of capital punishment—*even upon children.*

I find it particularly puzzling that Elisha himself, with all his magnificent, magical abilities, could not have resolved the situation by simply conjuring up an enormous bag of candy—a *never-ending* bag of candy at that—to befriend the children. Or, he could have done the Santa Claus trick and pulled toys from beneath his wizard's cloak, or won them over with a few sleight-of-hand tricks. At the very worst, he could have caused them all to spank their own little fannies. Yet he did none of these things. Instead, this Prophet of God, this miracle worker with powers beyond comprehension, universally revered and praised by every Western religion created by man, chose to curse the children "in the name of the LORD" and cause two she-bears to come roaring out of the woods and rip all forty-two of them to bloody shreds. What a far cry this is from gentle Jesus saying, "Suffer the little children to come unto me." (I guess we should be thankful he took after his *mother's* side of the family!)

I began this piece by saying the subject would be about bullying. Now, after seeing all the characters portrayed as three-dimensional people, we have to wonder just who the real "bullies" are. And yet, the term "bully" hardly even begins to describe the actions of Yahweh and his spiritual cohorts. There is another term we're hearing a lot these days—*TERRORIST*. These are individuals—usually motivated by their religious convictions—who blindly, obediently and enthusiastically inflict pain, destruction and death in the name of their god. Slaughtering innocent children doesn't even cause them to bat an eye. And why should it when their beloved, invisible "spiritual leader" has shown them by his own gory examples that it's perfectly OK?

As we have seen time and time again, when "true believers" find themselves in the embarrassing position of having to explain or defend one of these outrageously ridiculous yarns, they simply change the story a bit so as to make it a little more palatable. But seriously, how could anyone possibly change this abhorrent nightmare to make it any less abhorrent? The answer lies in blaming the victims. Or rather, *changing* the victims to make them seem less "innocent". That way, the reader won't feel so sorry for them.

Let's first examine the story as it appears in the King James Version (2 Kings, Chapter 2). It is a remarkably short piece, only three verses, a total of 94 words. It reads like this: "And he went up from thence unto Bethel: and as he was going up by the way, there came forth little children out of the city, and mocked him, and said unto him, Go up, thou bald head; go up, thou bald head. And he turned back, and looked on them, and cursed them in the name of the LORD. And there came forth two she bears out of the wood, and tare forty and two children of them. And he went from thence to Mount Carmel, and from thence he returned to Samaria."

Please note the use of the term "little children". When I think of "little children" I imagine youngsters between the ages of three and ten years old. All the children killed at Sandy Hook Elementary School were between six and seven years old. When we recall this horror we are sickened and outraged to our very core. But as I mentioned earlier, when most people seek comfort after a tragedy like this, they entreat the very fiend who unhesitatingly sent two bears to tear apart forty-two "little children".

Now here is the same story as it appears in the New International Version. "From there Elisha went up to Bethel. As he was walking along the road, some boys came out of the town and jeered at him. "Get out of here, baldy!" they said. "Get out of here, baldy!" He turned around, looked at them and called down a curse on them in the name of the Lord. Then two bears came out of the woods and mauled forty-two of the boys. And he went on to Mount Carmel and from there returned to Samaria."

Did you notice? The "little children" are now "some boys". Well, as everyone knows, boys will be boys. I suppose that's enough to justify turning them into bear burgers. Some other translations refer to them as "youths". I'm certain that before too long someone will re-re-write the "immutable word of God" so that the antagonists are morphed into a gang of meth-crazed motorcycle thugs. Then the believers will have just cause to actually be *glad* when these punks get their grisly comeuppance.

While writing this piece, I found myself wondering, just what was God thinking while those children were being mauled to death? What was he feeling when he heard their tortured screams and saw their little bodies being ripped apart, their flesh and organs being devoured? Since he did in fact cause it to happen as a form of punishment and retaliation, he certainly could not have felt any remorse or sympathy. Was it joy then? Smug satisfaction? Sexual titillation? There are monsters living among us, psychopaths who commit unspeakable atrocities against children for these all-too-human reasons. Why then should God be any different? He was, after all, created in *our* image.

David and Jonathan: A Forbidden Love Story
As Found in the Book of 1 Samuel, Chapters 8-31
and 2 Samuel, Chapter 1, Verse 26

Few topics get the Judaic, Christian and Islamic communities fired up more vocally—and at times violently—than that of homosexuality. If these three main religions cannot agree on anything else, they *will* agree that homosexuality is a Capital-S sin. Some will say it is even *the worst* sin two people can commit. (Even worse than beating and robbing a blind person or murdering someone's child?) *Yes! Even worse than those!*

This religion-based hatred of "H-chromosome" persons follows no rational thought process. But then, in order to believe all the other nonsense in the Bible one must by default *suspend* rational thought to the point of committing "intellecti-cide". The closest they can come to a logical reason for condemning the act is to claim it is "immoral". When pressed to explain *how* it is immoral, they quickly disengage the intellectual part of their brains and go right to the evasive default response, "Because God says so!"

One of my favorite scenes in Bill Maher's brilliant docu-comedy, *Religulous*, is where a young woman (a member of the notorious Westboro Baptist Church) is part of an anti-gay rally. With sublime sanctimony oozing from her every pore, she tells the interviewer, "*I* don't hate them (fags). *God* hates them." And it is this divinely ordained hatred that has empowered believers throughout history to commit atrocities of every unspeakable nature. (But that's nothing you didn't already know.)

So, if the Bible god hates homosexuals that badly one has to ask 1) Why did he create them in the first place? 2) Why doesn't he simply *un*-create them? 3) And most confusing of all, why did he allow his supposedly "inspired" editors to include in his Holy Manifesto a story that *overwhelmingly* describes a homoerotic relationship of—pardon the pun—*biblical proportions?* Now, of course religious apologists roundly and fervidly deny that there is anything either homo *or* erotic about the very special—and incredibly close—relationship between David and Jonathan. Gay activists, on the other hand, herald it as irrefutable scriptural proof that there is light at the end of the rainbow, and that Yahweh, despite his earlier condemnations, is revealing a softer, gentler, even conciliatory side, be it ever so obfuscated. What we are left with then is a kind of "Kramer vs. Kramer" battle for custody of the plotline.

As with all my stories, before I begin writing I read the actual biblical account in order to get to know my characters. I begin with the King James Version and crosscheck it with at least three other translations. If you've been paying attention so far, you know that there can be significant discrepancies from one version to the other (like the difference between 70 men killed and *50,000-and-70* killed by Yahweh in the "Holy Hemorrhoid" story).

What I found while researching this tale was no less incongruous. However, the thing that really put a twitch in my eyebrow was the seemingly deliberate, almost blushing way the various editors contrived to divert *any* hint of homoeroticism away from the main characters. It was if they were embarrassed to admit the KJV account ever existed! Ironically, they don't have a problem recounting how their celestial superhero repeatedly orders the indiscriminate slaughter of defenseless women and babies; yet when it comes to the topic of *hombre y hombre amor*, they suddenly scramble like penguins in an ice cube factory to erase, or at least dilute as many "intimate" details as possible. This alone has to make me wonder, if these people are the "scriptural experts" on everything biblical, then what do they know that I don't know...or more to the point, why are they trying so hard to disclaim it?

The story of David and Jonathan is actually a story of *three* men, the third being Saul, the first king of Israel. It is an epic tale to rival the literary magnitude of Shakespeare himself, complete with greed, jealousy, betrayal, war, obsession, revenge, sacrifice, unrequited love, heroism, madness, a ghost, a witch, a giant, more war, and of course, the *bro-mance*. It's a lot like *Hamlet, Macbeth, Richard III* and *A Midsummer Night's Dream* all rolled into one.

The first main character is Saul. Now, at this point in Bronze-Age man's history, the people of Israel were demanding a flesh-and-blood king to rule over them. The prophet Samuel (no doubt realizing that he was about to lose his prestigious position as "mouthpiece of the Almighty") grudgingly agreed to find them a human king. One day while Samuel was taking a stroll, he spied an incredibly handsome, very tall, young man walking toward him. The young man was Saul, and he was out looking for some ass (donkeys actually) that had wandered away from his father's house. Samuel's heart began to pound. *He's the one!*

the little voice inside his head cried. *He's the one you shall make their king!*

And so Samuel invited Saul into his house and seated him at his dinner table. Then Samuel placed an enormous piece of meat in front of Saul and told him to eat of it. And Saul ate. Afterward, Samuel took a flask of olive oil and poured it over Saul's head. The golden oil showered down Saul's rich crown of curly black hair, glistening in the flickering lamp light. Samuel drew close and kissed him, telling him, "You are now the ruler over the LORD's inheritance." And though Saul didn't really know what that meant, he knew he would be changed forever. (No kidding, this really is in the Bible!)

There is nothing particularly special about Saul in any way except that he was remarkably handsome and taller than any man in Israel; hardly what I would call prerequisites for kingship, but as cheap fiction goes, he was the stereotypical "tall-dark-handsome" storybook hero. The scripture also tells us that God gave him super powers that enabled him to prophesy. This really had to chafe old Samuel something awful; not only was he being ousted as God's judicial right hand man, but now this young upstart from the smallest tribe in all of Israel and the most insignificant family *in* that tribe had been endowed with the power of prophesying as well!

Before going into forced retirement, Samuel delivered a scathing farewell speech to the Israelite people, chastising them for their ingratitude and generally wicked ways, not the least of which was getting him canned. As a parting shot, he threatened, "I will call on the LORD to send thunder and rain! And you will realize what an evil thing you did in the eyes of the LORD when you asked for a king!" Then, with an air of self-righteous humility, he added, "As for me, far be it from me that *I* should sin against the LORD by failing to pray for you." Wow, what a guy!

Saul ruled Israel for forty-two years, right up to the point where he committed suicide by falling on his own sword rather than being captured by the "uncircumcised" Philistines. (I mean really, would *you* want to be captured by someone who wasn't circumcised?) Like all good biblical heroes, Saul was a vicious, bloodthirsty military leader who had no problem ordering the grisly slaughter of innocent women and children, and this, as always, pleased Yahweh no end. But then one day, during the genocidal battle against the Amalekites, Saul screwed up big time. Despite Samuel's very specific directive—which of course came from The Master of the Universe himself—to destroy every living thing (1 Samuel, 15:3) "Now go and smite Amalek, and utterly destroy all that they have, and spare them not; but slay both man and woman, infant and suckling, ox and sheep, camel and ass", Saul, in an inexplicable act of mercy, spared the life of the Amalekite king. He also saved some of the best cattle and lambs, which he intended to sacrifice to the LORD (as if slaughtering all those women, children, infants and sucklings wasn't "sacrifice" enough for the bloodthirsty war god).

When Samuel learned of this he blew a holy gasket and cursed poor Saul for his noncompliance, telling him that blind and total obedience—even if it meant shoving a sword through a tiny baby's body—was far better than any sacrifice from the heart. Furthermore, he told Saul he could kiss his precious crown good-bye, for another was to be chosen in his place. Saul was heartbroken and begged for clemency, but Samuel (still nursing that original grudge, I'll wager) offered only a sanctimonious sneer. He called for the Amalekite king to be brought forth and proceeded to hack him to pieces "in the sight of the LORD".

The last line in the chapter reads, "and the LORD repented that he had made Saul king over Israel." Maybe it's just me, but I find it awfully strange that an all-knowing, all-wise, all-powerful, perfect and unerring entity that can know the future long before it happens can also be such a colossal fuck up. After all, *God* chose Saul in the first place, right? So how come he didn't see this royal train wreck coming? It *had* to have surprised him or he would not have "repented" his choice in picking Saul. Ah well, I guess even the great Yahweh can be blindsided by a pretty face. And that brings us to the next major character in this passionate play, David.

Again under God's direct supervision, poor old Samuel was tasked with finding a replacement for King of Israel. God told him to go to Bethlehem and to the house of Jesse, who had several sons to choose from. Now, here's where it gets confusing again: Before they even got to Bethlehem, God told Samuel, "I have chosen one of his sons to be king," but God never said *which* son. Well, if God already knew the guy he wanted, then why waste everybody's time by going through the motions of a Hollywood cattle call? Why didn't God just say, "I picked David, and that's that." But noooo, God could never make things that simple. Next to the wholesale slaughter of babies, apparently "high drama" is what the Big Guy loves best. Or maybe he knew how much his homeboy, Samuel, loved looking at healthy young man-meat, and this was God's way of making up for the Saul debacle, by throwing the old codger "a bone", so to speak.

At any rate, when they got to Jesse's place, Samuel was at once smitten by a particularly comely lad and thought, "Yes, yes! Please, God, let it be him! *Oh, pleeease, let it be him!*" But God scolded Samuel and told him, (actual text, 1 Samuel 16:7 KJV), "Look not on his countenance, or on the height of his stature; because I have refused him: for the LORD seeth not as man seeth; for man looketh on the outward appearance, but the LORD looketh on the heart." OK, *time out!* Now, when Samuel chose Saul—again, under the personal directive of God himself—was it just a *coincidence* that Saul happened to be amazingly tall and drop-dead gorgeous? But now we see that God has basically told Sam to stop drooling over this pretty boy because that's not how the Heavenly Honcho rolls. I guess in a way it makes perfect sense: God realized that he really messed up the first time by choosing the "Sarah Palin" candidate, so he was determined not to let his holy hormones get the better of him the next time around.

After seven of Jesse's sons had been trotted out and paraded in front of an ogling Samuel like Chippendale dancers, Sam asked if there were any more to look at. Jesse said his youngest son, David, was out tending the sheep. Samuel ordered that the youth be brought before him. I can just imagine Samuel's reaction upon seeing the boy, for the Bible tells us (1 Samuel, 16:12 KJV), "Now he was ruddy, and withal of a beautiful countenance, and goodly to look to." In other words, *he was babe-a-licious!* At that moment the little voice inside Samuel's head, i.e. the LORD, popped up and told him that this child was the chosen one. (Well, so much for God claiming he wasn't going to use "looks" as a criteria for kingship anymore.)

Immediately Sam whipped out his horn and poured a golden shower of olive oil on the boy's head. *And the glistening beads shimmered through David's curly, auburn locks...dripping onto his strong, muscular young shoulders and arms...slipping in slow, serpentine patterns down his tan cheeks, his neck, his bare chest...his firm, bronzed abdomen. They lingered for an instant at the delicate hollow of his navel before disappearing into the fold of his low-slung loincloth...* OK, I added that part just for fun. But then the Bible says, "And the spirit of the LORD *came powerfully* upon David." Now, if that doesn't *just scream* "homoerotic imagery", I don't know what does! And so began the rags-to-riches story of David, the humble shepherd boy who rose to become King of Israel.

David is without a doubt one of the best known and most beloved characters in the Bible. He is beloved because the vast

140

majority of people who "belove" him don't know what a lying, conniving, arrogant, drunken, blackmailing, debauching, lascivious, womanizing, adulterous, backstabbing, treacherous, sexually deviant, animal-torturing, baby-killing son of a bitch he really is. (And this is the guy from whom *Jesus* is supposedly descended?!)

Speaking of descendants, David's great, great-grandmother was Rahab, the whore of Jericho, who sold out her own people to be genocidally slaughtered just to save her own precious skin. And Ruth, (a Moabite, a people cursed by God "to the tenth generation") was David's great-grandmother. She is famous for creeping into the bedchamber of Boaz and uncovering his legs ("legs" is Old Testament-speak for "genitals"). So, with relatives like these, it's no wonder David went a bit awry.

To back up a bit, when Saul lost favor with Yahweh for committing that egregious act of mercy on the Amalekite king, God stripped him of his holy powers and replaced them with an "evil spirit" to torture and torment him all his days. This Shakespearian-esque affliction manifests itself as bouts of severe depression, murderous rage and paranoid delusions. (The Bible calls these episodes "prophesying". We know them today as schizophrenia or bi-polar disorder.) Saul's wizened advisors convinced him that only sweet music would drive the evil spirit into abeyance. And so a young shepherd boy renowned for his harp playing was summoned. This is where Saul meets David for the first time. (Coincidence? Divine Providence? Or merely a very derivative plotline?)

Like Samuel, Saul was immediately smitten with the boy's beauty (1 Samuel 16:21) "And David came to Saul, and stood before him: and he (Saul) loved him greatly". It isn't clear how old David was when he first met Saul. That answer—like *all* mythological answers—depends entirely on *whose* interpretation you happen to consult, and these vary wildly from "He was too young to fight in the army" (*Judaism Online* website) and he was "an inexperienced boy" (*Jewish Virtual Library*), to he is "a brave man and a warrior" (NIV), and the ever-popular KJV which calls him "a mighty valiant man, and a man of war." Quite a big difference! All I know is, when I was in Sunday School, all the pictures we saw of David in our story books showed him as a kid like the rest of us. Besides, doesn't that make his feat of killing a *giant* seem so much more *awesome?*

The music did indeed have miraculous healing powers, and the king decided to keep the beautiful, young shepherd boy by his side forever and spent hours stretched out upon his royal lounge, gazing at him adoringly like in the painting, "David and Saul" by Julius Kronberg (1885). If we need more proof of Saul's love for David, we need only look at 1 Samuel 18:2, "And Saul took him that day, and would let him go no more home to his father's house."

Poor demonically possessed, love-struck Saul had no idea at this point that David had recently been tapped to be his replacement; and David, who must have realized what a sweet deal he had going, never let on. And so, not only did Saul take the comely lad into his house and his heart, he trained him in military ways and eventually put him in charge of his entire army. David soon won the admiration of soldiers and servants alike. But it was the admiration of Saul's own son, Jonathan, that blazed brightest of all.

It is the first, third and fourth verses in 1 Samuel, Chapter 18 that give us our first—and most revealing—clue: "And it came to pass, when he (David) had made an end of speaking unto Saul, that the soul of Jonathan was knit with the soul of David, and Jonathan loved him as his own soul." And, "Then Jonathan and David made a covenant, because he (Jonathan) loved him as his own soul. And Jonathan stripped himself of the robe that was upon him, and gave it to David, and his garments, even to his sword, and to his bow, and to his girdle."

This last verse is particularly evocative. I can just picture these two beautiful, virile, young men gazing at one another for the first time and knowing...*knowing* even then...that what they shared was something so special, so rare and so pure that it reached down to their very souls! They knew it was forbidden, even punishable by *death*. And yet they could not deny that it was also *so very real!* The Bible gives no specific timeframe or location, so we cannot know when and where this first encounter and subsequent disrobing took place. In fact, we are given very little at all to go on, except that Jonathan fell in love with David at first sight and only three short verses later is doing a striptease for him.

To fill in some of the blanks, let us imagine David's royal bed chamber. The hour is late. Jonathan stands poised in the doorway, a small oil lamp clutched in his trembling fingers. The quivering flame illuminates the stark yet regal trappings of a warrior. His heart pounds as he creeps closer to the bed. Curtains of deepest indigo trimmed with gold tassels surround the sleeping figure. A great yearning fills him. How he longs to reach out and caress those exquisite features...fingers delighting to the sensation of the rich, warm, auburn locks... *Can you know what I am feeling? Can you even begin to imagine the sweet agony that fills my heart...my soul...my body every time I look at you? Can you possibly feel the same?*

David stirs!

He opens his eyes. A look of confusion, surprise, and then delight washes over his countenance. "Jonathan? What are you doing here so late?" he whispers, his voice heavy with sleep. "Is something wrong?"

Unable to form the words for the tightness in his throat, Jonathan turns his head slowly from side to side. He draws a deep breath to steady himself. The sound of his thundering pulse is deafening! "I—I only wanted..."

Propping himself on one elbow, David smiles. "I think I know what you want, Jonathan. I think we *both* know." With a slow, deliberate motion he draws the bed cover aside, exposing the naked glory of his maleness.

Jonathan's breath catches in his throat. His hand begins to shake so that he nearly drops the lamp. The shivering light dances across the chiseled contours of David's body, revealing every ripple and angle and curve of his magnificent warrior's physique. Sweat stings Jonathan's flesh as he peers, transfixed, his own body responding with a throbbing desire.

As if he can sense Jonathan's anguish, David chuckles. "Come here," he says, patting the thick cushion. "Sit and tell me why you have come."

Without taking his eyes from those of his desired, Jonathan sets the lamp on a nearby table. "I would rather *show* you," he murmurs.

As David watches, Jonathan removes his robe and hands it to him. "This I will give to you," he tells David. Then he unbuckles the girdle which holds his sword and dagger and hands these to David. "These I will give to you." With nervous fingers, he unties the strings securing his other garments. One by one they fall away until he is standing completely naked, bathed only in the glow of the gently flickering oil lamp. A trembling smile upon his lips, he approaches the bed and whispers, "This *too* I will give to you."

Perhaps this isn't exactly what the ancient storytellers had in mind (or perhaps it *was*), but one thing is certain: The sensual chemistry that exists between David and Jonathan is undeniable. There are other passages later on that further indicate that this was no mere "man crush", such as Joe the Truck Driver might have for his favorite Pittsburg Steelers offensive tackle in some fantasy football league. Then too, I cannot imagine a dewy-eyed

Joe the Truck Driver removing his clothing piece by piece and handing them to Marcus Gilbert.

The repeated theme that runs through the first book of Samuel is one man's attraction to the physical beauty of another man. If you recall, Samuel was attracted to Saul for his remarkable height and handsome features. Samuel was later taken with the very *young* and stunning shepherd boy, David. Saul too was smitten by David; so much so that he refused to let the boy leave the palace. The attraction between David and Jonathan has already been described in vivid innuendo. Thus we have our cast of main characters and enough plot twists and complications that would make the Bard himself Avon green with envy.

You may have asked yourself at this point, "Were there no women in the lives of these men?" Indeed there were! The Bible tells us that Samuel had sons, but it says nothing about a wife. The sons, however, having inherited their father's insatiable lust for power and control, became corrupt and perverse, prompting Samuel to look outside the family for a ruler. Saul not only had a legitimate wife with whom he produced four sons (Jonathan being the eldest) and two daughters; he also had a concubine who bore him two sons.

Jonathan evidently married (or at least had intercourse with a woman), because he produced a single son that became crippled as a child. But nowhere in either the King James or New International versions does it actually mention a wife. His most intimate, passionate and well-documented relationship is, of course, with David. And this lasted for *fifteen years*.

After the deaths of Saul and Jonathan (sorry for the spoiler), David began collecting wives like crazy. By the end of his life, he had amassed between six and eight *known* wives, depending upon which "unerring" book of fables you choose to read. (Interesting side note: Apparently only the names of wives who had *given birth* were recorded, thus reaffirming that in the male-dominated world from whence the Bible is derived, a woman's only value, nay her very literary *existence*, depends on the service she provides to her husband as breeding stock.) In the second book of Samuel (Chapter 5, Verse 13) it says that while in Jerusalem "David took him more concubines and wives" but it doesn't say how many. In psycho-analytical terms, his sexually fecund activities could be considered a symptom of *over-compensation?* Whatever the explanation, one thing seems clear, after losing Jonathan, his love and soul mate of fifteen years, David's moral compass took a drastic plunge southward, and his personal and political dealings took on a pallor that would make even Caligula shudder. But more on that later. The purpose of this chapter is to focus on the interpersonal relationships between these men of biblical renown. However—as will become abundantly obvious—there seems to be much more going on here than the special love between David and Jonathan.

Right from the beginning King Saul loved David. But Saul became jealous of David's popularity and saw it as a threat to his crown. (How sadly ironic that losing his throne to this handsome upstart was already a done deal.) Saul was also intensely jealous of David's relationship with heir-apparent Jonathan. At one point, during one of his "evil spirit" episodes, Saul grabbed a javelin and hurled it at David, intending to literally nail him to the wall with it. This passage (found in 1 Samuel 18:10) is actually quite comical at best and utterly absurd at worst, for it states that Saul hurled not one javelin at David but *two*, missing him both times. And all the while David continued to play his harp.

Even more ridiculous, sometime later Saul, in a kinder, gentler mood, offered David his older daughter, Merab, in marriage. Perhaps not surprisingly, David turned down the offer. A few verses later Saul offered up the younger daughter, Michal. Again, David tried to get out of the deal by claiming he was too poor and not worthy of such an honor. Saul then told him all he had to do to win Princess Michal was to bring back one hundred Philistine foreskins—yes, I said *foreskins*. Saul, all the while, was secretly hoping the Philistines would do David in for him, which was a pretty good plan, considering what a rotten shot he was with a javelin even at close range. But the plan backfired and David returned in triumph with a basket of—not one, but—*two hundred Philistine foreskins!*

I'd like to pause a moment and try to imagine that gruesome scene: On a blood-soaked battlefield, littered with mangled Philistine bodies roasting in the desert heat, we see David and his Hebrew buddies going from corpse to corpse, reaching into sweaty breechcloths, grasping hold of a dead man's uncircumcised penis, pulling it out, and then slicing off the fleshy covering to be taken back as a form of bridal dowry. Assuming this perverse tale is true, what thoughts must have been going through David's mind as he is performing this grisly task? What was the purpose in collecting *two* hundred foreskins when only *one* hundred was required? *AND WHY FORESKINS IN THE FIRST PLACE?* Was he deriving some kind of sick pleasure from the mutilation of dead men's sex organs? Was it a particular form of retaliation against the Philistines themselves? Or against Saul for maneuvering him into a marriage that he didn't want in the first place? As I indicated earlier, this entire book of biblical nonsense is steeped in homoerotic imagery and innuendo. It is almost as if the writer had a personal obsession with male genitalia. To be sure, Sigmund Freud would have an absolute field day trying to unravel all the sado-sexual symbolism in this gory motif.

At any rate, David and Michal were married, and Saul's hatred of David grew even hotter. In desperation, the king tried to persuade Jonathan and his servants to kill David. But the ever-faithful Jonathan warned David and told him to hide while he tried to reason with his father. The appeal worked, and Saul welcomed David back into his home with the promise that he would no longer try to kill him. All was well once more, and David did what David did best: led his troops in bloody slaughter of the Philistines (although no foreskins were taken this time).

But then one day while David was sitting playing his harp for the king... "The evil spirit from the LORD was upon Saul, as he sat in his house with his javelin in his hand." (Can you guess what happens next?) That's right! Saul, in a fit of god-induced rage, chucked that javelin at David so hard that it impaled itself right into the stone wall! Happily for David, Saul's aim was just as good as it was the other two times, but this time David ran like hell.

Once again, I'd like to pause to examine the preposterous events in these verses. First off, just where the *hell* did Saul learn how to throw a javelin? Second, what happened to that oath he swore not to try to kill David? Third, just how *incredibly stupid* is David for hanging around a guy who keeps trying to turn him into a human shish kebab? Religious apologists will delight in pointing out that "God" was protecting David from Saul's attacks. OK, if that's true, then why does "God" keep precipitating these attacks by sending his "evil spirit" to torment Saul to the point of murderous rage? The answer to this question is perhaps the easiest of all, and we need not look any further than the obvious: The Bible god is a mean, petty, childish bully of galactic proportions who takes sadistic delight in torturing and killing creatures lesser than himself. You will find numerous references throughout the Bible where the LORD "hardened" someone's heart (like Pharaoh of Moses fame), deliberately causing that person to do evil so he could be smited later on by the "just and merciful god". As to the question of why

David kept coming back, I believe this answer too is quite simple: He wanted to be near his soul mate, Jonathan.

I think it is significant at this point to contrast David's relationship with Michal with that of Jonathan. It is stated early on that Michal loved David, but nowhere does it even come close to saying that he loved her in return. His reluctant taking of her as a wife and the requisite sexual mutilations of the dead Philistine soldiers (at least, let us *hope* they were dead!) seems less a demonstration of his feelings for Michal and more of an "in your face!" attitude toward Saul, the guy with the really lousy aim. David—as would soon be revealed in subsequent chapters—loves his position of power and authority, and the more he gets, the more extravagant and libertine his appetites become. Marrying Michal, therefore, is obviously a way to keep himself comfortably planted in the lap of luxury...despite those inconvenient times when his paranoid schizophrenic father-in-law is trying to skewer him.

The bond he shares with Jonathan appears, at least on the surface, to be rooted in nothing but the purest love. Yet even here David has positioned himself quite strategically. Jonathan is the natural heir to the kingdom of Israel, genetically speaking. And even though David, as a boy, was "anointed" by Samuel in preparation for ascending to the throne, David doesn't seem to realize that it is he, and not Jonathan, who is destined to become the next king. In this respect, David is nothing more than a poseur, a "groupie" that loves basking in the light of a royal rock star.

Then again, there is the argument that he and Jonathan were indeed homosexual lovers. Now, when you read further into the Bible and discover what an arrogant, hedonistic, disingenuous prick David ultimately becomes, it's hard to believe he could have tender, reciprocal feelings for *anyone*. And given his obvious love of palace life—in spite of those occasional life-threatening drawbacks—one would think that he is merely using poor love-struck Jonathan to further his personal agenda. Recall if you will, in 1 Samuel, Chapter 18:1-4, it was *Jonathan* whose "soul was knit with the soul of David", and it was *Jonathan* who "loved him as his own soul", and it was *Jonathan* who is mentioned first in the verse: "Then *Jonathan* and David made a covenant, because he (Jonathan) loved him as his own soul." And of course, it was *Jonathan* who stripped himself in front of David, not the other way around. First Samuel 19:2 tells us "*Jonathan* Saul's son delighted much in David". In nearly every instance you can find, it was *Jonathan* who was opining his love for David. Whether or not there was any actual "anal penetration" involved is irrelevant. By sucking up to the king's successor, David was not only able to continue his regal lifestyle, he was also cultivating a powerful political ally in Jonathan.

After that last indoor javelin event, David decided it might be in his best interest to leave the palace for awhile. With Michal's help he managed to escape into the night. Interestingly enough, there was no farewell scene between him and his wife. No hug, no good-bye kiss, not even a handshake. While on the lam, he took a brief sojourn with the old prophet, Samuel. But then he did something really strange: He returned to the palace under cover of darkness...not to see his wife...but to see *Jonathan!* Jonathan was of course overjoyed to see him. David then enlisted him to spy on his own father, even using a bit of psychological arm-twisting by reminding Jonathan of the special relationship they shared: "Therefore thou shalt deal kindly with thy servant (me, David); for thou hast brought thy servant into a covenant of the LORD with thee." (Yes, that *does* sound like a conjugal union.) And sweet, gullible Jonathan replied, "Whatsoever thy soul desireth, I will even do it for thee." (1 Samuel, 20:4). Modern translation: "Oh, David. I'll do whatever you want me to!" I don't care who you are or where you were raised, this is *not* the way two battle-hardened soldiers talk to one another—*even three thousand years ago!*

There is actually a considerable amount of very "heartfelt" dialog between the two men in Chapter 20, most of it in the form of David manipulating Jonathan into helping him. Then Jonathan remarked to David (perhaps taking him by the hand), "Come, and let us go out into the field." And they both went out into the field where David was to remain in hiding so that Daddy wouldn't find him. During their time in the field, Jonathan pleaded with David to show him unfailing kindness, i.e. protection, like "the LORD's kindness", as long as he lived so that he would not be killed. He also begged David to show kindness to his family so that they would not be killed. Then we are told Jonathan asked David to "...swear again, because he (Jonathan) loved him: for he (Jonathan) loved him as he (Jonathan) loved his own soul." That is a *LOT* of love. And *all* of it spewing forth from *Jonathan!* Not once does David acknowledge any love for Jonathan in return. For all intents and purposes, he appears to be using the king's lovesick son as a spy and nothing more.

By and by, Saul learned of his son's collaboration with David, and he unloaded a scathing tirade upon his firstborn. I have included the exact King James verbiage here. Like many biblical passages, it is rather hard to follow. "Then Saul's anger was kindled against Jonathan, and he said unto him, Thou son of the perverse rebellious woman, do not I know that thou hast chosen the son of Jesse to thine own confusion, and unto the confusion of thy mother's nakedness?" (1 Samuel 20:30). Then, in a murderous rage, he grabbed a javelin (they must have had those things just lying around everywhere) and hurled it at Jonathan. As usual, he missed, but Jonathan got the message and ran off to join up with David, who was hiding in the field.

I'm not going to pretend I know for certain what this convoluted tangle of Medieval doubletalk means, although I do find the part about "his mother's nakedness" a bit creepy. A key word here seems to be "confusion": Jonathan's own confusion and that of his naked mother. If you do a whole-Bible search you will find that in the majority of instances the word "confusion" refers to "shame". It certainly would not be unreasonable to imagine a tough, chauvinistic, warrior father like Saul shaming or *being* ashamed of his suddenly-outed gay son—even to the point of committing physical violence or murder. And while we live in (somewhat) more tolerant societies today, there are still many instances of extreme harassment and discrimination being perpetrated on gay and lesbian persons. How much *worse* would those prejudices have been in primitive Bronze Age cultures?

The word "confusion" appears in other contexts as well. In Leviticus 18:23 we're told that bestiality (having sex with animals) is "confusion". Then there's that part about "the confusion of thy mother's nakedness". That's another one of those strange KJV word groupings that can take on various meanings depending on the circumstances. Typically, to "uncover someone's nakedness" is to have sex with them, or at least to see their genitals. Alternatively, this can mean to put them to shame or dishonor as in Leviticus 20:11 "And the man that lieth with his father's wife hath uncovered his father's nakedness..." So, if you have sex with your mother (or stepmother) you have shamed/dishonored your father, i.e. "uncovered his nakedness".

Here's one that combines a little of both definitions: "And if a man shall take his sister, his father's daughter, or his mother's daughter, and see her nakedness, and she see his nakedness; it is a wicked thing...he hath uncovered his sister's nakedness..." (Leviticus 20:17). And now here's one with a twist: "And if a man lie with his daughter in law, both of them shall surely be put to death: they have wrought confusion..." (Leviticus 20:12).

What? "Confusion" instead of "uncovering someone's naked-ness"? Either way, they're still going to die. But why, I wonder, would the authors (or translators) choose one term over the other? As I said, both words can mean "shame". However, it is the *kind of shame*—and the kind of *sin*—that makes all the difference.

Here's the last part of Saul's rant again: "...the confusion of thy mother's nakedness". Once more, let's look at the key words. "Confusion" can mean shame but so can "nakedness". So, is Saul saying, "...the shame of your mother's shame"? Or is he telling his "confused/shameful" son that he is a disgrace to the "natural order" in which a man is only supposed to have sex with a woman, as in "uncover her nakedness"? Remember, "confusion" is also used to describe having sex with animals, another "unnatural" union in the same category as homosexuality—both of which are punishable by *death*.

As if you weren't "confused" enough, I'm going to compare the King James passage to that found in the New International Version: "Saul's anger flared up at Jonathan and he said to him, You son of a perverse and rebellious woman! Don't I know that you have sided with the son of Jesse to your own shame and to the shame of the mother who bore you?" See how much softer, simpler—and non-sexual—that sounds? (This might be off the subject, but I'm wondering why Saul should give a rip about Jonathan's mother's "shame" when at the very beginning of his tirade he refers to her as a "perverse rebellious woman". Perhaps that's the Old Testament way of calling someone a "son of a bitch".)

I think it's important that we examine a few other differences between the KJV and NIV translations. Remember Leviticus 20:12 (KJV), the "confusion" caused by having sex with animals? The NIV passage uses the word "perversion" instead. Similarly, the NIV editors use "perversion" to define the homosexual act. So in essence, they are equating bestiality with homosexuality by referring to both as "perversions". And as we've just seen in the case of Saul's tirade, they use "shame" to replace "confusion". This is fine and dandy, but *what if* the original authors (whoever they might be) *meant* to use the word "confusion"? What if they *meant* it in the "bestiality" sense? What if they *meant* for it to have a *sexual connotation?* If the NIV editors had used the word "perversion" in this case, the verse would read like this: "You son of a perverse and rebellious woman! Don't I know that you have sided with the son of Jesse to your own *perversion* and to the *perversion* of the mother who bore you?"

As we can see, cherry-picking the words you want to use in order to fulfill your own agenda can be a tricky business. Still, given these various definitions and applications, it seems suspiciously evident that Saul is accusing his son of having *some sort* of illicit liaison with David that is both unnatural *and* sexual. And while we're on the subject of motivation, let's not forget that "Saul loved David greatly" from the moment he laid eyes on him. We can just imagine how betrayed and rejected the poor old king must have felt, finding out that the object of his passion, i.e. David, had chosen his son instead!

I am reminded of a great plot complication in the movie, *American Beauty*, where the tough, jar-head ex-Marine father beats his teenage son to a bloody pulp, believing that he is having a homosexual affair with his adult neighbor. As it turns out, the ex-Marine father *himself* is a deeply-closeted homosexual, living the all-American lie. Tentatively, he approaches the presumed-gay neighbor with the intention of revealing his true identity. When the shocked and *confused* neighbor tells him, "I'm not gay!" the father gets his pistol and blows the man's brains out. Not a happy ending, but it makes the point.

Now, let's continue with our story. After the spear-chucking at the dinner table, Jonathan ran off to the field where David was hiding. Alone in the field, they fell together in the deep, soft grass. They held each other close and kissed... Overcome with emotion they began to weep in each other's arms, but David's sorrow exceeded that of his beloved friend. Then Jonathan whispered, "Go in peace, forasmuch as we have sworn both of us in the name of the LORD, saying, The LORD be between me and thee, and between my seed and thy seed forever."

David wiped the tears from his cheeks then got up and walked away. His heart breaking, Jonathan stared after him for a moment. Then he turned and headed back to the city. (As found in 1 Samuel 20:41-42). For some reason, the author of this verse wanted us to know that David's grief was greater than Jonathan's. We have to wonder, was this because he was genuinely distraught over leaving his beloved Jonathan, perhaps never to see him again? Or did it finally become apparent to him that he had lost his grand palace lifestyle forever?

Saul's fury at David was now in full-force and he spent a formidable amount of time, energy and resources trying to hunt him down and kill him. One has to wonder...what could possibly have happened between the two young men to make a father angry enough to want to murder one—or both—of them? The Bible tells us simply that Saul was fearful that David would usurp his throne. This hardly seems rational, considering that King Saul had massive armies at his command, while David made his escape with only a few hundred loyal men. Even if Saul were the spurned lover, as previously suggested, everybody eventually gets over a lost love. Still, we have to remember that Saul's mind was being influenced by the "evil spirit" sent from the LORD. (For all you "Trekkie" nerds out there—myself included—that sounds exactly like the plot from *Original Star Trek* Season 3, Episode 7: *The Day of the Dove*, where an invisible alien entity forces the Klingons and the crew of the Enterprise to fight one another in bloody combat against their will just for its own perverse pleasure. Does that remind you of some other "evil entity" we know?)

For the next couple of chapters David and Saul are running around the countryside, playing hide-and-kill with each other. Then one day Jonathan got out of bed and went out into the wooded wilderness of Ziph and found David. Just like that. No map. No compass. No fairy godmother giving him directions. He just got out of bed one morning and headed straight to where David was holed up. (I guess we're supposed to assume they had runners carrying secret love notes back and forth.)

Can you just imagine how delighted they must have been to see one another? It goes without saying that they kissed and embraced as before. Then Jonathan probably brushed the auburn curls from David's broad forehead and whispered (literally), "Don't worry. My father will never harm you. Someday you will be king over all Israel, and I will be right there at your side. Even my father knows this is true." Holding hands, they knelt, facing one another, and renewed their vows before the LORD. After this, David returned to his hiding place in the woods, and Jonathan returned to his house. (1 Samuel 23:16-18 NIV).

Here again we see that it is *Jonathan* who seeks out David. But more significant, Jonathan is relinquishing his claim to the throne, giving it to David, and taking for himself a subservient position such as would be reserved for a consort. It seems strange that through all these verses, David never utters a word; he just listens and accepts the love, honors and approbations that Jonathan heaps upon him.

A bit later on, David had a perfect opportunity to kill Saul while he was sleeping. Instead, he merely snipped off a piece of the king's robe and absconded with it. Feeling guilty, David then confronted Saul and told him, "See? I could've killed you in your sleep, but hey, no hard feelings, OK?" Saul was so moved—and relieved—that he wept and apologized for ever trying to kill David. He also acknowledged that David was the rightful successor to the throne. Then, a very contrite and humbled Saul begged David to swear "by the LORD" that he would not kill off any of his family when he became king. And thusly David swore. After that big emotional scene, Saul returned to his palace and David and his men returned to their stronghold.

(It was around this time that the prophet Samuel died. Yet, as we shall see, he is far from *dead*.)

David and his gang of freebooters were meanwhile roaming the countryside, extorting a living by offering "protection" to local farmers and herdsmen, whether they wanted it or not. When one farmer named Nabal refused to pay the shake down, David ordered his men to kill the man and plunder his goods. But word of the plot reached Abigail, Nabal's beautiful wife, so she loaded up several donkeys with provisions and took them to David, hoping to stop the attack with a bribe. The plan worked. However, God killed Nabal so David could take Abigail as his wife. (Just an FYI: Awhile back Saul, in one of his psycho-snits, gave David's first wife, Michal, to some other guy. She and David eventually got reunited, but she grew to hate him—and with very good reason.) Not that it has anything to do with our story, but around this time David also married a woman named Ahinoam. Never once does Jonathan enter his thoughts. It is as if David is making every effort to divorce himself from that former life.

Saul's hatred of David waxed and waned in direct correlation with his psychotic episodes, and before long he was back to the business of trying to hunt David down and kill him. David decided it would be in his best interest to hide out again, this time in the land of the Philistines, of all people. He befriended King Achish (who obviously hadn't heard of that little "foreskin incident") and eventually became Achish's personal bodyguard. David and his 600 henchmen remained in Philistine territory for about a year and a half, where they continued to live like sand pirates, attacking, destroying and plundering neighboring towns. Here is the full, colorful verse in 1 Samuel 27:8-12. I should note, I am using here the NIV Bible passage because I want my readers to get the rich, full-bodied flavor in the most unequivocal terms.

"Now David and his men went up and raided the Geshurites, the Girzites and the Amalekites. (From ancient times these peoples had lived in the land extending to Shur and Egypt.) Whenever David attacked an area, *he did not leave a man or woman alive*, but took sheep and cattle, donkeys and camels, and clothes. Then he returned to Achish. When Achish asked, "Where did you go raiding today?" David would reply, "Against the Negev of Judah" or "Against the Negev of Jerahmeel" or "Against the Negev of the Kenites." *He did not leave a man or woman alive* to be brought to Gath, for he thought, "They might inform on us and say, *'This is what David did.'*" And such was his practice as long as he lived in Philistine territory. Achish trusted David and said to himself, "He has become so obnoxious to his people, the Israelites, that he will be my servant for life."

I added the italics, not that I needed to. The gruesome details speak for themselves. Also, in verse 12, the KJV Bible uses the word "abhor", not "obnoxious". A loud-mouth talking on his cell phone in a movie theater is obnoxious. David was *abhorred*, i.e. hated, despised and detested by his own people. And this was just the beginning in the long and blood-soaked career of David, the "man after God's own heart", a foundation character beloved and revered by Jews, Christians and Muslims alike. Terrorist, murderer, pillager *against his own people*! Just for kicks, read those verses again, but this time substitute "Satan" for "Achish". A rose by any other name...

Back at the palace, Saul, still plagued by his personal demons, decided to enlist the help of a witch to conjure up the spirit of the dead Samuel for help. Trouble was, Saul—having followed Yahweh's "theocratic ethnic cleansing" directive—had put to death all the witches and wizards in the land. Ah, but there was one witch left, his advisors told him. (How lucky is *that*?) And so off they went, desperately seeking the aid of a woman who, according to Exodus 22:18, should have been killed along with the rest of her black-arted ilk.

Not surprisingly, she didn't trust Saul, fearing he would kill her too, but he swore not to harm her. And hey, if you couldn't believe the word of the psychotic King of Israel... At any rate, she agreed to do the conjuring, and a few bat wings and newt's eyes later, the Macbeth-ian ghost of Samuel magically appeared before them—and boy, was he *pissed!* "WHY HAST THOU DISQUIETED ME, TO BRING ME UP?" he moaned.

Saul entreated the apparition, asking to know why God refused to speak to him.

"Because you fucked up that Amalekite job, you fucking moron!" Samuel replied, maybe not exactly in those words, but that was the gist of it. He then dropped a steaming turd on poor, beleaguered Saul, telling him that God hated him and that Israel would fall to the Philistines, David would inherit the throne, and oh, yeah—"tomorrow you and your sons are gonna die."

Now, any other person might have packed his bags, collected his family and caught the next camel out of Dodge, but not Saul. Despite Samuel's dismal prediction, he prepared to do battle with the Philistines.

David, true to his traitorous nature, was with the Philistine camp as they too were moving into battle formation. But soon there was dissention in the ranks. Several of King Achish's military commanders reported that there was growing distrust of David and his men. They felt that once the battle was pitched, he would turn on them as he turned on his own people. (These Philistines were obviously pretty smart; probably also heard about that "foreskin thing" and didn't want to suffer the same kind of post-mortem cock docking.) They implored Achish to send the two-timing Israelites back to their home camp in Ziklag. Reluctantly the king conceded, and David and his goons were sent packing.

When they reached Ziklag they discovered that the Amalekites had attacked during their absence, plundered and burned the town and made off with the entire population, including David's two wives. David and his men were so upset that they sat down and cried like little girls until they were too exhausted to cry any longer. (Yes, that is exactly what the Bible says they did.) Then they pulled themselves together and did what they do best: They tracked down the Amalekites and brutally slaughtered every woman, child, infant, old, lame or blind person and most of the men. Only 400 Amalekite men escaped on camels. *Everyone else* was butchered with swords and spears and daggers in a blood-fest orgy fueled by genocidal vengeance and led by David, the "man after God's own heart".

This charming little Bible tale can be found in 1 Samuel, Chapter 30. In defense of David's actions, religious apologists will no doubt jump on the pulpit and cry, "He had a right to rescue his wives and kinsmen and regain their possessions! Wouldn't *you* have done the same?" Yes, I probably would. And yes, the Amalekites were sneaky shits for attacking in the first place. Equal guilt on both sides. But now let's look at one very fundamental difference between the Amalekites and David.

Here are Verses 1 and 2: "And it came to pass, when David and his men were come to Ziklag on the third day, that the Amalekites had invaded the south, and Ziklag, and smitten Ziklag, and burned it with fire; And had taken the women captives, that were therein: they slew not any, either great or small, but carried them away, and went on their way."

Did you catch that? *They slew not any, either great or small.* Plundering horde though the Amalekites might have been, they did not kill their captives, did not mistreat them in any way that the scriptures reveal. David, on the other hand, who made his living raiding and slaughtering *everything that moved*, did the same to the Amalekites in retaliation. So yes, while it can be argued that what the Amalekites did was bad, what David did was an act of utter depravity. But then, what's a little depravity when you are the "*most* beloved of God"?

And now a word about the Amalekites themselves. These people must have had some incredible regenerative powers. If you recall from Chapter 15, Saul initially slaughtered every Amalekite "man and woman, infant and suckling". Only the king did he allow to live, and Samuel dispatched *him*. So that pretty much means a 100% kill quota. In other words, *EVERY... AMALEKITE...ON EARTH...IS DEAD!* But then twelve chapters later, David and his bloodthirsty sand bandits are raiding and plundering—guess who—the *Amalekites* again, and again they "left neither man nor woman alive". Now, hold onto your hats... In only three more chapters those Amazing, Miraculous Amalekites are back and thriving as a full-blown society. But what's even *more freakin' miraculous* is that all this spontaneous regeneration took place in only *a few years!* David's genocidal counterattack destroyed all but 400 men who escaped riding camels. And in 1 Chronicles 4:43 we're told—in a mind-numbingly roundabout way—that the descendants of David wiped out the escaped Amalekites...or *did* they???

Enough of this genealogical nonsense. The Philistines now had Saul and his three sons surrounded on a hillside. Saul took several arrows to the vitals. His sons—including Jonathan—lay dead around him. Rather than be killed by these uncircumcised savages (yes, that was his primary fear, to be killed by some guy sporting a turtleneck penis), he fell on his own sword.

When David heard the news he killed the messenger, tore his clothes and fell into a deep depression. It is in 2 Samuel 1:17-27 that he sings his famous "Lament of the Bow" in honor of his fallen comrades. However, it is Verse 26 which has raised the most eyebrows on both sides of the "homosexual relationship" debate. Because of the obviously controversial nature of our subject, I'm going to show both the KJV and NIV Bible passages for comparison. But as you will see, they both say pretty much the same thing.

KJV: "I am distressed for thee, my brother Jonathan: very pleasant hast thou been unto me: thy love to me was wonderful, passing the love of women."

And now the NIV: "I grieve for you, Jonathan my brother; you were very dear to me. Your love for me was wonderful, more wonderful than that of women."

So, there you have it. David, the chosen of God, warrior, husband, future king of Israel, has just confessed, *in writing*, that Jonathan's love was "more wonderful" than the love of *any woman!* But please notice that here again, it is *Jonathan* who is doing the "loving". David is merely acknowledging that love; he is not saying that he loved Jonathan in return. Sure, he is sorry the man is dead, and using the term "brother" does indeed confer a kind of affection. But judging David's nature by the brutal, self-serving things he has done to other people, one would have to conclude that poor Jonathan, despite his own sincere and passionate feelings, meant little more to David than the family dog. And given the station of *women* in the Bible, proclaiming that a love is "more wonderful than that of women" isn't saying much.

The story about the love between David and Jonathan is arguably the most hotly debated book in the entire Bible because it deals with the most taboo of subjects: homosexuality. (The story of Ruth and Naomi is also thought to have some serious homoerotic overtones. If you're interested, it can be found in the Book of Ruth.)

As we have seen in numerous other works of scripture murder, rape, killing babies, plundering and committing all-out genocide are completely tolerable, forgivable, even laudable, *if* they are done in the name of your "loving god". But mention homosexuality and the religious world goes batshit crazy with condemnation. There are many taboos regarding sexual conduct; however, homosexuality is the only one referred to as an "abomination", *and* it is punishable by death per Leviticus 20:13. (Just an observation here, but considering how many so-called laws are punishable by death, I can't help wondering when that "Thou shalt not kill" commandment is supposed to kick in.)

Gays and supporters of LGBT (Lesbian, Gay, Bi-sexual and Transgender) rights have made the claim that Jesus never spoke against homosexuality. Well, not in so many words. However, in Matthew 5:17-18 (the famous "Sermon on the Mount") he tells the crowd, "Think not that I am come to destroy the law, or the prophets: I am not come to destroy, but to fulfill. For verily I say unto you, Till heaven and earth pass, one jot or one tittle shall in no wise pass from the law, till all be fulfilled."

So basically, what he is saying here is that all the Old Testament laws are still in play along with their denunciations and punishments...and that includes those pertaining to homosexuality. Also, in the first verses of Matthew 19 he schools the Pharisees on the terms of divorce, stating in Verses 4 and 5 "Have ye not read, that he which made them at the beginning made them male and female, And said, For this cause shall a man leave father and mother, and shall cleave to his wife: and they twain shall be one flesh?" But again, did Jesus specifically condemn homosexuality? No, he did *not*.

But even if Jesus didn't address the topic directly, the Apostle Paul of Tarsus most certainly did. Paul is credited with having written thirteen books in the New Testament, although this—like nearly everything else in the Bible—is unprovable and the subject of much academic disagreement. Still, three of these books, Romans, 1 Corinthians and 1 Timothy contain verses that speak to homosexuality and the "sinfulness" thereof:

(Romans 1:26-27) "For this cause God gave them up unto vile affections: for even their women did change the natural use into that which is against nature: And likewise also the men, leaving the natural use of the woman, burned in their lust one toward another; men with men working that which is unseemly, and receiving in themselves that recompense of their error which was meet."

(1 Corinthians 6:9) "Know ye not that the unrighteous shall not inherit the kingdom of God? Be not deceived: neither fornicators, nor idolaters, nor adulterers, nor effeminate, nor abusers of themselves with mankind."

(1 Timothy 1:9-10) "Knowing this, that the law is not made for a righteous man, but for the lawless and disobedient, for the ungodly and for sinners, for unholy and profane, for murderers of fathers and murderers of mothers, for manslayers, For whoremongers, for them that defile themselves with mankind, for menstealers, for liars, for perjured persons, and if there be any other thing that is contrary to sound doctrine."

Not only is Paul calling homosexuals *immoral*, he is lumping them in with the most vile of criminals. If it's of any consolation, Paul is also pretty disparaging toward women, blaming them for the downfall of man due to Eve's fruit fetish, and telling them they must submit completely to the will of their husbands. Then he goes so far as to tell the males of the world that they would be far better off not to pollute themselves by having sex with women. To him, marriage was only to be considered if the man just couldn't keep it in his loin cloth. (1 Corinthians 7:8-9) "I say therefore to the unmarried and widows, it is good for them if they abide even as I (celibate). But if they cannot contain (their lust), let them marry: for it is better to marry than to burn (in Hell)." I added the words in parenthesis for clarity.

It is difficult for rational, free-thinking minds to comprehend why homosexuals and homosexuality have been so demonized by the three main Western religions. A great many ancient and highly developed cultures, including Roman, Greek, Egyptian, Mesopotamian, Babylonian, Assyrian, Persian, Chinese and Japanese accepted homosexuality as part of normal human physical and emotional expression. Pacific Island, Eskimo-Aleut, and Native American cultures too were not only tolerant of homosexuals, but these "two-spirit" persons were often accorded special status in the village or tribe. Even those barbaric, uncircumcised Philistines demonstrated far more cultural sophistication in their view of homosexuality than their foreskin-phobic neighbors.

Perhaps it's the whole "sexuality" thing that causes the Abrahamic religions such Freudian shit fits. Sex is, after all, a really big deal, perhaps *the biggest* deal for every living thing on the entire planet. For without sex there would *be* no life, plain and simple. To ancient humans the whole reproductive process was the greatest of mysteries. Priests and prophets of biblical origins learned very quickly that by controlling this most basic—and pleasurable—aspect of human nature they would be able to control the masses, thereby ensuring their role as divine revelators *and* the plush living typically accorded such persons.

But how to accomplish this? Well, first make it sinful, shameful and dirty. Second, restrict it to the rigid confines of marriage (between a man and a woman *only*, of course). Third, make it exclusively for the purpose of procreation. Fourth, curse all babies born as a result of this foul union with the sin of their parents (but mostly the mother since it was Eve who seduced Adam and that's just what women do). Fifth, offer the guilt-ridden minions absolution...for a price. Sixth, threaten would-be nonconformists with grievous punishments, curses and even *death*. And these are just the ground rules for *hetero*sexuals!

Homosexuals are in an altogether different category. For starters, they don't procreate. They do what they do for one reason: *PLEASURE*—the most reprehensible reason of all! The very idea of having sex for pure pleasure seems incongruous, abhorrent, even antithetical to conventional biblical thinking. In fact, the authors who concocted the scriptures seem to have an almost paranoid fixation with sex and genitalia in general.

(Remember, it was Abraham, patriarch of the "Big Three" religions, who initiated that whole circumcision thing.) Slaughtering animals because your god loves the smell of burning blood, guts and hair is one thing; sexually mutilating a tiny baby boy—and in some cultures, little girls—is something else.

Of all the religions that have populated this planet from the dawn of recorded time, none has demonstrated such an unbridled and irrational hatred of the homosexual community as ancient Judaism, followed by Christianity and Islam. The "jealous god" of the Bible may speak of love, but he dishes out hatred in egregious acts of violence. We can be coaxed into forgiving the ignorance of Bronze Age peoples, saying they just didn't know any better. But even today, in the United States of America, a country where "all men are (supposedly) created equal", we still see glaring evidence of that same irrational and indefensible prejudice. Small wonder the people who continue to have the greatest difficulty accepting homosexuals as fellow human beings with the right to "life, liberty and a pursuit of happiness" are those still mired in fundamentalist religious dogma. Fortunately, attitudes *are* changing for the better. We see this in the entertainment industry; we see it in politics; we see it in independent research polls. And yes, believe it or not, we are even seeing it in some churches.

Now, in light of all the Bible-based gay bashing that has been going on for centuries, you may have asked, "So, just how *did* a story with such overtly homoerotic overtones ever find its way into the holy scriptures?" Consider this: Homosexuality has obviously been around from the dawn of time, as evidenced in ancient works of art. The homosexual presence might seem higher now simply because general acceptance for the most part is higher, and more people are "coming out". But logic would indicate that there were just as many homosexual persons 10,000 years ago, percentagewise, as there are now. In fact, recent studies by various groups estimate between 3% and 10% of the population is homosexual. (The vast difference between the numbers is likely due to a personal reluctance to answer the question honestly for fear of stigmatic reprisal.) Furthermore, an article in *US News and World Report*, dated July 29, 2013, mentioned a study that suggested up to 60% of all *Catholic priests* were gay...and that probably *included* the priests who took part in assembling the Bible.

Coincidence? Not hardly. They say the best place to hide something is in plain sight. So, if you were a homosexual man living during the dark rise of European Catholicism you learned at an early age to conceal your true self. What better camouflage than the priesthood? You could surround yourself with the objects of your ardor-ation—many of them having similar interests—and never have to explain to anyone why you "haven't gotten married and settled down to raise a family yet".

Given these statistics, let's take a trip back in time. The year was 397 CE. Emperor Theodosius I had recently made Christianity the official religion of the Roman Empire. (Failure to convert was typically punishable by death.) Trouble was, there were many different sects of "Christianity" floating around, each one claiming to have *the* purest and most accurate scriptures. To remedy the squabbling, the Third Council of Carthage was held to determine once and for all which supernal fairy tales would be compiled into the official Bible of the Roman Catholic Church. (To this day there is still much controversy and contention among other "Christian" churches, who claim *their* doctrines— omitted from the Catholic compilation—are the most complete and valid. And then there are the Jews and Muslims, who have their own take on the matter.)

It must have been a gargantuan task to wade through the mountains of letters, papyruses and scrolls to determine which of the holy scriptures were more "holier" than the others. Now, can you imagine the sheer joy of a sexually and emotionally repressed gay priest upon discovering the story of David and Jonathan? Without a doubt he would share its "spiritual significance" with his most trusted colleagues, who, like himself, could fully understand and appreciate the much deeper meaning hidden within the story. One can only wonder how many similar tales never made it to canonization...how many were destroyed outright for their explicit imagery...and how many wound up under the mattresses of horny priests for that special "midnight mass".

I don't suppose we'll ever know the intimate truth that lies hidden between the lines of the "David and Jonathan" story. Gay believers will continue to embrace this endearing tale as proof that God loves them for who they are, because, after all, he *made* them that way. Beautiful and quasi-logical as this concept is, it does not negate the fact that he refers to them as an "abomination" and wants them killed on the spot. (I've always wondered...wouldn't it be easier and a lot less messy to just *change* them? But I forget, Yahweh is a bloodthirsty war god that prefers senseless violence to simple solutions.)

Gay Christian believers assert that the kinder, gentler Jesus persona is the epitome of unconditional love and acceptance. Again, this sounds wonderful, and it certainly wouldn't be the first time a son broke with his father's parochial, outmoded beliefs and traditions. But then again, there is that "sexual morality" thing of which he makes no bones: 1) sex outside of marriage is immoral, and 2) marriage was made for man and woman. Quite a homosexual Catch 22.

Yet perhaps it wasn't what Jesus *said* but rather what he *didn't* say that might shed a ray of hope. Truth is, all we know about what Jesus said is what somebody *said* he said. Most of the people who wrote about Jesus never even met him, and *none* of the first person accounts can be authenticated. A few paragraphs ago I mentioned that it is a well-known and admitted fact that numerous books and other forms of scriptural literature were deliberately omitted from the final draft of the Roman Bible for one reason or another. What if some of that omitted material cast Jesus in an entirely different light? Perhaps a more... "*rainbow*-colored" light? There are dozens if not hundreds of books and articles available that make the argument that Jesus of Nazareth was very likely a homosexual. (For the love of trees I will not even try to list them here, but they are easy to find, thanks to the Blessed Internet.)

To begin with, Jesus was well past the age of majority yet chose to remain single in a society that virtually demanded that a man marry and begin fathering children. Moreover, in Judaic society of that period celibacy was *not* an honored state, but would have been considered a bit "queer", so to speak. Jesus obviously preferred the company of other men. Then there is that mysterious eighteen year gap in his life from age twelve to thirty. So either he did absolutely *nothing* of any importance, or he did something that the priesthood felt needed to be covered up.

In the Book of John 13:23, we find this curious passage: "Now there was leaning on Jesus' bosom one of his disciples, whom Jesus loved." The disciple is John, who is speaking of himself in the third person. This intimate form of address is not used in any other of the Gospels nor for any other disciple. What's more, John is singularly referred to as the "Beloved Disciple", and he is pictured in numerous classic works of art as the man provocatively laying his head against Christ's breast during the Last Supper. John—egotistical sycophant though he might have been—is also the only disciple who had the courage to show up at Jesus' crucifixion. Now *that* takes a special kind of devotion! And of course, he gallantly took care of Jesus' mother, Mary, in effect becoming her "son" (one might conjecture, her "son-in-law").

Sometime after Jesus' grisly death on the cross John apparently went a bit cuckoo and concocted the scary-tale, *Revelation*, which foretells the horrifically violent, monster-ridden, blood-drenched end of the world. (And who could blame him after witnessing his beloved tortured to death right before his eyes?) One verse in particular gives us a glimpse into where his sexual and psychological head was at: "These are they which were not defiled with women; for they are virgins. These are they which follow the Lamb whithersoever he goeth." (Revelation 14:4). He is talking about the 144,000 who will comprise the Lord's ruling class in Heaven. All virgin *men* (presumably young and beautiful), who have not been soiled and *defiled* by having had sexual intercourse with (ugh!) women. Need I say more?

If gay priests of yore were indeed responsible for the inclusion of the David and Jonathan story, it isn't unreasonable to think that straight priests would endeavor to conceal or even outright destroy any and all "controversial" depictions of their superhuman savior. There is but a thin line between conscientious editing and premeditated censorship. But if homosexuality is a "sin against nature", then so is celibacy, for neither is an act of procreation. So I guess straight Christians would rather believe that their gentle, androgynous Jesus wasn't getting *any* sex than getting the wrong *kind* of sex.

Now here's a bit of historical trivia that I find particularly insightful: James I of England was the famous king who sponsored the Bible compilation that bears his name. What most Christian believers don't know is that this king was also a *queen*. He was notorious for surrounding himself with an entourage of handsome young men. When his enemies tried to scandalize him for his open and unapologetic dalliance with a young George Villiers, the First Duke of Buckingham (whom James referred to as his "sweet child and wife"), James responded with this statement: "I wish to speak in my own behalf and not to have it thought to be a defect, for Jesus Christ did the same, and therefore I cannot be blamed. Christ had his son John, and I have my George."

Whether or not Jesus was gay is irrelevant. His message was simple and unequivocal: LOVE. It wasn't a suggestion; it was a commandment. So, the next time you encounter one of those simpering, sanctimonious, Bible-wielding, hate-speakers, you might lay a little Luke 6:37 on them: "Judge not, and ye shall not be judged: condemn not, and ye shall not be condemned: forgive, and ye shall be forgiven."

And if they come back with the classic rejoinder, "*Sodomy is a sin!*" tell them you couldn't agree more, then direct them to Ezekiel 16:49 for the *true* definition of "sodomy": "Behold, this was the iniquity of thy sister Sodom, pride, fullness of bread, and abundance of idleness was in her and in her daughters, neither did she strengthen the hand of the poor and needy." In other words, the four things that caused Yahweh to put the atomic smack down on Sodom town were arrogance, gluttony, laziness, and failure to help those less fortunate. Not a single word here about anal sex.

Now, toward the beginning of this story I made some pretty disparaging comments about David's character. I believe I called him a "lying, conniving, arrogant, drunken, blackmailing, debauching, lascivious, womanizing, adulterous, backstabbing, treacherous, sexually deviant, animal-torturing, baby-killing son of a bitch". Most of these infamous epithets I have already illustrated in the context of our story. But it's after he becomes firmly established as king of all Israel (2 Samuel) that he really gets his sado-sanctimonious freak on.

Remember the oaths he swore "by the LORD" to Jonathan and then Saul not to let any harm come to their family members after he became king? Well, as it turned out, Saul had one remaining son, Ish-bosheth, who was the natural successor to the throne. Israel was a divided kingdom, half following David, the other half loyal to Ish-bosheth. Two years after ascending to power, Ish-bosheth was assassinated. The Bible tells us that when the assassins came to David for a reward, he had them killed out of anger. Anger? Or was he simply getting rid of the witnesses? Either way, the road was now clear for David to take full control over all of Israel.

But Saul had two more sons through his beloved concubine, Rizpah. There were also five grandsons from Saul's eldest daughter, Merab. David—the man who swore an amnesty oath "by the LORD"—had all seven of them butchered and their bodies hung from a scaffold on the pretense of ending a three-year famine, which certainly justifies coldblooded murder. With these "genetic" obstacles out of the way, David was now uncontested in his full-blown grab for power.

I suppose I should mention that *technically* there was one survivor in the House of Saul: Jonathan's own son, Mephi-bosheth. The boy was only five years old when his father was killed. Upon hearing the news, his nurse dropped him, permanently crippling both his feet for life. He never married and thus produced no offspring (which probably would have been a good thing for him *and* them). Apparently seeing the child as no threat, David not only allowed him to live, but made him a ward of the state. Then too, if the young man bore a physical resemblance to Jonathan, David might have had *other* reasons for keeping him alive. I'll let you draw your own conclusions on that one.

Then there was the incident that took place while David was leading the procession that brought the Ark to Jerusalem. David was so happy (and drunk) that he stripped off all this clothing, leaving only his loincloth, and danced wildly, leaping and cavorting like a big Hebrew yutz, before the cheering multitude. His wife, Michal, Saul's younger daughter, was so embarrassed and disgusted that she gave him a thorough tongue lashing. He replied to her—and I can imagine his voice thick and slurred with liquor as he said— "Hey, I was dancing for the *LORD*. You remember the *LORD*? The guy who picked *me* to rule over Israel and not your *old man*, and not any of his *sons* either! Yeah, *that* LORD. So, I'll do whatever I *want*, you got that, sister? And furthermore, I plan on getting a whole lot more viler than *this*. In fact, I'm gonna get *so* stinkin' vile that I'm even gonna make *myself* sick of me! Whadaya think of *that*? And then I'm gonna find some maidservants—you know the ones I'm talking about—and I'll bet *they* show me a little respect, wink, wink!"

Dear readers, if you think I'm making this up, I encourage you to read 2 Samuel 6:20-23. I may have "modernized" the words, but the sentiment and the virulence is dead-on accurate. Regardless of the verbiage or the translation, King David was a colossal *dick*. This is why the last verse in the chapter declares, "Therefore Michal the daughter of Saul had no child unto the day of her death." Obviously, she hated him and refused to ever have sex with him again. Not that he would have noticed, as he already had numerous other wives and countless concubines to keep him occupied.

And speaking of sex, everyone is familiar with the story of David and Bathsheba, the woman he saw bathing on a nearby rooftop. (What pubescent boy hasn't been titillated by *that* religious imagery?) The story is a simple one: David, in true voyeuristic fashion, was watching a beautiful, naked woman bathe. He had her brought to him, they had sex. Many movies have portrayed Bathsheba as a willing participant, if not the actual seductress. Personally, I think this is more a bunch of macho-biblical-whitewashing aimed at cleaning up David's patently lascivious involvement in the affair. Whether or not it was consensual is irrelevant; he *was* the king after all, therefore she—like every other woman of that time—had no right to refuse. Add to this the fact that it was a case of double-adultery, which means, by Bible Law, they *both* should have been stoned to death.

At any rate, he eventually got her pregnant. Then, in true "Bible hero" fashion, he tried to blame it on her soldier husband, Uriah the Hittite, by recalling him from battle and repeatedly coaxing him to have sex with his wife. But Uriah was a good and loyal soldier, and he stanchly refused to enjoy the comforts of his wife's cooter while his men were suffering the privations of war. (An excellent question that rarely gets raised in this chapter is, why the hell wasn't David also at the battle leading his troops like a proper king instead of lounging about his cushy palace, ogling naked women on rooftops?)

Afraid that he would be found out—which makes no sense whatsoever, since *he was the freakin' king*—David then ordered poor Uriah sent to the frontlines and ultimately his death. The problem solved, David took Bathsheba as yet another one of his wives. Bathsheba gave birth to a son and they all lived happily ever after. Well...not exactly.

Apparently the whole sordid affair ruffled old Yahweh's feathers and he threw down a curse upon David, causing a dreadful sickness to befall the infant, which died a few days later. Here again we see a fine example of Divine Justice: David commits adultery and murder, so God evens the score by torturing to death an innocent baby. Never mind that Yahweh the Maleficent could have, at any time, prevented any and all of these events from ever taking place; instead, he chose to wait until there was a tiny, newborn baby to kill. (Just an FYI: For some odd reason, this entire tale does not even appear in the Books of 1st and 2nd Chronicles, which are basically a "Reader's Digest Condensed Version" of human history as per Bible lore. I wonder what *those* editors were thinking?)

After the death of his son, David's "sado-psychotic" brand of warfare really kicked into overdrive. In 2 Samuel, Chapter 8, Verse 2 he attacks and vanquishes the Moabites. And then, just for fun, he makes all the people—young, old, male, female, children and babies—lie down on the ground side-by-side, and he measures them off with a piece of rope. Everyone that falls within the first two measurements is put to death. In this fashion he casually and systematically slaughters two-thirds of an entire population. The "lucky" surviving third are made slaves and forced to pay tribute.

This lovely little verse demonstrates not only David's sick sense of humor but also his perfidious ingratitude. He was, after all, related by blood to the Moabites through his great-grandmother, Ruth. More shocking, it was the Moabites who protected David's father and mother while he was hiding out from Saul's armies. And so in return, David slaughters 66% of the Moabite population in a perverted little game of "eenie, meenie, minie—*murder!*"

But David's deeds of misdoing didn't stop there, and they were not confined to humans. In 2 Samuel, Chapter 8 he is back to committing glorious acts of slaughter against several different peoples. But it is in Verse 4 that he turned his sadism against one of the most noble and useful animals known to mankind. The verse reads, "And David took from him (king of Zobah) a thousand chariots, and seven hundred horsemen, and twenty thousand footmen: and David houghed all the chariot horses, but reserved enough of them for an hundred chariots."

The verb "houghed" translates as "hamstrung". It means to slice through the tendon in an animal's hind leg just above the hock joint. Here's what Wikipedia says about it: "Hamstringing is used primarily to incapacitate a human or animal and render them incapable of effective movement. The severing of the hamstring muscles or tendons results not only in the crippling of the leg, but also in tremendous pain common to heavy laceration. For this reason hamstringing has been used as a form of torture, often resulting in the death of the victim."

When we consider that this "man after God's own heart" could systematically and without any form of remorse butcher women and children, it's no stretch to imagine him mutilating by slow torture a mere beast. (And just so you know, Joshua did the same thing at the LORD's request.)

But it gets even better! In 1 Chronicles, Chapter 20 his armies are in the process of destroying the city of Rabbah. Verse 3 tells us what David then did to the survivors: "And he brought out the people that were in it, and cut them with saws, and with harrows of iron, and with axes. Even so dealt David with all the cities of the children of Ammon. And David and all the people returned to Jerusalem."

Cut them with saws, and with harrows of iron, and with axes! Even worse, 2 Samuel 12:31, which says basically the same thing, adds the chilling line: "...and made them pass through the brick-kiln." *An oven!*

The New International Version Bible, which does its pathetic best to dilute some of those "ickier" passages, offers this watered-down milksop translation: "...and brought out the people who were there, consigning them to labor with saws and with iron picks and axes, and he made them work at brick making. David did this to all the Ammonite towns. Then he and his entire army returned to Jerusalem." Now, given everything we know about the great and gruesome King David so far, which translation are *you* more inclined to believe?

While David is perhaps no worse than any other god-loving, baby-killing genocidal maniac the Old Testament can offer up as proof of its theocratic superiority, he most assuredly is no *better* despite his grandiose scriptural stature. Simple-minded, puerile apologists love to turn to the Psalms of David for comfort and reassurance. Here is a favorite: Psalm 101: "I will sing of mercy and justice; I will behave wisely in a perfect way. I will walk within my house with a perfect heart. I will set nothing wicked before my eyes; A perverse heart shall depart from me; I will not know wickedness."

King David is considered to be one of *the most* revered, beloved and pivotal figures in all of Judaism, Christianity and Islam, ranking right up there with Abraham, Jesus and Mohammed. He was God's "most beloved", his prototype of what a perfect king should be. But now that we have seen him in all his blood-drenched, sadistic glory, perhaps that list of notables should instead include: Genghis Khan, Ivan the Terrible, Joseph Stalin, Mao Zedong, Pol Pot, Adolf Hitler, and various other war criminals. It is no small wonder then that theologians from popes to Sunday School teachers have chosen to simply ignore "those" parts of the story. Interestingly, if you search "King David's sins" on the Internet, you will find countless Christian websites that list 1) his affair with Bathsheba and resulting death of her husband, and 2) he took a census of his people when God told him not to. That's it; not a peep about torture or mass murder of civilian populations.

I understand how people can adore this iconic figure when they don't know what he did. What I find profoundly disturbing are the ones who *do know* and adore him in spite of it. These people are downright scary, in my opinion, because they have in effect disengaged the part of their brain that recognizes egregious turpitude. They have been conditioned to believe, without doubt or question, that any atrocity, no matter how perverse or grisly, can be overlooked, accepted, even applauded if it was done in the name of God Almighty. Once people are able to do this, it isn't a far leap to justify burning women at the stake, throwing children into ovens and flying jet liners into skyscrapers.

Lucifer:
The Evil-ution of a Scapegoat

In the very first story we met God's horny, hedonistic, incorrigible sons. We learned that it was because of their lascivious exploits—i.e. banging the Earth babes, which created a race of giants, who in turn began screwing animals, which resulted in a bunch of perverted, cannibalistic offspring—that God decided to wipe out every living thing on the planet with the exception of Noah, his family, a few dozen "untainted" animals, some dinosaur eggs, and several 450-foot tall giants, who somehow miraculously managed to escape detection and survive the flood. But then the whole mess started all over, proving again that 1) Yahweh is *not at all* omniscient, since he apparently didn't know that was going to happen, or 2) he deliberately *allowed* it to happen because he just loves to see living things suffer in tortuously hideous ways like some galactic spoiled brat.

Now, to the rational mind this Hebrew god of misery and mayhem would have to seem like the very incarnation of evil itself. And he is, but only if one has a rational mind. To the *irrational* mind the concept of "evil" becomes highly subjective; the so-called "moral compass" takes on the attributes of a spin-the-wheel game. Ripping open pregnant women and hacking children to death with an axe morphs into a glorious duty, if your god tells you to do it. Boiling heretics in oil, launching an unprovoked attack on a foreign country and decapitating journalists become noble acts, if Yahweh/Jehovah/Allah is on your side. So, if these are some of the shining examples of the Bible-based "morality" that believers love to crow about, what—or who—on earth could possibly be considered *IM*-moral? Or more to the point, *EVIL?*

As a child raised in a Christian environment I learned about the "big three" figures in the Bible: God, the Father; Jesus, the Son; and Satan, the Devil. The descriptions and attributes of each were pretty simple and straightforward (they would have to be in order to be absorbed by a child's mind or someone with the mind of a child). Problem is, children grow, and with growth comes curiosity, and with curiosity comes questions, questions such as, "If God is all-powerful, why didn't he just kill Satan in the first place?" and "If God loves us, why does he allow Satan to do such horrible things to us?"

Pure, simple, logical. The answers, however, are anything but. With simpering self-satisfaction the religious will tell us, "God has a perfect plan," followed by the intellectually insulting, "We're not smart enough to understand his plan." And if that isn't enough to crush the wondering spirit, there is that thinly veiled threat, "To question God's plan is to question God himself, and to question God is to incur his wrath!" (And we all know what *that* means.)

These types of puerile, nonsensical, ambiguous answers have served the various clergy well over the centuries and helped them amass king-sized fortunes by selling the equivalent of "afterlife insurance policies" to the sick, the forlorn, the bereaved, the gullible and the easily frightened. And if gentle psychological persuasion didn't work, there was always the threat of death by some gruesome torture to bring the sheep back into the fold. Evangelical? Or just plain Evil? Let's spin that moral compass and find out.

The subject of this story is Lucifer. He is known by several names: Satan, the Devil, the Beast, the Destroyer, Beelzebub, the Dragon, Prince of Darkness, the Serpent, the Deceiver, the Seducer, the Tempter, Dark Angel, Fallen Angel and on, and on, and on. In short, he is the worst of the worst; the supreme King of the Despicable; even worse than Darth Vader, Adolf Hitler and the Grinch-Who-Stole-Christmas all rolled into one. If God is perfect goodness, then Lucifer is perfect badness. Or so the Judeo-Christian fear peddlers would have you believe. And yet, if you take a closer look, judge these two morally diametric entities by their *actions* (as Jesus recommended, ironically), that stark black-and-white distinction between "good" and "evil" starts to get a bit fuzzy. More interesting still, it actually becomes rather difficult to tell them apart.

Since something cannot come from nothing, as creationists will gleefully maintain, so it must follow that Lucifer had to come from something, i.e. he was created. But by *whom?* This question is not meant to be facetious. The identity of Lucifer, Satan, the Devil, et al, is in itself a study of evolution—*literary* evolution. As good little Christian children we were told that God made Lucifer along with all the other angels. But Lucifer became jealous of God's power (or God's special relationship with Jesus, or with that of mankind; it kind of depends upon which church you went to, as they all have their own "spin" on the matter, and the Bible itself doesn't offer any clear

171

explanations). At any rate, Lucifer got a third of the angels to side with him in a failed *coup d'état*, after which they were tossed out of Heaven and banished to Earth where they were allowed to run wild all over the place, wreaking havoc with the locals while God just stood by and didn't lift a finger to help.

Just a side thought here, but that must have been one (pardon the pun) *HELL* of a battle, the likes of which all the creative geniuses at *DC, Dark Horse* and *Marvel Comics* combined couldn't conceive! And yet, ironically, there is no account of it at all in the Bible. The only clues we get that it even happened are bits and pieces scattered throughout much later scriptures; almost as if those latter writers needed something to "punch up" their own particular stories in order to make them salable to the masses. Still, you would think that a political upheaval of such Hollywood proportions—and with such cataclysmic implications for all of humankind—would deserve an entire book all to itself. But no.

Interestingly, the best descriptions we have of Lucifer's fall and the place called Hell come from some very *human* authors, most notably Dante Alighieri, who, in the 14th Century, wrote the terrifyingly detailed poem, *Inferno*, and John Milton, who gave us the satanically sympathetic, *Paradise Lost* (1667). It is from these two classic sources, and numerous others—*not* the Bible—that many, if not most, of our concepts of Heaven, Hell and Lucifer derive. That aside, the vast majority of theological sources I have found seem to agree that the cosmic battle and the unceremonious casting out took place before humans (or at least Adam and Eve) inhabited the Earth.

All right, let's get back to the actual identity/creation of Lucifer. He was purportedly the most beautiful of all the angels. A resplendent creation. Perfect in every way. What, then, went wrong with his wiring to make him turn evil? If this sounds like a familiar theatrical plotline, there's a reason for that. The concepts of "good" and "evil" have been fundamental to every human culture, great or small, from time immemorial. Even our earliest cave-dwelling ancestors must have conceptualized good and evil in terms of their physical environment: fire "good", lightning "evil"; healthy baby "good", deformed baby "evil". Every dramatic saga from Shakespeare to spaghetti westerns, folktales to Saturday morning cartoons revolves around the "good guy/bad guy" scenario. The hero must have a villain, the protagonist an antagonist, the knight a dragon, the old man a sea. In other words, the men who wrote the Bible stories were simply following the same trite formula that had been handed down through ages and generations of storytellers. Lucifer's only reason for existing, therefore, is to act as the adversarial counterpoint, "perfect evil", to Yahweh's (or Jesus') "perfect good".

That's a mighty powerful role to play. You would think a character of such malevolent magnitude would receive frequent and formidable mention throughout the Bible. You would be wrong. In fact, in the entire King James Version Bible the name Lucifer, for all of its vile, loathsome and wicked connotations, only appears *once!* In the Old Testament the moniker "Satan" appears in only four books. Stranger still, in the New International Version Bible "Lucifer" appears *not at all*, and Satan shows up in a paltry 3 Old Testament books. Now, in the *New* Testament of both Bibles you will find nearly *forty* mentions of Satan, encompassing twelve separate books. (If you include references to demons, devils and evil spirits, that number jumps to nearly *600!*) OK, so what happened between the Old and New Testaments to cause such a literary population explosion of "Satans" and his gangs of ghoulies? And how come Lucifer, the Supreme King of the Diabolic, only gets one lousy mention in the KJV and *none at all* in the NIV? That alone should be cause for suspicion, so let's begin our forensic investigation with that.

I'll start by defining his name. *Lucifer* is Latin for *Day Star*, *Morning Star* or *Brightest Star*, an epithet for the planet Venus and the Roman goddess of love and beauty. *Love and beauty?!* It can also mean *bringer of light* or *illuminating*, depending on whether it is being used as a noun or an adjective. That doesn't sound so scary, and certainly not very *evil*. Since it is used only once in the KJV Bible, let's look at that passage. It appears in the Book of Isaiah, Chapter 14, Verses 12-15. It reads: "How art thou fallen from heaven, O Lucifer, son of the morning! how art thou cut down to the ground, which didst weaken the nations! For thou hast said in thine heart, 'I will ascend into heaven, I will exalt my throne above the stars of God: I will sit also upon the mount of the congregation, in the sides of the north: I will ascend above the heights of the clouds; I will be like the most High.' Yet thou shalt be brought down to hell, to the sides of the pit."

Well, that would probably convince any jury that Lucifer was indeed the arrogant, rebellious "Fallen Angel" we were all told about in Sunday School. Here now is the same passage from the NIV Bible *without* Lucifer: "How you have fallen from heaven, morning star, son of the dawn! You have been cast down to the earth, you who once laid low the nations! You said in your heart, 'I will ascend to the heavens; I will raise my throne above the stars of God; I will sit enthroned on the mount of assembly, on the utmost heights of Mount Zaphon. I will ascend above the tops of the clouds; I will make myself like the Most High.' But you are brought down to the realm of the dead, to the depths of the pit." Note the use of the term *morning star*, which is the *accurate* translation from Latin. In the KJV *Lucifer* seems to be a proper name. In the NIV it is only a title.

Given the discrepancies between the two passages, a competent detective would insist on some further investigation. If we do that—that is to say, if we read Chapter 14 from the beginning—we soon realize that the narrator is very clearly and specifically talking about the tyranny and subsequent downfall of the King of Babylon—*NOT* Lucifer, a.k.a. Satan! This is true for both versions of the Bible. Here are Verses 3, 4 and 5 (KJV) as evidence: "And it shall come to pass in the day that the LORD shall give thee (Israel) rest from thy sorrow, and from thy fear, and from the hard bondage wherein thou wast made to serve, That thou shalt take up this proverb against the king of Babylon, and say, How hath the oppressor ceased! the golden city ceased! The LORD hath broken the staff of the wicked, and the sceptre of the rulers."

In Ezekiel 28:12-14 there is another passage that quote-mining Christians like to use because they believe it describes Lucifer/Satan's physical attributes. (I will use only the NIV verses for brevity; there is virtually no difference in the KJV.) "You were the seal of perfection, full of wisdom and perfect in beauty. You were in Eden, the garden of God, every precious stone adorned you: carnelian, chrysolite and emerald, topaz, onyx and jasper, lapis lazuli, turquoise and beryl. Your settings and mountings were made of gold; on the day you were created they were prepared. You were anointed as a guardian cherub, for so I ordained you. You were on the holy mount of God; you walked among the fiery stones."

Yes, once again this definitely sounds like our Mr. Iniquitous, at least the image that we had branded into our small, innocent brains. The problem is, as it was in the other example, they are conveniently leaving out the first few lines of the passage which tells—as Paul Harvey would say—the *rest* of the story. Here is the *beginning* of Verse 12: "Son of man, take up a lament concerning the king of Tyre and say to him: 'This is what the Sovereign LORD says...'" Just like in the Isaiah verses, this is *NOT* about Lucifer/Satan; it is about a very nasty and very mortal *human* ḳing!

Since the introductory verses of these chapters make the meaning so undeniably clear, it's curious why the authors would use so many lovely connotations to describe a couple of shitty monarchs? (I can only presume they were speaking sarcastically.) Nevertheless, Christians have for centuries *erroneously* used these intentionally truncated verses as their "proof positive" that Lucifer is in fact the fallen angel, Satan, as mentioned so often in the New Testament. They will even try to back this up by cherry-picking a verse in Luke where Jesus is talking about Satan's downfall. (Luke 10:18 reads, "And he said unto them, I beheld Satan as lightning fall from heaven.") All this "proves" is that Jesus told a whopper of a lie based on a few lines he read in the Hebrew Scriptures, just so he could impress a flock of gullible groupies.

Speaking of Hebrew Scriptures, the actual word-in-question is הֵילֵל (or heylel in the transliteration), and it means—you guessed it—*day star!* So naturally, when the Hebrew writings were translated into Latin, the word quite literally followed. It did not become a capital "L" proper name until the Early Christian Period in the first few centuries after the death of Jesus. Why the change? If you recall, I mentioned that the Old Testament portions of the KJV and NIV Bibles contain very few mentions of "Satan"; yet the New Testaments of both contain *dozens*. Again, you can blame Jesus (or his biographers) for this. His ministry was packed with lurid images of Hell and torture and warnings about demons, evil spirits and, of course, *Satan!* Oddly enough though, he never once referred to any malevolent entity as "Lucifer".

Just a fun little bit of trivia here: If you skip ahead to Revelation 22:16 you will read where Jesus is doing what Jesus does best—flaunting himself—and he says, "I Jesus...am the root and the offspring of David, and the bright and morning star." Let's read that sentence again, using the Latin term for "bright and morning star". It would go something like this: "I am the root and the offspring of David, and (I am) *Lucifer.*" So, either Jesus has just confessed that he is in fact Satan incarnate, or the Latin word means what it means and nothing more.

At this point you might be wondering, if the Old Testament Bible went from Hebrew to Latin to English, how come that one particular Latin word got left in? (Remember, this applies only to the KJV and a few obscure others.) The answer is elementary. The translators-*all Christians*—set out to deliberately obfuscate the true meaning of the older texts, thus creating the literary illusion that the Satan/Devil in the New Testament is the same diabolical dude being talked about in Isaiah; a self-fulfilling prophesy, you might say. *Lucifer*, being a completely foreign word to an English-speaking (and largely illiterate) population, would seem formidable and frightening, especially when coupled with the very *real* forms of torture being meted out to sinners and heretics in those early dark days.

Another morsel of trivia pertaining to translations and translators: In 1382 a brilliant Oxford university professor, philosopher, theologian and political activist named John Wycliffe, along with his likeminded associates, began the daunting task of translating the entire *Latin Vulgate* (Catholic Bible) into English. He believed the common man had a right to read God's word for himself. More to his credit, Wycliffe was an outspoken critic of the Roman Catholic Church's opulence, greed, corruption and unjust laws. In retaliation the Church began rounding up his collaborators and burning them alive at the stake as heretics. Wycliffe escaped the horror of the stake by dying of a stroke. Though nothing remains of his masterwork, he is considered a champion of the Protestant cause and is referred to as "The *Morning Star* of the Reformation". In other words, he was *Lucifer!*

Now, if you want to keep your kids in line and give them screaming nightmares in the process, read them the Book of Revelation. It is here that we get the first visual picture of Satan (again, *not* Lucifer) in several of his vividly grotesque embodiments. It is also in Revelation that we are told—*for the very first time*—of the battle in Heaven between the good angels and the bad angels and how Satan (a.k.a. "the Dragon") and his sinful ilk were cast out. This psychotropic fairytale (courtesy of a few psilocybin mushrooms, which grew in abundance on the Isle of Patmos where John was exiled during his "visions") also asserts that it was *Satan* in the Garden of Eden, not merely a garden variety of garden snake, who corrupted Eve and brought about mankind's downfall. There are also several references to bizarre visions and monsters found scattered throughout the Old Testament. And once again we see that timeless storyline of "good guy" Jesus vs. "bad guy" Satan in a winner-take-all gorefest. I have to wonder though, given all this wildly graphic and categorically conclusive information about Satan, why was it kept mum until the very *last* book of the Bible?

Obviously Revelation, which was supposedly written by a *very old* (and very stoned) Apostle John approximately 100 years *after* Jesus died, is nothing more than a specious, retrospective way to tie up loose ends and cobble together a house-of-cards explanation to "prove" that Jesus was who he said he was, and that the Lucifer in Isaiah and the "seal of perfection" in Ezekiel are testaments to the fallen angel Satan. This shameless case of "evidence tampering", coupled with grisly accounts of screaming demons, multi-headed monsters, rivers of blood and eternal fiery torture was—and still is—the Christian church's way of controlling the masses and keeping the coffers full. Thus we see a prime example of using psychological terrorism in the name of religion.

All right, we have ascertained that Lucifer isn't Satan, but here's another puzzle to ponder: Satan isn't Satan either. Confused? You're certainly not alone. A few paragraphs back I used the term "evolution" in relation to Lucifer's development as a character. Let me start by saying, there is *nothing* original or special about any story or character in the Bible, and that includes Yahweh, Jesus and Satan. Like hand-me-down clothing, every one of these events and personifications has been pieced and patched and trimmed and hemmed and modified from other much older sources and mythologies. If we go back far enough in time, we will find that every ancient culture the world over has had its demons, devils, elves, imps and assorted evil spirits. This simply stems from mankind's innate need to pin the blame on someone else when things go wrong and find a way to keep the spiritual universe in balance.

Looking at the Mesopotamian region alone, we see a colorful assortment of gods, goddesses and their contumacious coun-terparts. Interesting though, whether the culture be Assyrian, Babylonian, Arabian, Egyptian, Persian, Greek or Roman, there are striking similarities in the physical attributes of their demonic deities. Horns, hooves, claws, fangs, tails and wings seem to be the most commonly occurring features. The reason for this is twofold: Animals have always held a special fascination for us. We admire, envy, love and fear them— especially the ones with the horns, hooves, claws and fangs. It's only natural that our ancestors would idolize and demonize them, sometimes in the literal sense. Then too, as waves of soldiers, settlers, merchants and nomads washed over the lands, they inevitably deposited traces of their own cultures while absorbing some of the native fare. What we wind up with is a montage of mythological creatures who look like they all share a common ancestor. And they do! It's called *Homo Imaginatio*.

As children raised in a Christian culture we were indoc-trinated to believe there is only one god, and the Jews invented him. Actually, what they "invented" was a belief that *their* god was the *real* god, and everybody else's gods were demons. This kind of self-serving sanctimony comes in handy when you're giving yourself the moral justification to slaughter your neighbors into extinction because you want their land, women and other valuables.

We also learned a new big word: *Monotheism.* In a nutshell that means "one god"—*period.* Well...one god, plus his sons, plus all the angels, but basically one—and *only one*—all-powerful, all-knowing, jealous, wrathful, vengeful and generally cranky, undisputed ruler of the universe. The problem with a monotheistic system is that the "one and only god", like an overworked single parent, must be not only the benevolent caregiver to his children, but also the disciplinarian. That means handing out punishment as well as reward. And as we've seen, there are numerous examples in the Old Testament of Yahweh meting out some pretty cruel and gruesome punishments to his so-called "children". Quite truthfully, if a mortal parent resorted to even a mere fraction by degree of the corporal castigations inflicted by the "god of perfect love", he would find himself doing some hard prison time for child abuse.

This was a serious contradiction inherent with monotheism; the solitary god had to play the role of "good cop" *and* "bad cop". Then again, it was a socio-superstitious construct that lent itself well to the establishment of a theocratic dictator, i.e. prophet and later the clergy. One god, one prophet, one set of rules. "God told me to tell you, do as I say or suffer the consequences!" Then of course if famine, drought or disease should strike, there was the all-encompassing comeback, "I *told* you so!"

Monotheism had another unique advantage in keeping the masses under control simply because there were no other gods a person could turn to. In the belief system of ancient Greece, for instance, if Apollo didn't answer your prayers you could always throw in with Dionysus or perhaps Aphrodite. In a pinch, Pan would do. Truly, this was the essence of freedom of religion. Not so with My Way Yahweh. His Rule #1 is, "Thou shalt have **no other gods** before me!" In other words, my American readers, according to the Bible you can throw that First Amendment right out the window.

So, what is the one-and-only god to do when someone needs a good smiting? He hires—or rather, *creates*—a hit man, of course. In Genesis God did his own killing: first the flood, then a seven year worldwide famine, then the towns of Sodom and Gomorrah, plus several individuals who happened to piss him off. That's a lot of death and destruction to be responsible for in just *the first book*. Obviously, he needed some help. God the father was about to become God the *Godfather*.

It is in Exodus 12:23 that we first encounter "the destroyer". In Hebrew he is called *mal'ak hamashit*, which means "angel of destruction" (sometimes simply *mashit* for "destroyer"). God's first assignment for this grim reaper is to kill the firstborn son in every Egyptian household that does not have lamb's blood smeared on the doorframes. God oversees the killings, but it is his angelic assassin who actually wields the sword of death, thus keeping his master's hands clean of innocent blood.

This marks an important paradigm shift for a monotheistic culture that believed their god was the sole and direct cause of everything, good *and* bad. There are several other passages throughout the Old Testament where the LORD sends out "the destroyer" or "angels" to do his killing. Make no mistake, he still does his fair share of plaguing, maiming and slaughtering; some habits are just too hard—or *fun*—to give up completely. But now we are beginning to see the emergence of "the *other*".

In case you're interested, here are a few more places where "destroying angels" can be found: 2 Kings 19:35, "And it came to pass that night, that the *angel of the LORD* went out, and smote in the camp of the Assyrians an hundred fourscore and five thousand: and when they arose early in the morning, behold, they were all dead corpses." And 2 Chronicles 32:21, "And the LORD sent *an angel*, which cut off (killed) all the mighty men of valor, and the leaders and captains in the camp of the king of Assyria." And Job 33:22, "Yea, his soul draweth near unto the grave, and his life to the *destroyers*." And Psalm 78:49, "He cast upon them the fierceness of his anger, wrath, and indignation, and trouble, by sending *evil angels* among them." (NIV calls them *destroying angels*.) And lastly, the Apostle Paul in 1 Corinthians 10:10 attributes the plague mentioned in Numbers 16:46 to *the destroyer*, the angel sent by God.

So, when does Satan actually come in? To fully understand who and what he/it is we need to define the word itself. "Satan" (spelled in lowercase and pronounced sah-TAHN) is a Hebrew word that simply means an adversary or accuser. It can also be an obstruction or punishment. The term can refer to a human being *or* a celestial being. (It is important to understand that in the Hebrew writings—the *original* writings from whence the Christian Bible derives—there is no person named "Satan" *per se*, neither is there an independently active devil. In fact, Judaism has neither the concept of a Satan/Lucifer/Devil nor that of a fiery Hell where sinners are subjected to eternal torture. These mythical horrors are entirely the works of *Christian* writers who were promoting their own theological interests.

If you search Hebrew scripture you will find *hasatan*, which literally means "*the* satan", or *HaSatan*, which means "the *Satan*". I know that seems confusing. (This is just one of the myriad reasons Bible translations have been argued over for centuries.) The former is nothing more than a title, a station or an office, *not* a personal name. The latter is the person *holding* that office. For instance, you could say, "Mary is the president (*hasatan*) of the boosters club," compared with "President Mary" (*HaSatan*). Understanding just this little bit of ancient Hebrew sheds an entirely different light on the meaning of the Christian scriptures.

The Book of Numbers, Chapter 22 contains one of the most absurd stories in the entire Bible. Remember Balaam and his talking ass? (Some of you probably still find this worth a giggle.) Basically, God tells Balaam not to take a journey, but Balaam goes anyway. (Obviously, he was unfamiliar with God's penchant for smiting disobedient people.) So God sends a sword-wielding angel to stop him. The KJV calls the angel an "adversary". The NIV says the angel was sent "to oppose" him, but it means the same thing: God sends a *satan* to do his bidding with the directive to kill Balaam if he doesn't move his ass.

The first actual appearance of capital "S" *satan* is in 1 Chronicles 21:1. It reads, "And Satan stood up against Israel, and provoked David to number Israel." This is the story wherein King David incurs Yahweh's wrath simply for taking a census that Satan coaxed him into taking, kind of bizarre in itself. But here's the *really* bizarre thing: This same story takes place in 2 Samuel 24—a book written nearly 100 years *earlier*—but this time the villain is *not* Satan, it is Yahweh himself. "And again the anger of the LORD was kindled against Israel, and *he moved David* against them to say, Go, number Israel and Judah." (I added the italics for emphasis.)

The passage in 2 Samuel clearly makes God out to be a vindictive, duplicitous douche bag who deliberately set David up for failure just so he could smite the hell out of him. He does this by forcing David to choose his own punishment between A) three years of famine, B) three months of fleeing from their enemies, or C) three days of a hideous plague upon his people. David chose the plague, and so Yahweh the Compassionate allowed 70,000 innocent people to perish by a slow, agonizing death.

But there's a bit more to it than that. You see, it wasn't actually *God* who slaughtered all those people. Once more, he sent an "angel" to do his dirty work. The passage in Verse 16 says, "And when the angel stretched out his hand upon Jerusalem to destroy it, the LORD repented him of the evil, and said to the angel that destroyed the people, It is enough: stay now thine hand." So basically, Yahweh had a twinge of conscience about his "evil" actions and stopped his ectoplasmic enforcer from killing even more people. This story alone should convince anyone of what a bi-polar, sadistic psychopath the Bible god really is. Small wonder the writer of 1 Chronicles replaced him with "Satan"... *nearly a century later!*

As I said, the term *satan* can also refer to a mortal person or even a situation. If you recall from my *David and Jonathan* story, David turned traitor against his own people and joined up with the Philistines for awhile. The Philistine officers didn't trust him and told their king, (1 Samuel 29:4) "...let him not go down with us to battle, lest in the battle he be an adversary (a *satan*) to us." The NIV says, "...turn against us," but again, it means the same thing. And after reading a few of the gut wrenching atrocities David committed, I think it can be safely argued that he was fully deserving of the title "Satan" by *anyone's* definition.

The same phraseology occurs three times in 1 Kings 11:14-25. This wonderful chapter begins, "But king Solomon loved many strange women..." Talk about an attention grabber! Naturally, the idea of a man enjoying his god-given gonads really infuriates old Yahweh the Jealous, and he sends adversaries (*satans*) to thwart Solomon's plans. You can check this against Hebrew Bibles; they use the actual word *satan*. In any case, the word here refers to purely *human* adversaries.

One of the most famous and sadistic stories in the Bible takes place in the Book of Job. It is here that HaSatan—yes, "The Satan"—finally gets a co-starring role alongside The Big Yahuna. The plot is a simple one. God is bragging to HaSatan about what an righteous and obedient man Job is. HaSatan counters by saying Job is only that way because God has given him wealth, servants, livestock, a great family, etc. HaSatan suggests that if God were to take away Job's earthly possessions, Job would hate him. God, who thinks nothing of gambling with the lives of puny mortals, takes the bet and gives HaSatan free rein to destroy everything Job has, including his ten children! HaSatan, how-ever, is not permitted to harm Job.

When, after all this horror, Job's faith remains resolute,

HaSatan asks God to up the stakes by letting him put the hurt on poor Job himself. Naturally, God agrees but with the caveat that Satan cannot *kill* the man. Now the real fun begins, and HaSatan bombards a hapless Job with excruciating boils from head to foot. As you recall from Sunday School Job never does blame God, and in the end God proves what a great guy he is by giving Job double the wealth and possessions he had in the first place...except for his ten murdered children. To be fair: God *did* give him ten more children, which was kind of like placating a bereaved child simply by replacing ten dead goldfish with ten new goldfish. Still, it was his poor old wife who had to crank them out (the children, not the goldfish).

For centuries Jews, Christians and Muslims have heralded this deplorable fairy tale as proof that if you stay loyal to an abusive deity, he will give you twice the riches you currently have. The same "moral" argument can be made in the case of a man who beats his wife to a bloody pulp; then afterward he buys her an expensive diamond ring, all the while professing his undying love. Job is the very definition of an "abused spouse", blaming himself for his wretched misery and refusing to leave the heartless bastard who permits him to be terrorized, tortured and his children murdered. In fact, Job is so afraid of angering his violently vindictive benefactor, that he performs burnt offerings on behalf of his children, just in case one of them inadvertently did something to offend the thin-skinned deity.

I would like to mention a few key points that are frequently overlooked in this story. The interaction between God and Satan begins in Chapter 1, Verse 6: "Now there was a day when the sons of God came to present themselves before the LORD, and Satan (HaSatan) came also among them." Remember those obnoxious "sons of God" from my first story? Well, here they are again! Biblical scholars will insist these are simply angels, and since we know how much God hates sex, and since there are no female angels for him to get jiggy with, I guess we'll just go along with that. But notice how Satan now stands apart from these run-of-the-mill angels. That's because he is not just Satan, he is *The* Satan, The Accuser, the astral adjudicator that God uses—let me repeat that: *God uses*—to torment his mortal minions.

The next verse reads, "And the LORD said unto Satan, Whence comest thou? Then Satan answered the LORD, and said, From going to and fro in the earth, and from walking up and down in it." This single passage is HUGE because it demonstrates two critical issues: God *cannot* be "all-knowing" or he would not have to ask where Satan had been. But more important, this is the *very first time* we learn that Satan is able to travel back and forth between Heaven and Earth on his own volition. He is no longer constrained by Yahweh's leash. Also, he has begun to demonstrate a nascent thought process. He can think and reason and conjecture and have interactive conversation. Still, he is not yet a sovereign being. Like his precursor identity, he cannot act on his own accord; he can only carry out his master's gruesome orders. But he is developing a rudimentary independence nonetheless. In other words, he is *evolving.*

(For those of you who might be interested in an actual body count: In the Old Testament Satan is credited with killing only ten people, Job's children. Yahweh, on the other hand, killed nearly 2.5 *million*, according to a tally performed by Steve Wells, author of *Drunk with Blood, God's Killings in the Bible.* I highly recommend this humorous look at unbridled homicide.)

The next book and chapter to mention Satan by name is Psalm 109. King David is bemoaning the fact that some people don't like him (I can't imagine why). So, he asks God to intervene against one in particular: "Set thou a wicked man over him: and let Satan stand at his right hand." That was the King James Version version. Interestingly, the New International Version puts an entirely different spin on it: "Appoint someone evil to oppose my enemy; let an *accuser* stand at his right hand." So which is it: "Satan" or a human prosecutor? I'm going to add the same passage from the translated Hebrew Orthodox Bible as a tie breaker. It says, "Set Thou a wicked man over him; and let HaSatan (the Accuser) stand at his right hand."

What David is requesting, therefore, is for God to send some malevolent muscle against his enemy, and he wants him tried and condemned by the Ultimate Prosecutor. Here again, Satan is nothing more than an instrument for carrying out Yahweh's orders. He may hold a higher office than any other angel, but he is still just a servant.

The last book of the Old Testament to use the term "Satan" is Zechariah. Zechariah is a man given to prophetic hallucinations. In Chapter 3, Verses 1-2 he is receiving telepathic intel from an angel: "And he shewed me Joshua the high priest standing before the angel of the LORD, and Satan standing at his right hand to resist him. And the LORD said unto Satan, The LORD rebuke thee, O Satan; even the LORD that hath chosen Jerusalem rebuke thee. Is not this a brand plucked out of the fire?" Here again, to get an accurate translation we must go back to the original Hebrew, which uses the term *HaSatan.* In this scenario, per Zechariah's vision, the high priest Joshua, who was covered in metaphorical "filth", is being evaluated by God. HaSatan is merely fulfilling his role as the accuser, adversary or even counsel for the prosecution; basically the same function David requested of God earlier. (And FYI: Even up to this point, he has still *NOT* been cast out of Heaven. Rather, he is an integral part of the divine judiciary process.)

But here's another point to ponder. Satan is standing at the *right hand* of the angel of the LORD. In Biblical terms, there is no higher honor or station than to be at someone's "right hand". If Satan were indeed the bad guy in this story he certainly *would not* be so positioned. I think what we're seeing in this story is a courtroom-style battle between "the angel of the LORD" and Satan over the guilt or innocence of the defendant Joshua. One thing is certain, however: For the first time in the Old Testament Yahweh and Satan are at odds with one another. It will only be a matter of time now before their two personalities diverge completely.

How and when and why did this cosmic falling out take place? Like all the other books of the Bible, no one knows for certain when Job, Zechariah, et al were written or by whom. It is widely accepted, however, that they were written in the 6th Century BCE, during what is referred to as the Second Temple Period (the time frame when King Solomon's Temple in Jerusalem was being rebuilt for a second time, roughly 530 to 200 BCE). But something far more noteworthy and influential was happening in Mesopotamia at that time. In the year 522 BCE Darius the Great became the ruler of the expansive Persian Empire. Rare among emperors, Darius was renowned not only for his tolerance of other cultures and beliefs but also for his generosity. He provided considerable funding to help the Hebrews rebuild their temple. This alone earned him the unbounded appreciation and loyalty of the Hebrew population.

Darius was also a very spiritual man, having adopted the religion of Zoroaster, which he established as the state religion. Darius did not force this religion on his subjects, but as in the story of *The Emperor's New Clothes*, if you wanted to be considered one of the really "cool people" you became a believer. (A bit of Zoroastrian trivia here: Though no one is really sure when Zoroaster lived or died, according to legend he was born of a virgin who was impregnated by "a ray of divine reason". As a young boy he astonished the wise men of his day with his knowledge of all things spiritual. He was baptized in a river. At age 30 he began his humble ministry. He baptized his followers with "holy wind" comprised of water and fire. He told of an apocalyptic End Time when the forces of Good and Evil would wage a final battle for control of the earth. The evil doers—followers of the Dragon, who was cast down from Heaven—would be consumed in rivers of lava, while the followers of the Good Spirit would live in eternal peaceful bliss on a newly created earth. Zoroaster also claimed he would return in the form of his three sons, each born a thousand years apart to virgin mothers, conceived from his celestial semen. I swear I am *not* making this stuff up!)

In a geographical region with dozens of diverse cultures and probably thousands of gods, Zoroastrianism offered a revolutionary alternative to standard polytheism. It had only two gods: one good, one evil. Ahura Mazda, the "Good Spirit" created the heavens and the earth and everything pleasant. Pictured as half-man, half-eagle, he embodies wisdom, truth, benevolence, charity, justice, etc. To his followers he offers peace, love and an afterlife filled with eternal happiness. Conversely, Angra Mainyu, the "Bad Spirit" is a god of darkness, disease, destruction, death (you get the picture). His goal is to tempt and corrupt mankind. Angra Mainyu is pictured as a terrible snake or dragon with menacing fangs and often horns. He rules a dark, sinister lair where sinners go after death. According to the tenets of Zoroastrianism mankind was given freewill to follow either god, with the predictable consequences. Both Ahura Mazda and Angra Mainyu have legions of assistants to help carry out their respective agendas (angels and demons?)

At its height the Persian Empire reached from Egypt to India, the Balkan Peninsula to the Caucasus Mountains. Now, imagine if you will the immense socio-politico-spiritual melting pot that must have existed at that time. New ideas, customs and beliefs were rich, abundant and free-flowing. Imagine too a Jewish populace, many of them living in exile in foreign lands, having been taken as slaves during the previous Babylonian invasion. Lost and forsaken—once again—by their capricious one-and-only god who hands out punishments as easily as rewards, their faith had undoubtedly taken a serious beating.

Now, enter Ahura Mazda, a deity of peace and joy; a deity who, by his very nature, *cannot* cause pain or plagues or pestilence. This is not a jealous, smiting god. This is a truly *loving god*. It would not take much of a leap in faith for a people already accustomed to worshipping a single god to transpose the beneficent attributes of this new god onto their existing deity. Simultaneously they could dump his nastier characteristics onto the evil entity. And remember, the Jewish people were already deeply obliged to Emperor Darius for his magnanimous contribution toward restoring their most holy of holy places. What greater honor—not to mention political coup—than to adopt the religion (or at least some of its aspects) of their benefactor?

Obviously the godly personality split didn't take place overnight, and it certainly was not a clean break. Even today the "new and improved" Yahweh still gets credit for causing devastating earthquakes and tsunamis. So we see that the Judaic-Christian-Muslim "god of perfect love" retains some pretty nasty tendencies. As for Satan, it is during this transitional period that his metamorphosis really begins, not only in function but in form as well.

Following the Second Temple Period of writings came a span of about 300 years known as the Intertestamental or Apocalyptic Period (approximately 200 BCE to CE 100). In a nutshell, this was the literary epoch between the writings of the Hebrew Old Testament and the Christian Gospels. During this time there was a renewed energy, perhaps even a frenzy of "inspired" texts being written. Many of these were lost or intentionally destroyed; some found their way into Roman Catholic, Eastern Orthodox, Islamic and various other religious canons. The universal theme of these writings was the ill-deserved demonization of HaSatan. In them he is referred to by several new names: Mastema, Sammael, Azazel, Satanail, Belial, Semyaza and of course, the Devil.

In some texts his primary job is still to tempt mankind on God's behalf. To do this he asks God for a cadre of demons to assist him, and God complies. He is also now credited with entreating God to test Abraham by making him sacrifice his son (similar to the Job story). Again, God complies. This "new-and-improved" demonic being is basically a rehashing of "the accuser" but with far more cognitive abilities, not the least of which is being able to talk God into granting his requests, which in essence implies that Satan has the power to manipulate God himself.

In addition to these qualitative alterations, the authors of these defamatory writings unabashedly hijacked several Old Testament stories and placed Satan at the scene of the crime. For instance, in the Old Testament book of Exodus 4:24 when God meets Moses at the inn and decides to kill him (for no specified reason, I might add), the author of the Apocryphal Jubilees (48:1) changes the would-be assassin to Satan. So, even before Jesus made his earthly début, the cosmic personality split between Yahweh and HaSatan was well underway. And by the time the Gospels were written (70-100 years *post*-Messiah) our demonic anti-hero had been morphed into a character of Iliadic proportions. Master of demons and devils, avowed destroyer of mankind, supreme ruler of Hell, direct and sole cause of disease, pain and suffering, and of course, arch nemesis of the Christ, he was no longer a mere manifestation of Yahweh's evil alter ego, he was no longer the *satan* of Hebrew lore. He was *SATAN!*

As I mentioned earlier, the Book of Revelation gives us the first mental images of the Evil One. Greco-Roman mythological influences helped to shape perceptions of Hell/Hades. An important fact to remember here: There is no "Hell" or tortuous afterlife in Judaism, past or present. There is, however, a place called *Sheol*, a "waiting room" of sorts where everybody goes, regardless of the kind of life he or she has led. And while—quite strangely—Hebrew scripture says virtually nothing about this place or what happens there, some believers think of it as a kind of classroom where a sinner is taught the error of his ways before being allowed to journey on to the next level or incarnation. One might call it the ultimate *"Halo"* game.

In short, everything we know about Satan and Hell is nothing more than the delusional ramblings of 1st and 2nd Century *Christian* word-smithers who reworked the ancient texts to fit their "Jesus agenda". They transmogrified Satan into a stand-alone creature of monstrous proportions. They renovated his lair into a place of molten agony and eternal torture. But it was not until Medieval times that the physiology of Satan himself came blazing to life. He grew scaly wings, horns, hooves, fangs, claws and even a tail, all of these taken from "demons" found in other religions. He became the resplendent epitome of Evil Incarnate!

I hope this clears up any confusion or misconceptions you might have had about the origins of Lucifer/Satan. As the title of this chapter alludes, he was invented by ancient Hebrews and later *reinvented* by early Christians as a scapegoat to bear the brunt of blame while rabbis and priests were hard at work remaking their heretofore vindictive god's political profile. We can look at those fanciful (albeit grotesque) images and marvel at the simple, superstition-ridden minds that created them. Over the last few centuries, as an ever widening swath of society began to embrace the fundamentals of science, medicine and education in general, religious dogma and the terrible power it exercised over the masses began to wane. Satan himself softened, took on a more vulnerable, genteel, even comical aspect as can be seen in literature, advertisements and cartoons of the late Nineteenth and early Twentieth Centuries.

And yet even today, in our supposedly "enlightened" culture, there are still people who genuinely and fervidly believe this piecemeal Prince of Darkness *literally* exists and is working feverishly 24/7 for the destruction of the human race. It would be easy enough to dismiss these individuals with a chuckle and a wave of the hand, until we are reminded that some of them have—or are trying relentlessly to obtain—access to nuclear weapons. As we have seen throughout history and even in our modern world, *evil* is not a manifestation of some demonic supernatural being; it is wholly in the mind of the *believer*. All that is required to ignite the holocaust is a spark of inflammatory rhetoric delivered from the pulpit, the podium or the minbar. The French Enlightenment writer and philosopher, Voltaire, summed it up nicely. "Those who can make you believe absurdities can make you commit atrocities." Amen!

But I would like to close this chapter on a lighter note with another quote from the late great comedian Mr. George Burns. "And God said: 'Let there be Satan, so people don't blame everything on me. And let there be lawyers, so people don't blame everything on Satan.'"

Morality, What A Concept!

A main theme of this book is *morality*. If you ask five different people what the word means, you'll likely get five similar answers. If you ask five different religions, you'll probably get the same answers but with the explanation that since theirs is the only "true faith" their morals and laws are the ones that should be adhered to. Then too, when it comes to the treatment of people of other faiths, often what is sauce for the goose is not always sauce for the gander. A lovely example of this occurs in Deuteronomy 14:21. God has commanded his people, "Do not eat anything you find already dead. You may give it to the foreigner residing in any of your towns, and they may eat it, or you may sell it to any other foreigner. But you are a people holy to the LORD your God." I imagine this could apply not only to dead animals but any other sort of business transaction. Kind of kicks that old "do unto others" rule right off the porch.

As we have seen numerous times throughout this book "morality" is a very subjective subject. We are told killing is a sin! But committing genocide in the name of God is laudable. Stealing is a sin! But taking plunder after slaughtering your neighbors is cool. Do not commit adultery! But kidnapping little virgin girls and forcing them to be your "wife" is perfectly acceptable. Honor your father and mother! But you *must* kill them if they try to worship another god.

The examples of man's immorality—not to mention his hypocrisy—toward his fellow man are far too numerous to elaborate on here. If you have access to radio, television, newspapers, Internet or simply a group of well-informed friends you know what I mean. But this chapter—nay, this entire book—is not about *man's* immorality. Rather, it is an indictment of the Abrahamic god and his bloody reign of terror masquerading as love and justice. In fact, his entire theocratic manifesto can be summed up with one simple sentence: "Worship me, or *I will kill you!*" That's certainly straightforward enough, but is it really *moral?*

Believers are forever claiming that morality comes from the Bible, and that if you don't believe in the Bible you can't possibly be a moral person. From what we've observed in the preceding chapters this is laugh-my-ass-off ridiculous. Now, if we were to ask those same believers to list what they considered *IM*-moral in order of severity, the results might look something like this: murder, rape, child abuse, animal abuse, torture, slavery, stealing, adultery, lying.

That's some pretty heavy-duty stuff, and every one of those things rightfully deserves to be on the list. Next, ask the believers whom do they consider to be *the most* immoral or evil person that ever existed? Far and away they will say Adolf Hitler, followed by a host of other human fiends commonly found in everyday history books. And again, these are all very correct answers. If you then ask these same believers *why* said persons should be considered immoral/evil, they will first, look at you as if you are a complete idiot, then second, give you a ready laundry list of the grisly atrocities committed by the reprobate in question. Now ask them, "Would you ever consider following a leader like that?"

"No!" they will exclaim.

"Would you ever donate money to their cause?"

Again, "*No!*"

"Could you ever love a person that behaved like that?"

"*NO!*"

(Pause for a moment then ask,) "Then why do you worship a god that admittedly has done—or ordered his people to do—all of those things and *worse*?"

I had a conversation very much like this with a former coworker. By all accounts he was a very intelligent man; a professional civil engineer. He was also a born-again Christian. During our encounter, I gave him some examples of God's inhumanity to man. I'll never forget the all-too-familiar look on his face, first shock then affront then suspicion, when he asked me, "Where does it say that?" Like the vast majority of believers, he too had never ventured beyond those "feel good" passages that speak so glowingly about eternal life and God's uncon-ditional love. I was only too happy to reach into my desk and hand him a prepared list of verbatim biblical quotes complete with chapter and verse. His brow furrowed as he read them over carefully. (I could almost see the wheels turning.) Shaking his head dismissively, he said, "You can't just take passages out of context like that."

Excuse #1: Believers love to claim we're always taking these things "out of context".

I replied, "In what context would it *ever be OK* to butcher babies?!"

Then came Excuse #2: "Well, that's just the way things were

back then."

"But these were supposed to be God's *chosen* people," I countered. "Shouldn't they have been setting a higher moral standard?"

The mental wheels began turning again. Squaring his shoulders with an air of triumph, he folded the paper in half, handed it back to me and uttered Excuse #3, the religious apologist's theological panacea: "Hey, none of us can understand God's Plan. If he did it, he must've had a good reason."

So there you have it; murder, rape, child abuse, animal abuse, torture, slavery, stealing, adultery and lying are all perfectly acceptable, justifiable, even obligatory if God tells you to do it. And as we all know, failure to obey God's orders, like failing to obey the orders of any psychotic dictator, carries very, *very* odious consequences. It makes me wonder though... If God can do all these things and still be considered "good", what *would* he have to do in order to be considered "*evil*"?

In August of 2014 the world was appalled and outraged by the sadistically gruesome atrocities committed by the Islamic terrorist group known as ISIS (Islamic State in Iraq and Syria). I will never forget my reaction to hearing President Obama speak of the grisly beheading of *GlobalPost* journalist James Foley. He said, "No faith teaches people to massacre innocents. No just god would stand for what they did yesterday and what they do every single day."

The president was partially correct; no "just god" *would* stand for it. But the god found lurking in the pages of the Tanakh, the Bible and the Koran is *far* from just. He is by every connotation of the word *EVIL*. And to say that, "No faith teaches people to massacre innocents" is to admit that you are completely and unforgivably ignorant of the very doctrine that you hold up as a compass not only for steering your own moral course in life, but for making policy on how others should steer theirs.

If believers wish to insist that man was created in God's image (bloodthirsty ghoul that he is), then how can we condemn and hold guilty those who act on his behalf and employ the same methods described in his "moral handbook"? If we choose to believe that the Bible is in fact the unerring word of God, then how do we know he *didn't* speak directly to ISIS ringleader, Abu Bakr al-Baghdadi, as he has to his other prophets, and tell *him* to launch this blood-drenched jihad? Perhaps God also guided the hand of Osama bin Laden in orchestrating the 9/11 attack on the World Trade Center. And all those parents you have read about in the news who murdered their own children, claiming, "God told me to do it." How can we be certain he *didn't*? How can we possibly prosecute these people for simply carrying out God's orders as Moses and Joshua and Samuel did? Just because we puny humans cannot understand his Divine Plan certainly does not give us the right to sit in judgment of their actions.

I promise you, dear readers, nothing being perpetrated by these mortal monsters is in any way worse than what their god—be he Hebrew, Christian or Muslim—has perpetrated on a much grander and more horrific scale. Hypothetically speaking, if these fiends are the embodiment of what a civilized society has come to regard as pure evil, yet their atrocities are committed in the name of their like-minded god, does it not follow that God himself must be the *root of all evil*?

After learning the true nature and methods of the Bible god, I encourage you to make your own compilation of readily available verses to give to your disbelieving believer friends. Here are a few more quotes right out of the "Good Book" to prove that old Yahweh doesn't really give a plug shekel upon whom he brings pain and destruction.

• (Exodus 32:27-29 NIV) "Then he (Moses) said to them, 'This is what the LORD, the God of Israel, says: Each man strap a sword to his side. Go back and forth through the camp from one end to the other, each killing his brother and friend and neighbor.' The Levites did as Moses commanded, and that day about three thousand of the people died. Then Moses said, 'You have been set apart to the LORD today, for you were against your own sons and brothers, and he has blessed you this day.'"

• (Leviticus 26:27-29 NIV) "If in spite of this you still do not listen to me but continue to be hostile toward me (God), then in my anger I will be hostile toward you, and I myself will punish you for your sins seven times over. You will eat the flesh of your sons and the flesh of your daughters."

• (Numbers 31:17 KJV) "Now therefore kill every male among the little ones, and kill every woman that hath known man by lying with him. But all the women children, that have not known a man by lying with him, keep alive for yourselves."

• (Deuteronomy 13:6-11 NIV) "If your very own brother, or your son or daughter, or the wife you love, or your closest friend secretly entices you, saying, 'Let us go and worship other gods'...do not yield to them or listen to them. Show them no pity. Do not spare them or shield them. You must certainly put them to death. Your hand must be the first in putting them to death, and then the hands of all the people. Stone them to death, because they tried to turn you away from the LORD your God, who brought you out of Egypt, out of the land of slavery. Then all Israel will hear and be afraid, and no one among you will do such an evil thing again."

- (1 Samuel 15:1-3 KJV) "...but slay both man and woman, infant and suckling."
- (Job 9:22 NIV) "He (God) destroys both the blameless and the wicked. When a scourge brings sudden death, he mocks the despair of the innocent. When a land falls into the hands of the wicked, he blindfolds its judges. If it is not he, then who is it?"
- (Isaiah 45:7 KJV) "I (God) form the light, and create darkness; I make peace, and create evil; I the LORD do all these things."
- (Hosea 13:16 KJV) "Their pregnant women shall be ripped up!"

Now, I know I tend to come off a bit heavy-handed on some issues regarding religion. And in all fairness, there are indeed some very beautiful passages and stories to be found in the Bible. So, in keeping with the subject of morality I would like to close by offering a quote that pretty much puts the whole thing into perspective: "Reading the Bible for morality is like digging through shit for sweet corn. Sure, there's some, but is it really worth it?" (Author Unknown)

The REAL Ten Commandments
As found in Exodus 34:11

Whenever I hear believers, especially those with a political motive, opining about how we need to get this country back to Bible Law and adhere to the Ten Commandments, I am reminded of how pathetically little they actually know about their righteous rules and regulations. The vast majority of these folks, while they claim these pearls of wisdom are the bulwark of our society's moral structure, cannot name half of them and almost never get them in the right order. But here's the funny part: The Ten Commandments—I'll call them the "Classical Ten"—that we have all seen chiseled in stone blocks or placarded on the walls of justice buildings and libraries throughout America are not even the real Ten Commandments. So, what *are* the real Ten Commandments? you ask. Let's don our investigative reporter's cap and do some scriptural sleuthing.

It should come as no surprise by now that the Ten Commandments, like nearly every other story in the Bible, have been altered, amended and reworked to fit the agenda of whatever group of religious spin doctors were the last to lay their hands on these sacred texts. What *is* surprising is that the answer is spelled out quite definitively in the Bible itself. Yet for thousands of years priests and rabbis have been touting the same erroneous legislative litany to their unsuspecting congregations.

Our investigation begins in the Book of Exodus. This is the story about the Israelites wandering around in the desert for forty years after gaining their freedom from Pharaoh. Every Sunday School child knows how Moses went up on the mountain and got the first stone tablets, but when he returned and saw that the people had constructed a golden calf idol, he threw a hissy fit and smashed the tablets to bits. Then he had to go back up the mountain and get another set which, of course, became the Classical Ten Commandments...or so you were told. As always, there are some interesting little nuggets hidden in these verses that somehow never seem to make it to the pulpit. Let's begin by looking at the two main characters in this story: Moses and his brother Aaron.

According to fable, Moses was chosen by Yahweh to lead the Israelites to the Promised Land. In a blatant example of nepotism, Moses appointed Aaron as high priest to rule over the people while he was up on the mountain receiving instructions from the invisible talking head. When nearly a month and a half passed and Moses still hadn't returned, the people got antsy and implored Aaron to make them a god they could see and worship (kind of a gilded nuknuk to pacify them). He told them to bring him all their gold earrings, which he then melted down and fashioned into the famous golden calf. This is a pretty damn amazing feat in itself, given these people were not much more than a mob of tent dwelling vagabonds, likely without the kind of forge it would have taken to generate the 1,947 degrees of Fahrenheit needed to melt gold. But even more amazing is the fact that they possessed enough gold earrings to make a calf-sized idol! Apologists will argue it could have been thinly beaten gold *foil* laid over a straw model. Sorry, folks, but the Bible specifically says he made "a molten calf" and "fashioned it with a graving tool." (Exodus 32:4).

Regardless, that's not even the biggest curiosity here. Remember, it was *Aaron*, the high priest and keeper of the faith who called for the gold and made the idol to appease his frightened people. Then, after making the golden calf he constructed an altar in front of it and told everybody to prepare for a great feast and celebration. And that's exactly what they did. And as we all know, nobody parties like pagans!

Now, when the cosmic killjoy Yahweh saw what was going on down below he blew a holy gasket and told Moses he was going to destroy the entire lot of them. But Moses pleaded on their behalf and got the Big Guy to back off; more than just back off, Verse 14 says, "And the LORD repented of the evil which he thought to do unto his people." The two very significant words here are *repented* and *evil*. In essence, God, the all-powerful, the all-knowing, the most compassionate, is admitting that he lost control like a brat in a toy store, and he regretted that he nearly blasted his chosen people into camel dust. Further, he is acknowledging that to do so would have been *evil*. Another important point to make here is the fact that Moses, a mere mortal, was able to talk him into relenting, just as Satan was able to talk him into torturing poor Job. This is stand alone irrefutable *PROOF* that God is *NOT* perfect, nor is he omnipotent. He can't even control his own temper. At the first sign of trouble he wants to go on a mad killing spree.

After forestalling Yahweh's murderous tantrum Moses headed down the mountain with the first set of stone tablets. (You know what happens next.) Upon seeing the golden calf, he threw his own version of a galactic shitfit, smashed the tablets on the ground and destroyed the idol. He then turned to his brother Aaron and said, "What the fuck is going on down here?" (except in Hebrew). Now remember, it was *Aaron* who told the people to bring him their gold, and it was *Aaron* who constructed the idol, and it was *Aaron* who built the sacrificial altar and told the people to "party hearty!" So, when confronted with his brother's wrath Aaron replied, "Let not the anger of my lord wax hot: thou knowest the people, that they are set on mischief (NIV says "evil"). For they said unto me, make us gods, which shall go before us: for as for this Moses, the man that brought us up out of the land of Egypt, we know not what is become of him. And I said unto them, whosoever hath any gold, let them break it off. So they gave it me: then I cast it into the fire, and there came out this calf." (Exodus 32:22-24).

Notice how this high priest, this holder of the most sacred office, managed to shift the bulk of the blame onto those "mischievous/evil" people? Even better, he completely sidestepped the fact that *he personally* created the idol and carved it, a task that must have taken considerable time and effort. But in *his* version of the story, he simply tossed the gold into the fire and *POOF!* out came a fully formed golden calf.

Still plenty steamed at this point, Moses, the mouthpiece of God, called together all the men of the tribe of Levi and said to them, "Put every man his sword by his side, and go in and out from gate to gate throughout the camp, and slay every man his brother, and every man his companion, and every man his neighbor. And the children of Levi did according to the word of Moses: and there fell of the people that day about three thousand men." (Exodus 32:27-28).

You would think that the butchering of 3000 men in cold blood would satisfy even the likes of Yahweh, but no. The last verse in this chapter says that the LORD cursed the people with a plague because of the calf that Aaron had made. As for his part in the matter, Aaron got off scot-free. In fact, some rabbinical sources along with the Qur'an tell a very different tale wherein poor Aaron, fearing for his life should he interfere, did *not* fashion the golden calf, but instead was merely a helpless bystander.

What we see from these passages is that the commandments, this divinely inspired blueprint for mankind's morality and eternal salvation, were conceived in a fratricidal bloodbath.

Remember this the next time you read Commandment #6: "Thou shalt not kill."

Now, nobody knows what was actually written on those first two tablets because Moses smashed them. The first hint we get comes in Exodus 24:12. "And the LORD said unto Moses, Come up to me into the mount, and be there: and I will give thee tables of stone, and a law, and commandments which I have written; that thou mayest teach them." Notice, the passage mentions "a law" and "commandments". However, it must be emphasized that *at no time* is the list referred to as "The *Ten* Commandments". In fact, there is no "list" at all; it is just Yahweh rambling on and on and on—*for seven entire chapters!*—about how to build the Ark and the Tabernacle and their trappings (all made of gold, of course), adorn the priests, feed the priest, bathe the priests, slaughter and disembowel sacrificial animals, prepare incense, beat your slaves, sell your daughter into slavery, kill witches... And let's not forget the "Atonement Money" (Exodus 30:12). In addition to other forms of precious tribute that must be given to "the LORD" by way of the priests, every person had to cough up some cash as "ransom for his soul" to keep the Big Boss in the Sky from smiting him with a plague—or *worse*. In short, this is not so much a list of commandments as it is a manifesto for racketeering. It isn't until Chapter 31, Verse 12 that the Sabbath is even mentioned. And of course, the punishment for violating it—like nearly everything else—is *death*.

Finally, in Chapter 34, after the calf incident, God tells Moses to chisel out two more stone tablets upon which he will write the same exact words as before. So once again, up the mountain Moses goes, lugging these two granite slabs with him. Here's something I'll bet you didn't know: The tablets were inscribed on *both sides*, not merely the face. (Exodus 32:15) "And Moses turned, and went down from the mount, and the two tables of the testimony were in his hand: the tables were written on both their sides; on the one side and on the other were they written." This in itself makes me wonder, if the "Classical Ten" we're used to seeing are only the *front* half, what was on the *back* half?

At long last in Chapter 34 we begin to see some familiar ordinances; specifically the ones about not worshipping any other gods and not making idols and keeping the Sabbath. And of course old Yahweh, who can't say one word when ten will do, has to blather on and on about how people of other religions are to be treated. (Exodus 34:13) "But ye shall destroy their altars, break their images, and cut down their groves." There's also a bunch of other stuff that could only be described as race hatred, and calling their daughters "whores", but I digress. The point is, the Hebrew god is indeed spouting off a lot of rules in this chapter, many of which are just plain *weird*, such as: "But the firstborn of an ass thou shalt redeem with a lamb: and if thou redeem him not, then shalt thou break his neck." (Exodus 34:20) It's a pity none of the commandments say anything about animal cruelty.

It is not until we get down to Verse 28 that we finally—and for the *very first time*—see the term "*THE* Ten Commandments" used to describe the laws given to Moses. I will show them in order below. They can be found in Exodus 34, Verses 14-26 of the King James Version Bible. FYI: This is a very condensed format. The full text is quite lengthy and might easily have taken *both* sides of the two tablets to contain. One can only assume Moses used a kind of Hebrew shorthand.

1) For thou shalt worship no other god: for the LORD, whose name is Jealous, is a jealous God.
2) Thou shalt make thee no molten gods.
3) The feast of unleavened bread shalt thou keep. Seven days thou shalt eat unleavened bread, as I commanded thee, in the time of the month Abib: for in the month Abib thou camest out from Egypt.
4) All that openeth the matrix is mine; and every firstling among thy cattle, whether ox or sheep, that is male.
5) Six days thou shalt work, but on the seventh day thou shalt rest: in plowing time and in harvest thou shalt rest.
6) And thou shalt observe the feast of weeks, of the first fruits of wheat harvest, and the feast of ingathering at the year's end.
7) Thrice in the year shall all your men children appear before the LORD God, the God of Israel.
8) Thou shalt not offer the blood of my sacrifice with leaven; neither shall the sacrifice of the feast of the Passover be left unto the morning.
9) The first of the first fruits of thy land thou shalt bring unto the house of the LORD thy God.
10) Thou shalt not seethe a kid in his mother's milk.

"And the LORD said unto Moses, Write thou these words: for after the tenor of these words I have made a covenant with thee and with Israel. And he was there with the LORD forty days and forty nights; he did neither eat bread, nor drink water. And he wrote upon the tables the words of the covenant, "**The Ten Commandments**."

So there you have it, in black and white, the *REAL* Ten Commandments as spelled out in the Holy Bible itself. But trust me, these are not the only so-called commandments you will find. If you count *all* the laws in *all* the books of the Pentateuch (first five books of the Old Testament) you will come up with 613 "commandments"; 248 "thou shalls" and 365 "thou shall nots". (Some sources place those numbers even higher.) This leaves us with a couple of perplexing questions: Just where did the "Classical Ten Commandments" come from? And why were they changed?

The first answer lies in Chapter 20 of the Book of Exodus. Here you will find God, enveloped in a black, roiling cloud, speaking directly to the trembling Israelites gathered at the base of Mount Sinai. He takes only a moment to remind them that "I am the LORD thy God, which have brought thee out of the land of Egypt, out of the house of bondage" before he lays down the "classical" laws—one through ten—in no uncertain terms. However, these were *spoken* laws. They were *not* written down, not on paper, not on leaves, and not on stone. But most important, they *were never called* the Ten Commandments. (A note about the New International Version Bible. The editors of this modernized translation have added headings to foreshadow the content of an upcoming chapter or verse. Predictably, they put "The Ten Commandments" at the beginning of Chapter 20. This is *WRONG* and intentionally *MISLEADING*.) There is only one place in the entire Bible where the text actually specifies and describes "The Ten Commandments", and that is in Exodus 34:28—*PERIOD*.

That brings us to our second question: Why were they changed? The answer to that is really pretty obvious. *BECAUSE THEY ARE FREAKING RIDICULOUS!* This fact was evidently clear to the writer of Deuteronomy, a book written hundreds of years later, because he took the liberty of reworking the original texts to reflect his own preference. But in doing so, he not only contradicts himself, he contradicts the scriptures in Exodus. For instance, in Exodus 34:27 God instructs Moses to "Write thou these words" on the stone tablets. In Deuteronomy 10:4 the author claims that God did the writing. OK, that's a minor point. We can believe the Jolly Green Giant did it for all that matters. It is the rest of the passage that gives a clue to the *human* writer's intentions. "And he (God) wrote on the tables, according to the first writing, the ten commandments, which the LORD spake unto you in the mount out of the midst of the fire in the day of the assembly: and the LORD gave them unto me (Moses)."

Wow! Did you notice the knuckle-curve-ball he just threw? In essence, he did the biblical version of cut-and-pasting two completely separate pieces of scripture together to make them *appear* to be one and the same. "And he wrote on the tables, according to the first writing, the ten commandments" refers to Exodus 34 and the *real* (or really *weird*) Ten Commandments. The next part, "which the LORD spake unto you in the mount out of the midst of the fire in the day of the assembly" harkens back to Exodus 20, the "Classical Ten". But remember: These earlier statutes were only *spoken*. They were not written down, not by God, not by Moses, not by the Jolly Green Giant. The anonymous author of Deuteronomy—like so many others—has simply, shamelessly and deliberately altered the much older texts to obscure an embarrassing piece of whacky scripture that no sane person could find any value in at all. "Thou shalt not seethe a kid in his mother's milk." *Really?* I mean, was that a serious enough problem at one time that they needed a law to *prevent it?*

Considering that for centuries the Bible has been hyped as the perfect, complete and unerring word of God, it sure is funny how many contradictions there are and how many changes have been made over time. Even today there are over 40 different English versions alone, each one with just the slightest degree of difference to make the silliness inside a bit easier to swallow. (Please visit the website Biblegateway.com for an excellent list.) I am reminded of one of the many great lines comedian Bill Maher has delivered on the subject: "I tell ya, religion? It's like Wikipedia. Anyone can write something in."

Take the Catholic faith for example. We've all seen their resplendent, gold-plated cathedrals with their statues of Jesus (with or without his crucifix accessory), the Virgin Mary and an assortment of saints to whom believers pray for help and guidance. Many Catholics even wear Saint Christopher medals for protection, like carrying a lucky rabbit's foot or nailing a horseshoe above the door. All of these three-dimensional material objects and icons clearly fall under the category of manmade "idols" and "images". So, how does the Catholic Church reconcile this practice with the Second Commandment forbidding the worship of graven images? Easy! They just got rid of it. In order to round out a full ten they split the last one into two parts: #9 "Thou shalt not covet thy neighbor's wife." #10 "Thou shalt not covet thy neighbor's property."

In my chapter on morality (and the Bible's lack thereof) I listed several behaviors that pretty much everyone would agree are immoral: murder, rape, child abuse, animal abuse, torture, slavery, stealing, adultery and lying. Let's throw vandalism in there to make it an even ten. Now, isn't it odd that while the vast majority of ordinary human beings would agree this is a very good list of things *not* to do, the Bible god only finds fault with four? And even then, he turns a blind eye to those, provided they are being committed by his "chosen people" at his behest. Seems a tad hypocritical. Then too, the first four commandments have nothing whatsoever to do with moral or civil offences; they exist simply to flatter the Almighty's colossal ego. Makes me wonder... What does this tell us about the ethics of human society vs. religious dogma?

To say that the Ten Commandments—whichever set you choose to believe is the real one—are the foundation of our moral, social and political structure is absurd. To say that mankind needs religion to *be* moral is even more absurd. Many of the Mosaic Laws, as we have seen in this and other stories, are little more than the cruel dictates of a misogynistic, homophobic, xenophobic, baby-killing, desert-dwelling blood cult. Even the nobler of the laws are simply derivations of the centuries older Babylonian Code of Hammurabi. Yet even the seeds of Hammurabi's enlightened laws can be traced 300 years further back in time to the Mesopotamian Code of Ur-Nammu. And FYI: The Codes of Hammurabi and Ur-Nammu are very *real* and on display in several museums around the world, most notably the Louvre, Paris. Don't you think it's peculiar that *no trace whatsoever* remains of *THE MOST FAMOUS* set of "laws" known to Western religion? But hey, I mean, it's not like they were carved in stone.

Quotes from Famous
(or Completely Unknown) Freethinkers

I would like to share some really thought-provoking and humorous quotes and sayings that I have gleaned from various sources.

- "Calling the Bible a source of moral direction is like saying Adolf Hitler was a great motivational speaker." (Yours Truly)
- "All thinking men are atheists." (Ernest Hemingway)
- "The Government of the United States is not in any sense founded on the Christian religion." (President John Adams, 1797)
- "The most detestable wickedness, the most horrid cruelties, and the greatest miseries that have afflicted the human race have had their origin in this thing called revelation, or revealed religion. It has been the most destructive to the peace of man since man began to exist. Among the most detestable villains in history, you could not find one worse than Moses, who gave an order to butcher the boys, to massacre the mothers and then rape the daughters. One of the most horrible atrocities found in the literature of any nation. I would not dishonor my Creator's name by attaching it to this filthy book." (Thomas Paine, *The Age of Reason*)
- "It's almost as if the Bible was written by racist, sexist, homophobic, violent, sexually frustrated men instead of a loving God. Weird." (Ricky Gervais)
- "Humanity without religion is like a serial killer without a chainsaw." (Unknown)
- "Religion is excellent stuff for keeping common people quiet. Religion is what keeps the poor from murdering the rich." (Napoleon Bonaparte)
- "Don't you know? There ain't no devil, it's just god when he's drunk." (Tom Waits)
- "Once something has been approved by the Government, it's no longer immoral." (Reverend Lovejoy—*The Simpsons*)
- "Is God willing to prevent evil, but not able? Then he is not omnipotent. Is he able, but not willing? Then he is malevolent. Is he both able and willing? Then whence cometh evil? Is he neither able nor willing? Then why call him God?" (Epicurus)

202

- "If it turns out that there is a God, I don't think that he's evil. But the worst that you can say about him is that basically he's an underachiever." (Woody Allen)
- "Men never commit evil so fully and joyfully as when they do it for religious convictions." (Blaise Pascal)
- "In Christianity neither morality nor religion come into contact with reality at any point." (Friedrich Nietzsche)
- "It ain't the parts of the Bible that I can't understand that bother me, it is the parts that I do understand." (Mark Twain)
- "Why should I allow that same God to tell me how to raise my kids, who had to drown his own?" (Robert G. Ingersoll)
- "The philosopher has never killed any priests, whereas the priest has killed a great many philosophers." (Denis Diderot)
- "History, I believe, furnishes no example of a priest-ridden people maintaining a free civil government." (Thomas Jefferson)
- "Extraordinary claims require extraordinary evidence." (Carl Sagan)
- "I distrust those people who know so well what God wants them to do, because I notice it always coincides with their own desires." (Susan B. Anthony)
- "I say quite deliberately that the Christian religion, as organized in its churches, has been and still is the principal enemy of moral progress in the world." (Bertrand Russell)
- "I regard monotheism as the greatest disaster ever to befall the human race. I see no good in Judaism, Christianity, or Islam—good people, yes, but any religion based on a single, well, frenzied and virulent god, is not as useful to the human race as, say, Confucianism, which is not a religion but an ethical and educational system." (Gore Vidal)
- "They said God was on high and he controlled the world and therefore we must pray against Satan. Well, if God controls the world, he controls Satan. For me, religion was full of misstatements and reaches of logic that I just couldn't agree with." (Gene Roddenberry)
- "Religion. It's given people hope in a world torn apart by religion." (Jon Stewart)
- "You either have a god who sends child rapists to rape children, or you have a god who simply watches and says, 'When you're done, I'm going to punish you.' If I could stop a person from raping a child I would. That's the difference between me and your god." (Tracie Harris)
- "Live a good life. If there are gods and they are just, then they will not care how devout you have been, but will welcome you

based on the virtues you have lived by. If there are gods, but unjust, then you should not want to worship them. If there are no gods, then you will be gone, but will have lived a noble life that will live on in the memories of your loved ones." (Marcus Aurelius)

- "Religion has convinced people that there's an invisible man living in the sky, who watches everything you do every minute of every day. And the invisible man has a list of ten specific things he doesn't want you to do. And if you do any of these things, he will send you to a special place of burning and fire and smoke and torture and anguish for you to live forever and suffer and suffer and burn and scream, until the end of time. But he loves you. He loves you. He loves you and he needs money." (George Carlin)
- "The so-called Christian nations are the most enlightened and progressive...but in spite of their religion, not because of it. The Church has opposed every innovation and discovery from the day of Galileo down to our own time, when the use of anesthetic in childbirth was regarded as a sin because it avoided the biblical curse pronounced against Eve. And every step in astronomy and geology ever taken has been opposed by bigotry and superstition. The Greeks surpassed us in artistic culture and in architecture five hundred years before Christian religion was born." (Mark Twain)
- "When I think of all the harm the Bible has done, I despair of ever writing anything to equal it." (Oscar Wilde)
- "Who will say with confidence that sexual abuse is more permanently damaging to children than threatening them with the eternal and unquenchable fires of hell?" (Richard Dawkins)
- "It is the inevitable effect of religion on public policy that makes it a matter of public concern. Advocates of religiosity extol the virtues or moral habits that religion is supposed to instill in us. But we should be equally concerned with the intellectual habits it discourages." (Wendy Kaminer)
- "It seems to me that the idea of a personal god is an anthropological concept which I cannot take seriously. I also cannot imagine some will or goal outside the human sphere... Science has been charged with undermining morality, but the charge is unjust. A man's ethical behavior should be based effectually on sympathy, education, and social ties and needs; no religious basis is necessary. Man would indeed be in a poor way if he had to be restrained by fear of punishment and hope of reward after death." (Albert Einstein)

- "The god of the Old Testament is arguably the most unpleasant character in all fiction." (Richard Dawkins)
- "Don't wonder at those who are good without God. Pity those who need God to be good." (Unknown)
- "As a source of objective morality, the Bible is one of the worst books we have. It might be the very worst, in fact, if we didn't also happen to have the Qur'an." (Sam Harris)
- "Religion has caused more misery to all of mankind in every stage of human history than any other single idea." (Madalyn Murray O'Hair, Founder of American Atheists)
- "When his life was ruined, his family killed, his farm destroyed, Job knelt down on the ground and yelled up to the heavens, "Why god? Why me?" and the thundering voice of God answered, 'There's just something about you that pisses me off.'" (Stephen King)
- "Imagine there's no heaven. It's easy if you try. No hell below us. Above us only sky. Imagine all the people living for today. Imagine there's no countries. It isn't hard to do. Nothing to kill or die for, and no religion too. Imagine all the people living life in peace." (John Lennon)
- "God blesses you with free will, then strongly encourages you not to use it." (Unknown)
- "If only I wasn't an Atheist I could get away with anything. You'd just ask for forgiveness, and you'd be forgiven. It sounds much better than having to live with guilt." (Keira Knightley)
- "When a man is freed of religion, he has a better chance to live a normal and wholesome life." (Sigmund Freud)
- "One of the great tragedies of mankind is that morality has been hijacked by religion. So now people assume that religion and morality have a necessary connection. But the basis of morality is really very simple and doesn't require religion at all." (Arthur C. Clarke)
- "We keep on being told that religion, whatever its imperfections, at least instills morality. On every side, there is conclusive evidence that the contrary is the case and that faith causes people to be more mean, more selfish and perhaps above all, more stupid." (Christopher Hitchens)
- "Morality is doing what is right regardless of what you are told. Religion is doing what you are told regardless of what is right." (Unknown)
- "I'm an atheist, and that's it. I believe there's nothing we can know except that we should be kind to each other and do what we can for each other." (Katharine Hepburn)

- "Eternal suffering awaits anyone who questions God's infinite love." (Bill Hicks)
- "When I hear from people that religion doesn't hurt anything, I say really? Well, besides most wars, the crusades, the inquisitions, 9-11, ethnic cleansing, the suppression of women, the suppression of homosexuals, *fatwas*, honor killings, suicide bombings, arranged marriages to minors, human sacrifice, burning witches, and systematic sex with children, I have a few little quibbles. And I forgot blowing up girls' schools in Afghanistan." (Bill Maher)
- "Religion doesn't give you answers, it gives you excuses." (Unknown)
- "Reason is to religion what sunlight is to vampires." (Unknown)
- "God is an ever-receding pocket of scientific ignorance." (Neil deGrasse Tyson)
- "Science flies you to the moon. Religion flies you into skyscrapers." (Bumper Sticker)
- "*Faith* is the other F-word people use when intellect and reason fail them." (Again, Yours Truly)

Informational Sources I Highly Recommend

Books

1. American Atheist Press, *The Bible Handbook*
2. Annie Laurie Gaylor, *Woe to the Women, the Bible Tells Me So*
3. Anonymous, *The Holy Bible*
4. Christopher Hitchens, *God is Not Great*
5. C.J. Werleman, *God Hates You, Hate Him Back*
6. John G. Jackson, *Christianity before Christ*
7. Ken Smith, BA, *Ken's Guide to the Bible*
8. Madalyn O'Hair, *An Atheist Looks at Women and Religion*
9. Paul Farrell, *Illustrated Stories from the Bible*
10. Richard Dawkins, *The God Delusion*
11. Russell Shorto, *Gospel Truth*
12. Sam Harris, *End of Faith*
13. Steve Wells, *Drunk With Blood, God's Killings in the Bible*
14. Thomas Paine, *The Age of Reason, Part III, Examination of the Prophesies*
15. T.J. Wray and Gregory Mobley, *The Birth of Satan*

Video Artists and Commentaries Available on YouTube

1. 43Alley (Various Commentaries and Animations)
2. Atheistcoffee (Various Commentaries)
3. Bill Maher (Anything on Religion)
4. CultOfDusty (WARNING: Strong Language!)
5. DarkMatter2525 (Animated Humor)
6. Darryl Sloan, *Satan*
7. Eddie Izzard, *Jesus and the Dinosaurs* (Animated Version by 43Alley)
8. George Carlin (Stand Up Comedy: Religion)
9. Pat Condell (Commentaries on Religion)
10. Pop Lar, *Good Christians: The Cathars and Their Beliefs, Gnosticism and Dualism*
11. TheThinkingAtheist (Various Commentaries and Animations)
12. TheVeganAtheist (Various Commentaries)
13. Underlings (Proving God is Evil)
14. ZeEthiopia, *The History of Satan the Devil*

Websites

1. Biblegateway.com
2. EvilBible.com
3. DwindlingInUnbelief.com
4. TheBrickTestament.com
5. Atheists.org (Official *American Atheist Magazine* website)
6. AtheistSites.net

DVDs

1. Bill Maher, *Religulous*
2. *Star Trek II, The Wrath of Kahn*
3. *Raiders of the Lost Ark*
4. *Star Trek* (original TV series) Season 3, Episode 7: *The Day of the Dove*

About the Author

CL Putnam is a retired Highway Engineering Quality Specialist, who lives in the picturesque Rogue River Valley of Southern Oregon. While employed with the Oregon Department of Transportation, she was asked to write the narratives for three major infrastructure projects that had been nominated for national recognition. Due to her writing skills, all three won the "Gold Award" for their category.

In 1977 she graduated from El Camino College in Torrance, California with a degree in history. Her special interests include anthropology, psychology and comparative religions. As a freelance writer, she has had articles published in *Western Horseman*, *Equus* and *American Atheist* magazines, along with numerous other publications. (She also has nearly 300 "Letters to the Editor" to her credit.) She is currently working on her fifth novel.

When not at the keyboard, she enjoys hiking, cycling, cross-country skiing, snowshoeing, tennis, kayaking, horseback riding and scuba diving. An accomplished horsewoman, she has bred, trained and shown registered Quarter Horses and Arabians. For sixteen years she raised meat goats (along with various other kinds of livestock) on her one-woman mini-farm. When time permits, she loves to travel. Her favorite "travel adventure" was the pilgrimage she made to the Holy Land...during a Lebanese rocket attack.

She is active in several charitable organizations, including the MS Society, Diabetes Association, Habitat for Humanity, and Jackson County (Oregon) Historical Society. For seven years she was a volunteer and board member for HOPE (Horses Offering People Excellence), a therapeutic horseback riding facility for physically and emotionally challenged children and adults. At present, she is a "foster mother" to abandoned cats and kittens for the CATS (Committed Alliance To Strays) organization of Medford, Oregon. She is an outspoken advocate for LGBT rights and teaches self-defense for women and children. Her life motto is, *"Well, there's always Plan B."*

Made in the USA
Monee, IL
09 June 2022

97738487R00118